Sreeram Chaulia is Vice Dean of the Jindal School of International Affairs (JSIA) at the OP Jindal Global University in Sonipat, India. He is also a columnist on international current affairs for the Hong Kong-based *Asia Times* and the New Delhi-based *Financial Express*.

INTERNATIONAL ORGANIZATIONS AND CIVILIAN PROTECTION

Power, Ideas and Humanitarian Aid in Conflict Zones

SREERAM CHAULIA

I.B. TAURIS
LONDON · NEW YORK

Published in 2011 by I.B.Tauris & Co Ltd
6 Salem Road, London W2 4BU
175 Fifth Avenue, New York NY 10010
www.ibtauris.com

Distributed in the United States and Canada
Exclusively by Palgrave Macmillan
175 Fifth Avenue, New York NY 10010

Library of International Relations 54

ISBN 978 1 84885 640 0

A full CIP record for this book is available from the British Library
A full CIP record for this book is available from the Library of Congress

Library of Congress catalog card: available

Printed and bound in Great Britain by CPI Antony Rowe, Chippenham
Camera-ready copy edited and supplied by the author

To fearless peacemakers who dare to dream of a war-free future

CONTENTS

LIST OF ILLUSTRATIONS

LIST OF TABLES

LIST OF ABBREVIATIONS

AFP	Armed Forces of the Philippines
AusAID	Australian Government Overseas Aid Programme
BDA	Bangsamoro Development Agency
CAFGU	Citizen Armed Force Geographical Unit
CFA	Ceasefire Agreement
CIDA	Canadian International Development Agency
CVO	Civilian Volunteer Organization
DFID	Department for International Development
DS	Divisional Secretariat
DSWD	Department of Social Welfare and Development
GA	Government Agent
GRP	Government of Philippines
GSL	Government of Sri Lanka
ICRC	International Committee of the Red Cross
IGO	Intergovernmental Organization
IHL	International Humanitarian Law
INGO	International Non-governmental Organization
IO	International Organization
JICA	Japan International Cooperation Agency
JVP	Janata Vimukti Peramuna
LGU	Local Government Unit
LTTE	Liberation Tigers of Tamil Eelam
MDAP	Multi Donor Assistance Programme

MILF	Moro Islamic Liberation Front
MNLF	Moro National Liberation Front
MOA-AD	Memorandum of Agreement on Ancestral Domain
NDCC	National Disaster Coordinating Council
NPA	National People's Army
ODA	Overseas Development Assistance
RDCC	Regional Disaster Coordinating Council
SCF	Save the Children Fund
SCSL	Save the Children in Sri Lanka
SLA	Sri Lankan Army
TMVP	Tamil Makkal Viduthalai Pulihal
TRO	Tamils Rehabilitation Organization
UNDP	United Nations Development Programme
UNICEF	United Nations Children's Fund
UNV	United Nations Volunteers
USAID	United States Agency for International Development

FOREWORD

When European colonialists invaded and occupied African societies, they did not present themselves as colonisers. Instead, they claimed to be carrying out humanitarian work. Untold atrocities were committed in the name of spreading Christianity, civilization and commerce. These colonisers competed among themselves to see which could be the most brutal, and up to this time, the genocidal violence of many is still covered up.

Adam Hochschild has brought out one episode in his exposure of the role of the Belgians in the Congo. Under the monarch of Belgium, colonial administrators killed more than ten million civilians and yet, King Leopold managed to shrewdly cultivate his reputation as a great humanitarian.

Humanitarianism then and the humanitarianism of today dictate that serious scholarship contributes to lifting the veil off militarism that represents itself in a charitable guise. Nowhere was this more blatant than in the recent fiasco in Iraq, when the former US President George W Bush represented the occupation and destruction of the society as a humanitarian act.

From King Leopold II to George W Bush, the cry for new scholarship echoed through the ages. Now, Indian scholar Sreeram Chaulia has broken the silence on the criminal actions that often get disguised as humanitarian acts. His study brings out the intellectual and ideological basis of contemporary humanitarian actions in the Philippines and Sri Lanka. While his work concentrates on these two Asian cases, general lessons can be drawn for war-torn societies all over the planet.

Throughout war-affected parts of the world, one notices the quiet resistance of groups of humans to hierarchical structures of militarism, dominance and exploitation which prolong their misery and suffering. Courageous local movements of women, peasants, workers, students et al have arisen in response to the brutality and fear that are imposed via unjust structures through wars. The fact that a few profiteers nested in iniquitous international structures of capitalism and patriarchy make hay during wars while the mass of society- women, men and children- get trampled is well understood by observers of the 'political economy of war'.

Questions of peace with justice figure prominently in the struggles of human beings to lead a life of material dignity and spiritual well-being. The human endeavour to create spaces of security that are free from violence and oppression is an age-old quest that takes new forms and means with changing times. Concern for fellow humans, the community and the environment have driven peace movements to apply local variants of the universal philosophy of ubuntu, an African concept elaborated by Bishop Desmond Tutu as 'knowing that one belongs in a greater whole and is diminished when others are humiliated or diminished.'

Collective thinking and action drawing on the ubuntu principle of 'my humanity is caught up and is inextricably bound up in yours' has proven to be an important reservoir of strength for people's movements against the structures that entrench hierarchies, divide human beings and reduce the value of life. It is the only self-sustainable and indigenous means for salvation, redemption and emancipation of civilians caught up in wars that are not of their making.

There are no substitutes or shortcuts to grassroots action and human agency motivated by optimism and fortitude to end wars and impunity. The road to peace is mined heavily with dangers and risks, but communities that have mobilised and formed virtuous networks to alter the balance of forces stand testimony to the efficacy of popular interventions that are well timed and deeply rooted in moral courage.

The examples of anti-colonial liberation struggles in Asia, Africa and Latin America, which persevered against great superior military powers, ushered in a period of political independence. Yet, after failing to destroy freedom movements, the former colonial overlords devised schemes of overseas development and aid to perpetuate their cultural and economic influence.

Currently, the foreign aid business is a multibillion dollar enterprise to ensure the extraction of surpluses from the former colonised territories. Although scholars such as David Harvey have written on 'Accumulation by Dispossession', mainstream political scientists continue to use language of 'donors' and private- public partnerships to disguise contemporary imperial plunder. In this phase of neocolonialism, international non-governmental and governmental agencies have become the frontline forces for imperial penetration.

Today, charity and humanitarianism are favourite covers for financial capital and the military-industrial machine to advance their geopolitical and geo-economic interests in nominally 'independent' parts of the world. The sophistication with which neo-liberalism has taken on humanitarianism as its disaster zone cousin in order to prolong wars, persecution and extraction of strategic minerals needs deeper understanding and exposure.

The proliferation of NGOs and expatriate-led aid agencies in impoverished and war-hit areas is a consistent strategy of neoliberal structures to weaken the role of governments and popular movements and then use the vacuum to entrench male chauvinistic values and the 'free market' which militate against the basic principles of ubuntu. Unfortunately, the predominance of Western liberalism in the academe has meant that this sinister nexus between charity, humanitarianism and imperialism have not been adequately addressed.

Political scientists are especially guilty of complicity in justifying and finessing the charity model of international organizations, which are portrayed in a sympathetic fashion as angels for civilians in distress who face 'moral dilemmas' and 'hard choices'. The literature has not ventured into the ideological linkages between academic constructs and paradigms like rationalism and constructivism on the one hand and the extreme bodily, mental and spiritual violence that is perpetrated in wars. Instead of probing the violent structures that permeate and drive actions of the so-called 'international community', social scientists have championed humanitarianism and offered correctives to improve it.

Grassroots mass movements and radical thinkers have seen through the charade of humanitarian aid and keep questioning the causes, consequences and processes by which charity has trumped justice in war theatres. One only has to spend time in an area plagued by armed conflict to appreciate how the academe has skipped the will of populations to shed dependency on aid agencies and to engage in political activism to change their own circumstances.

The manipulation of humanitarian organizations by states, violent non-state actors and corporate megaliths is well understood by civilians on the ground who are desperate to find protection for themselves and their communities. That the humanitarian slogan of 'saving lives' can be a profitable business in which civilians are turned into sacrificial lambs, statistics and depoliticised masses is an intricate reality that needs to be confronted and explained by political scientists.

In this book, Sreeram Chaulia has managed to pierce the superficial veil of Western liberal academia by developing a political scientific critique of humanitarians and international organizations in general. Scarcely any study exists in the literature that uses paradigms of political science to understand the root motivations, intentions and impacts that govern humanitarian behaviour in wars.

The author, my student and long-time academic comrade, has combined intense personal knowledge of ground realities in the war-battered regions of Sri Lanka and the Philippines with theoretical reflections on the nature and purpose of international organizations. This book raises the level of debate about humanitarianism by revolving around the key issue of why they fail to assist local movements committed to protecting civilians. By delving into the 'rational' and 'cultural' aspects of decision-making in humanitarian organizations and their derivation from hierarchical global structures, the author has broken fresh ground on the politics of charity.

How can the era of liberal imperialism and humanitarianism be overcome by people whose honour and capacity to determine their own political fates have been robbed in war? The author reposes faith in radical activist networks within the war-scarred communities of Sri Lanka and the Philippines and proposes an agenda for international organizations to be decolonised. Democratic international relations can only be achieved if the foundational institutions and organizations of world order are reclaimed in the interests of the victims of countless wars and market-based impositions.

Genuine cooperation and solidarity-based linkages between local and global activists are the concrete bases for protecting civilians and ushering in peaceful coexistence in divided societies. For such an eventuality to transpire, humanitarianism and its associated militarism, greed and masochism will have to go. Academics must shed mental slavery to humanitarian ideals and rethink how justice could be the end goal of their intellectual outpourings. Chaulia's book is a step in that direction.

Horace G Campbell
Professor of Political Science
Maxwell School of Citizenship and Public Affairs
Syracuse University

ACKNOWLEDGEMENTS

This book would not have seen light of day without the eternal encouragement of my mentor, the pan-African activist scholar Dr. Horace Campbell. At every step — from loss of innocence about a 'dream UN job' to formulating my research questions and applying theory to facts from a pro-people perspective — I owe it to him. By writing the Foreword to this book, he has added to my debts. His belief that ancestors brought me to him has begun to convince me.

I also owe massively to professors at the Maxwell School in Syracuse University who offered constructive advice while this book was germinating in its dissertation avatar. Dr. Francine D'Amico, Dr. S.N. Sangmpam, Dr. Mark Rupert and Dr. Subho Basu spotted a variety of problems in my PhD thesis and suggested means to tackle them. The coherence and flow of this book stem from their collective wisdom.

My former colleagues at Nonviolent Peaceforce have been invaluable for me to discover ground realities in war zones. Their insights and actions in protecting civilians taught me more than any social science book. The radicals among them (unnamable here because of their present professional commitments) disabused me of myths about the inherent nobility of humanitarianism and converted me away from the liberal virus.

I have been blessed with a highly conducive family environment that stressed erudition and excellence. My parents, Dr. Prafulla Kumar Chaulia and Mrs. Chandrakala Chaulia, sowed in me since childhood an unquenchable thirst for international affairs and saved me from the coils of parochial vision. In no small measure, whatever I am today is thanks to their ideal upbringing.

Tolerance and absolute love from my wife, Usha Rani Damerla, kept me afloat during the uncertain times when research funding and encouragement from my graduate school were running dry. Usha's unquestioning support for my workaholic ways and sagacious advice at critical junctures deserve a big salute. I resolve to dedicate my next book singly to her.

Last but not least in the 'thank you' list is my long-time mentor, friend and inspirer, C. Raj Kumar, the dynamic Vice Chancellor of the one-of-its-kind OP Jindal Global University in India. The spark he lit has kept my flame burning. I am grateful for the extraordinary institutional support of the talented Research Associate, Sulbha Rai, of OP Jindal Global University for diligent assistance in polishing this manuscript.

PREFACE

In 2003, when I set out as a callow 24-year-old to eastern Sri Lanka as an international civilian peacekeeper for Nonviolent Peaceforce, a new international NGO dedicated to protecting civilians and strengthening local peacemakers, I was forewarned about embarking on a life changing experience. The two years I spent in Valachchenai, Batticaloa district, in association with extraordinarily courageous local activists and voluntary organizations, opened my eyes to a reality that had been clouded by a lifetime of Westernised education in elite institutions and training in posh headquarters of international humanitarian organizations.

I learnt first-hand the meaning of fear, suffering and resistance to violence and wondered why not a single book I had read in academia highlighted the seminal role of local civil society in protecting civilians and ending wars.

Nonviolent Peaceforce grew in time to start a second civilian peacekeeping mission in south-western Philippines. I was present at the creation of this venture and spent close to one year in a comparably ghastly setting in Cotabato province of Mindanao, mingling with a visionary breed of local activists. From the radical civil society leaders of Mindanao, I learnt how the violence imposed on civilians by collusion of foreign and domestic forces could be countered through organised human agency that is moderate but disciplined.

The direct experience of armed conflict in Sri Lanka and the Philippines, which included exposure to many close shaves in risky situations, reshaped my career priorities as well. During undergraduate years, I used to be one of those starry-eyed aspirants who yearned to work for the United Nations in one of its field-based aid organizations. Spending three years in war zones with ordinary people wizened me considerably and pushed me to think critically about the impact of gigantic humanitarian organizations on conflict.

In 2005, I returned to graduate school in search of theoretical works on this subject and sensed I was onto something that had not been written about at all — a political scientific critique of humanitarianism. This work, which draws upon over three hundred interviews and conversations in the field between 2003 and 2008, is intended to fill the lacuna in political science of theoretical works about aid agencies and their relationship to the violent international system.

I personally faced the brunt of the Sri Lankan state's propaganda machine when its high level functionaries tried to disparage my research about civilian suffering in Eelam War IV that was published in an article in *Asia Times* (Civilians Caught in Sri Lanka's 'Clean War', September 11, 2008). Rajiva Wijesinha, the then head of the Sri Lankan government's Peace Secretariat wrote a long diatribe in the state-dominated mouthpiece, *The Island*, arguing that I was misguiding the world about the reality of his state's 'war on terrorism' ('Chaulia of Syracuse Regrets', September 16, 2008). More insinuations followed against me by Sinhalese chauvinists in the Sri Lankan media alleging that I was an agent for the anti-state guerrillas, the Tamil Tigers. Wijesinha went to the extent of lodging a formal complaint through the Sri Lankan embassy in Washington D.C. to my graduate school in Syracuse University, saying that I was indulging in baseless slander against the Sri Lankan state's just war and that I should be gagged or worse. Unlike thousands of hapless victims of that brutal war, I survived this sneak attack and am here now to present the true story of how aid organizations and murderous regimes like that of Sri Lanka combine to violate the bodies and souls of civilians in war.

The views expressed here are solely mine and do not in any way represent the positions of my former employer, Nonviolent Peaceforce. I speak my mind and my heart in equal measure in this book because it is meant to be both a contribution to theory as well as a tribute to the indomitable spirit of local peacemakers and human rights defenders who peg away at repressive structures in the shadows, often unrecognised. I have not personally named these exemplars due to the danger of their exposure to violent state and non-state actors who kill at will. But the basic intent of writing this book is to show that the hope of ushering in justice to war-torn areas lies in supporting their kind of self-organised local activism rather than the colossal racquet called international humanitarian aid.

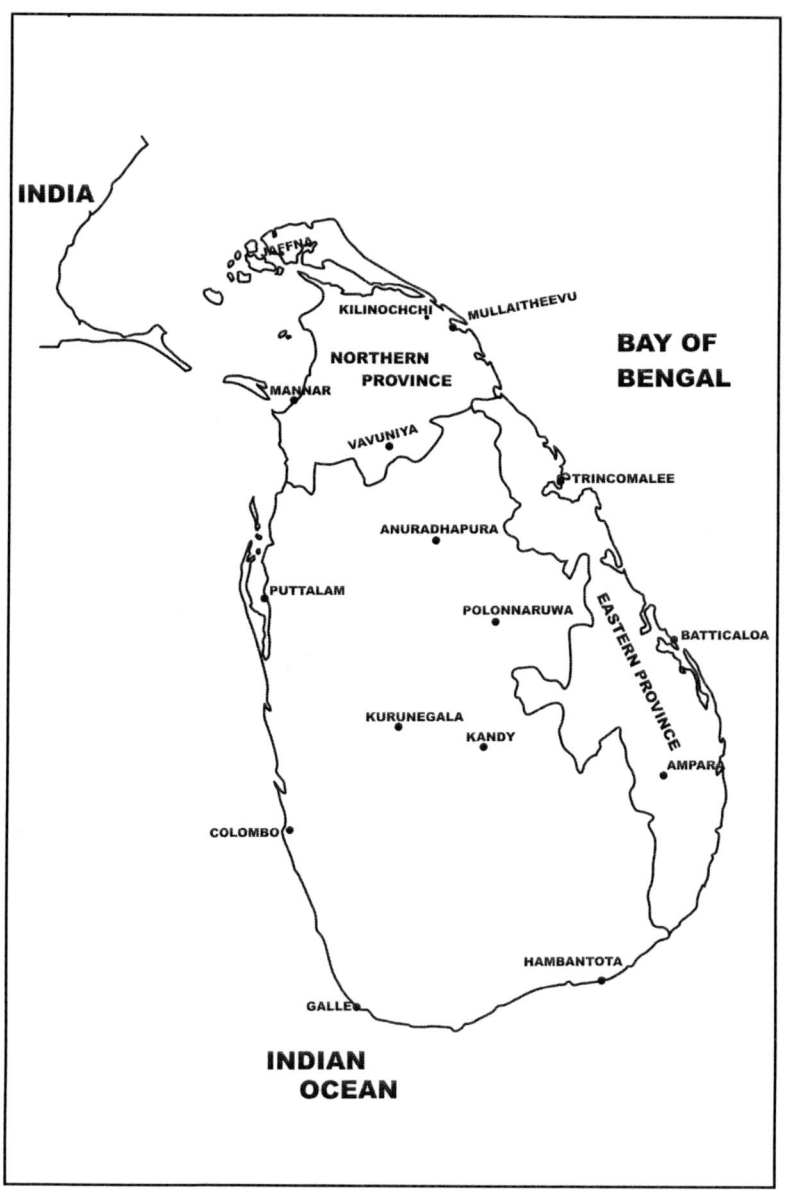

Figure 1. Map of Sri Lanka, highlighting the North and East.[1]
Source: Custom drawn art by Damerla Usha Rani and M.S. Harikrishna

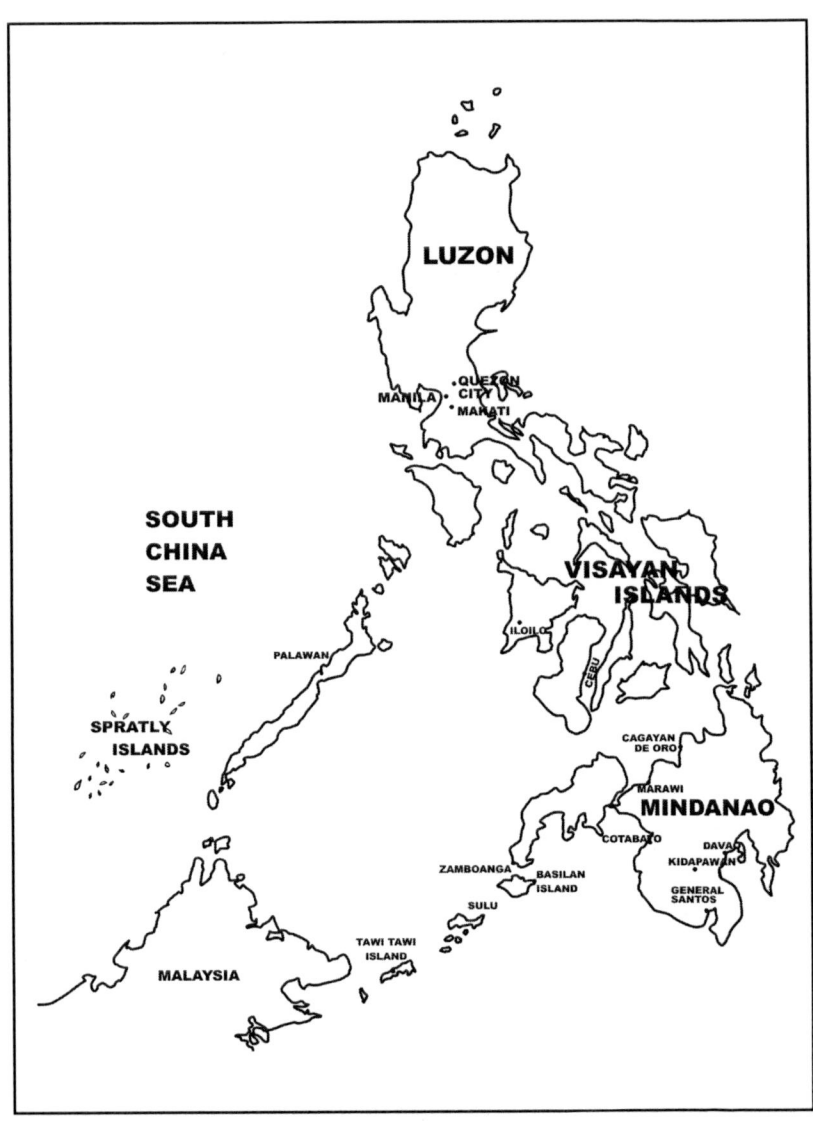

Figure 2. Map of the Philippines, highlighting the South-West.[2]
Source: Custom drawn art by Damerla Usha Rani and M.S. Harikrishna

INTRODUCTION

Charity is no substitute for justice withheld.
Saint Augustine.

Barons of Morality

The landscape of charity in the contemporary world is inhabited by a recognisable form channelling donations to the needy — the humanitarian organization. It is a registered non-profit entity that acts as intermediary between supposedly benevolent givers and desperate receivers weathering natural or human-made disasters. Hardly any disaster zone exists on the planet where humanitarian organizations do not ply their wares of relief goods and services that are, on paper, apolitical products of sympathy and kindness.

Where political barriers are erected to the access of these organizations, their champions raise a hue and cry and remind the blockers of their obligations under international law to allow 'neutral aid' to reach the suffering victims. As witnessed after Cyclone Nargis in May 2008, not even hermetically sealed societies like military-ruled Burma have managed to fully shut off their terrain from the army of humanitarian aid organizations.

The universality of the international aid agency, with its conspicuous emblems, uniformed specialist personnel, inventories of food, medicines, plastic tents and transportation equipment, is a constant reminder that the 'world' is involved wherever there is mass displacement and deprivation of basic needs. By commanding plentiful stocks of essential items, humanitarian organizations frequently play the double role of arbiter of the destinies of civilians floored by disasters and of consort to different shades of local, national and international authorities.

Aid organizations are vectors of not only international concern but also of vested interests that dwell in the nooks and corners of world politics. A core duality — the moral impulse to 'save lives' in emergencies and the practical impulse to influence the political fate of disaster-affected regions of the world — is embedded organically in the aid agency, however much it portrays itself as purely driven by altruistic ideas. Although morality and might seem conceptually distant in legal discourses for limiting the use of force in international relations[1], humanitarian organizations reflect both and often display the primacy of the latter over the former.

Political scientists, who are disciplinarily better attuned to spot power relations compared to their peers in the rest of the social sciences, should approach the study of aid agencies with this duality in mind. Unfortunately, not many scholars have attempted a political scientific treatise on humanitarian organizations that enhances theoretical knowledge about their basic purpose and effects in international affairs. The reason for this neglect is primarily ideological. Humanitarian organizations appeal to the liberal instincts that permeate the Western academe and hence do not receive adequate critical treatment from a theoretical angle.

Many well-meaning academics and lay persons spellbound by liberal ethos start with the assumption that aid agencies do wonderful work and help people in distress. Their minds are ideologically open to limited criticism aimed at reducing the inefficiency of these organizations, but not to proposals for structural overthrow of humanitarianism as a system. The Good Samaritan narrative, which humanitarian organizations themselves carefully nurture in their public relations and fundraising drives, conveniently hides the unequal power relations and injustices that underpin the aid enterprise. It legitimises these organizations as noble but imperfect and necessary but slightly flawed.

This book transcends Polyannaish delusions about aid agencies and instead tries to sensitise political scientists and general readers to viewing the macro-level recolonising impact of humanitarianism. It fills the gap in literature by testing alternative political science explanations for the behaviour of field-based international humanitarian organizations in war zones. It harnesses the incompatibilities and overlaps among four rival camps in political science to frame research questions and break fresh ground on the barons of morality who have become dispensers of the fate of millions of vulnerable civilians.

The Kernel of Political Science: A Will O' the Wisp

A political scientific study of humanitarian organizations has to first elaborate the identifiable features of the feuding camps of the discipline before entering into specifics of the research puzzle, methodology, empirical findings and deductions.

What constitutes the core of political science as a discipline? There are differing viewpoints about its most important theme or motif. Essentially, one can divide them into four paradigms — *rationalism, culturalism, institutionalism* and *structuralism*. Although each camp has a distinct emphasis, there are several overlaps in issue areas among the four. The same empirical event, say war, can be a favourite topic of research by all four camps, although the causal emphasis will be placed on different factors by each.

These camps have fought over the entire territory of the discipline for decades, waxing and waning in their popularity but never giving in to the other by admitting defeat. The lively exchanges among the four paradigms make political science what it is — a contested domain in which there is no possibility of finding a real silver bullet or Physics-like 'general theory of everything' that can explain all known phenomena. Political scientific testing of competing theories of humanitarian behaviour can proceed only after clearly adumbrating the distinctness of each of these camps.

Rationalism

A number of political scientists belonging to the 'rationalist camp' see the discipline as one big canvas for the articulation, coordination and clash of interests among actors. In the purest rationalist sense suggested by micro-economic theory, actors are understood as individuals (Becker, 1978). But larger macro-social units like community, region, nation, class, state, occupation, gender, organization et al can be categorised as actors having their own interests. Typically, actors possessing interests are understood to be acting upon them by means of information gathering, alliance formation or tussles with other actors with the objective of maximising their respective utility or power.

To this camp, the key behind political causation is the rational calculation of interests by individual or collective actors. Drawing from Western philosophical roots, many rationalists conceive politics as the pursuit of power by different actors endowed with defined or changing interests (Thommessen, 2003). Power itself is most commonly defined as the ability to influence the behaviour of others, with or without resistance. Actors pursue power either as a means to acquiring some concrete gains or as an end in itself. To many rationalists, the pursuit of power is viscerally related to action based on self-interest. The rational desire for utility maximisation can therefore be reframed as an attempt at altering the relevant power balance in one's desired direction.

One of the founding fathers of the rationalist paradigm, the eighteenth century English philosopher Jeremy Bentham, designed the 'Panopticon'— a new model prison where the jailor could maintain surveillance over prisoners without the latter being aware that there were under watch. Prisoners of the Panopticon had to also perform hard menial labour to make the concept financially viable. Bentham touted this rational cost-saving architecture as 'a new mode of obtaining power of mind over mind, in a quantity hitherto without example' (Bentham, 1995:29). The Panopticon model was commissioned by the British parliament to be constructed en masse in the Indian subcontinent, thereby tying rationality to the needs of colonial punishment.

Irrespective of whether an actor is relatively powerful (e.g. the colonial state vis-à-vis its subjects) or powerless (the peasant rebel vis-à-vis the extractive revenue collectors), she is understood by rationalists to be acting on the basis of self-interest in an effort to either preserve the status quo or to change it in her favour. It follows from this exegesis that any empirical political behaviour, outcome, or puzzle can be attributed to the interplay of self-interested stakeholders who cooperate, compete, obey, command, assist and harm each other from time to time.

Culturalism

Political scientists influenced heavily by sociology, anthropology and the interpretivist method accord primacy to factors like norms, culture, knowledge and values as the main determinants of political behaviour. The contention of culturalists is that political phenomena must be situated in their social ambience and explained in terms of their 'socio-cultural context' (McGlynn and Tuden, 1991:3). Among the multiple definitions of 'culture', anthropologist Clifford Geertz mentions the following as useful for social science: 'a way of thinking, feeling, and believing', 'a set of standardised orientations to recurrent problems', 'a mechanism for the normative regulation of behaviour' etc (Geertz, 1973: passim).

Several culturalist political scientists champion ideas as the essential theme of the discipline. Social and political behaviour is said by this camp to derive from a set of ideas (e.g. causal beliefs, principled beliefs and ontological worldviews) held by actors (Goldstein and Keohane, 1993). Ideas are viewed as a product of past history, the prevailing socio-cultural environment or the state of knowledge about the world in which actors operate. Culturalists claim to be superior or ontologically prior to rationalists because they say that the very definition of interests by an actor is an outcome of the prevailing norms and ideas (e.g. about development, progress or sovereignty) that surround the actor.

If some rationalists stress power, self-interest and objective material pressures as causal factors for political behaviour, sociological and cultural political scientists emphasise non-material beliefs and inter-subjectivity as the main causes. As will be elaborated in Chapter 2, this debate has become central to International Relations theory and is generating the master frames of current academic research.

Power is not the central concern of all rationalist accounts and ideas are not the default interpretive tools of all culturalists. But these two themes feature regularly on two sides of a theoretical wall in political science. Rationalists, keen on the primacy of power and material self-interests, dismiss the significance of ideas and culture in general as determinants of political behavior and outcomes (Popkin, 1979; Elkins and Simeon, 1979). Michael Desch has derisively downplayed the heuristic value of ideas by saying, 'the best case that can be made for cultural theories is that they are sometimes useful as a supplement to realist theories' (Desch, 1998:142). Culturalists have also joined issue by attacking rationalists at every available opportunity and accusing them of 'beginning at the end by assuming interests (as fixed and exogenously given)' (Wildavsky, 1987:5).

By turning into the showpiece contest in political science, rationalism vs. culturalism has spilled over into two other camps — institutionalism and structuralism — and suffused the two to the extent of engendering theoretical compounds like 'cultural/sociological institutionalism', 'rational institutionalism', 'ideational structuralism' and 'economistic structuralism'.

Institutionalism

Scholars who discern habitual action and regularity of behaviour consider the heart of politics to be nothing but an illustration of institutions, which are elaborated as rules, norms, conventions, procedures, moral codes, expectations and traditions. This camp sees institutions and rule-following behaviour as ubiquitous in every social or political setting. It claims that institutions are the fountainheads of both interests and ideas and that they set the constraints or limits within which politics is played out. Institutions can be formal (e.g. related to the state and its appurtenances or to the private sector) or informal (e.g. customs and practices that are deeply rooted in society), and the balance between the two types of institutions are considered crucial for political stability or the lack thereof (North, 1990).

Structuralism

While some scholars confine the pillars of political science to the 'Three I's — Interests, Ideas and Institutions (Garrett and Weingast, 1993; Irwin and Kroszner, 1999; Varshney, 1989) — a fourth paradigm insists on the seminality of structures. Political scientists of the structuralist camp visualise a map of dynamic relationships among actors and hold it to be the *sine qua non* of the discipline. The interaction among humans, societies, states and other socio-economic forces generates structures that can be conflictual or cooperative or a mixture of both, thereby giving rise to structural forms of domination, subordination, asymmetry, exploitation, cooperation, harmony etc. To structuralists, actors behave in a certain manner not in isolation but in consideration of their relationships and relative positions vis-à-vis other actors.

A common theme among structuralists of all shades is to conceive structure as a complex of constraints that guide political behaviour along designated paths. Neorealist Kenneth Waltz, defines structure as a 'set of constraining conditions' that determines behaviour 'through socialisation of the actors and through competition among them' (Waltz, 1979:74). Structuralists consider political behaviour to be delimited by the roles, positions and ranks decided by the system. For example, feminists see patriarchal structures achieving female subordination by designating specific roles for behaviour on gender lines (Walby, 1990).

Radical structuralists concentrate on how relationships determined by socio-economic modes of production solidify into 'world systems' of domination or oppression (e.g. capitalism, patriarchy, hegemony). The same systems are believed to be transformable into emancipatory modes through technological, economic, demographic and productive developments or revolutionary mobilisation by agents of change (Wallerstein, 1990; Robinson, 2004). Progressive structuralists argue that systems must be placed within a meaningful and dynamic historical context instead of being over-generalised as 'grand theory' of Parsonian ilk (Cox, 1981). They criticise structuralism inspired by Easton (Easton, 1990) as mechanistic for assuming that all political systems are essentially the same and subject to eternal laws of 'stimulus' and 'response' or inputs and outputs. The goal for activist theorists such as Antonio Gramsci is to parse the unique characteristics of an exploitative system and thence find strategies for overthrowing it (Gramsci, 1971).

Like institutionalism, structuralism has been subjected to the material power vs. cultural ideas dichotomy. Complex versions of realism and Marxism give equal explanatory weight to ideational and material factors in the formation and evolution of structures. Robert Cox depicts 'historical structures' as compounds of ideas, institutions as well as material capabilities (i.e. interests of the powerful) (Cox, 1981: 141). Similarly, as a proponent of agency that can change structures, Wallerstein attaches prominence to ideas, ideologies and beliefs in propping up the capitalist world-system, defined as a 'multicultural territorial *division of labour* in which the production and exchange of basic goods and raw materials is necessary for the everyday life of its inhabitants' (Chase-Dunn and Grimes, 1995: 389).

Wallerstein's concept of the world-system was fixated on the designated roles of different nation-states in a global order of industrial production and exchange. But the present-day superseding of industrial capital by finance capital (Sweezy, 1994) begs for a qualification. Wallerstein originally classified states as *core*, *semi-peripheral* and *peripheral* on the basis of their contributions to capitalist production. Now, the central *core* state of the system — the USA — is largely de-industrialised and 'captured' by financial capitalists (Johnson, 2009). The *semi-periphery* now contains late industrialised states that depend on financing from the *core* but also have a commercial/financial elite of their own to organise extraction of raw materials from the *peripheral* regions within and outside their nation-state boundaries. We shall return to this qualified version of the world-system later with regard to the warmongering oligarchs of the Philippines.

Irrespective of whether it is industrial or finance capital at the helm, the world-system emits a liberal ideational glue that holds the structure together and lubricates its outreach. Wallerstein identified the hegemonic ideology of liberalism as the guiding cultural framework or 'geoculture' of the capitalist world-economy (Wallerstein, 1991). Liberal geo-culture is also the ideological potion of humanitarianism, a keynote I shall return to in subsequent chapters.

This book gives due weight to progressive structuralist theories like Marxism and feminism, which have been sidelined by International Relations theorists in the US as unscientific or beyond the pale[2] due to ideological power play and shifts in funding patterns since the end of the Cold War. Without taking on board the merits of structuralist Marxism and feminism, the causality of rationalism and culturalism is devoid of explanatory depth.

The structures limned in this book as 'conditions' for rationalist and culturalist causes to combine and determine humanitarian behaviour are not so totalising to prevent organizational or individual agency from escaping or undermining them. By resurrecting flexible structuralism as an essential toolbox for understanding the behaviour of humanitarian organizations, this work challenges the hegemony of the Three 'I's in political science. In the process, it corrects lacunae in the 'Third Debate' of International Relations theory and proposes a more rounded picture of the behaviour of field-based international organizations which sustains structures of domination and injustice.

Progressive structuralist theories have a cachet of raising the question of justice and its upholders in national and international systems. Unlike theories from the Three Is, Marxism and feminism are critical of existing forms of rule and have a firmer grasp of empire — a central tenet in understanding humanitarian rationality and culture.

This book will demonstrate why failing to credit progressive structuralist theories and yet claiming to explain political behaviour is to limit knowledge about phenomena and deny the undeniable. The Three Is can at best identify immediate causes of an outcome but cannot go from the 'what' to the 'why'. Why are humanitarians motivated by interests and ideas? Is it because these two categories have intrinsic causal merit of their own? This book takes the investigation to a deeper level of abstraction by contextualising interests and ideas within longstanding structures of injustice.

Neo-Gramscian Robert Cox said famously that 'theory is always for someone and for some purpose' (Cox, 1981:207). None of the researchers on humanitarianism in the social sciences has looked below the surface for systemic forces that need to be restructured, not reformed, for victims of violence to find justice. Whose 'purpose', in Cox's language, is being served by the hegemony of the Three Is in analysing humanitarian behaviour and in political science as a whole? This book challenges the deliberate neglect of structuralism by theoreticians and practitioners of humanitarianism and restores the due importance of Marxism and feminism.

Humanitarians: At the Crossroads of 'Power' and 'Ideas'

To recap from the preceding section, there is no agreement among political scientists about what lies at the heart of the discipline — interests, ideas, institutions or structures. The recurring feature in our *tour d'horizon* of the four paradigms is the Power vs. Ideas duel, an overlapping refrain that promises rewards as the thematic fulcrum of this book. In view of the high incidence of this contest in the discipline, using it to design research promises to unravel strengths and weaknesses of all four paradigms. This book's subjects — international humanitarian organizations — exist at the crossroads of 'Power' and 'Ideas' and flower from the fountainhead of patriarchy and the capitalist world-system.

In general parlance, the word 'humanitarian' denotes one who wants to promote human welfare and reduce human suffering. These meanings are clearly in the domain of ideas, stemming from religious morals like kindness, philanthropy and service. Modern usage of the term 'humanitarian' began with individuals in early nineteenth century England who pressurised the Parliament during the industrial revolution to alleviate the exploitative conditions faced by factory workers. Hailing from the professional middle class, they acted out of sympathy for the unprotected proletariat (Roberts, 2002).

Yet, liberal Victorian middle classes were also agitating for a range of constitutional reforms to enhance their own power in the British political system. As Donna Loftus puts it, humanitarian policy proposals for reform 'promoted middle-class values and helped to cement middle-class leadership and authority' (Loftus, 2001). Thus, right from the etymology of 'humanitarian', there was interplay of 'Power' and 'Ideas'.

Since the humanitarian impulse and initiative arose from a particular class of Western Europeans at a specific stage in industrial capitalism and male domination over society, one must also note the underlying structures of exploitation and injustice out of which the charity model of dealing with the downtrodden arose. Instead of delivering justice to the labouring masses toiling within European societies and those at the mercy of imperial masters in the colonies, the Victorian middle classes devised a 'humanitarian' solution to their class anxieties.

Today, humanitarians are understood by lay persons to be succouring victims of warfare. The evolution of international humanitarian law and the rise of humanitarian organizations is a saga of encounters between 'Power' and 'Ideas'. The Hague Convention of 1899, the first formal international humanitarian treaty that prohibited certain destructive technologies in war, was the result of Russian initiative at a time of intense arms races among great powers in Europe. Czar Nicholas II struck upon the idea of an international treaty of this nature because 'Russia, at that time striving to modernise its industries and communications, was feeling the costs of armaments more painfully than Germany and Austria-Hungary, its principal enemies' (Best, 1999: 622).

If great power motives for embarking on humanitarian rule building were materialistic and self-interested, then their internationally conscious publics were playing their part with the script of ideas and values. A panoply of peace societies, associations and organizations belonging to a 'humming transnational civil society' also pressurised their respective governments to attend the Hague conference and sign the Convention (Best, 1999: 620).

The same mixture of 'Power' and 'Ideas' makes an appearance in historical trajectories leading to the four Geneva Conventions. If treaties strengthening *jus in bello* (acceptable conduct in war towards soldiers and civilians) were fulfilments of the beliefs of activists repulsed by the horror of war, they were simultaneously pragmatic agreements in a Europe where balance of power guaranteed huge military losses from hostilities for all belligerent states.

The proliferation of humanitarian laws to mitigate the most brutal aspects of warfare created an international 'humanitarian regime' prescribing rules for states and non-state actors. For rationalists, regimes are not causes of actor behaviour but rather intervening variables sandwiched between 'basic causal variables (most prominently, power and interests) and outcomes and behaviour' (Krasner, 1982: 189). But in the history of humanitarian regime, ideas, beliefs and values also played a role in its inception and spread. The act of convincing states to sign on to the corpus of humanitarian laws was accomplished by 'norm entrepreneurs' like Henry Dunant.

Yet, there is more to the story than just interests, ideas and institutions. The contemporary humanitarian regime is a product of specific global structures of exploitation and inequality. Instead of ending wars of colonial domination and forced integration of the Global South into a capitalist world economy, humanitarians from Dunant onward concentrated on making war more humane. They never questioned the legitimacy and justifiability of war and occupation by European states during the high noon of formal empires. A typical instance is Bentham, who put himself at the service of Her Majesty's government to suppress Indians under *Pax Britannica* but paraded as a humanitarian whose heart bled for Christian minorities in Europe (Price, 2008).

Many present-day humanitarians continue to maintain double standards about imperial aggressions and claim that it is too 'political' or impractical to advocate for ending wars and abuses (*jus ad bellum*). Instead, they prepare themselves for the wars with food and non-food relief items to distribute to civilians. The wars, consequently, get a long lease since humanitarians can always be counted upon by capitalist donor states, masculinist counter-insurgent states and rebel forces to temporarily relieve the suffering of civilians.

International organizations (IOs) — both intergovernmental (IGOs) and non-governmental (INGOs) — sit across an intersection of 'Power' and 'Ideas' as key actors of a structured tragedy. A central tenet of this book is that the rational 'Power' and cultural 'Ideas' that drive these IOs are not ahistorical starting points but derivatives from patriarchy and the capitalist world-system.

Humanitarian IOs reify the clash and coexistence of ideas, interests, institutions and structures and are fascinating subjects for research on the relative explanatory power of the four paradigms. The ensuing chapters of this book will test hypotheses that pit 'Power' against 'Ideas' as determinants of the behaviour of humanitarian organizations and restore structuralism to its deserved place in the pantheon of paradigms.

Prolegomena

The ontological genesis of this book is my own philosophical version of the social world as peopled by human beings who are struggling for life, liberty and dignity — the three eternal pursuits. War is a phenomenon that sanctions extreme physical, material and ideational suppression of human dignity and is a threat to these core aspirations of the inhabitants of the social world. My interest in studying protection of civilians in wars is not only a theoretical investigation but also an activist intervention calling for decolonising collective international organizations so that they can champion the dignity of the human person. As a peace activist trying to end the violence and impunity of war, I am inherently opposed to the charity model of international humanitarian organizations which leaves little scope for justice and perpetuates indignities again civilians. Normatively, I am motivated by Martin Luther King Jr.'s vision that 'the arc of the moral universe is long, but it bends toward justice' (Clayborne, 1997: 486). The activist in me is driven by a quest to wean international organizations away from humanitarianism and set them on the path of justice.

The empirical puzzle driving this study is variation in 'mainstreaming' of civilian protection by humanitarian IGOs and INGOs. Why are some IOs more actively occupied with protecting civilians in war zones compared to others? What motivates some humanitarian IOs to advocate for and act in favour of civil and political rights of civilians even as their peers restrict themselves only to distributing material relief items? The radicalism of some humanitarians stands in contrast to the conservatism of others. This book aims to explain such variance through qualitative structured-focussed comparisons of ten IGOs and INGOs in two different war zones — the North and East of Sri Lanka and south-western Philippines. The empirical parts of this work are organised through paired dyadic comparisons between two or more IGOs and INGOs — first within each of the two countries, and later across countries.

The richness of empirical details brought to the fore by my research affords readers a transparent window into the thinking, argumentation and values of humanitarians which rarely escape the confines of their air-conditioned offices. Through my experience as an international civilian peacekeeper in the war zones of Sri Lanka and the Philippines and the personal associations I developed with humanitarians on the ground, I could fully extract the benefits of the paired comparison method and weave an empirically dense story laced with concrete incidents and illustrations.

A further contribution of this book lies in operationalising independent and dependent variables, viz. 'Power', 'Ideas' and 'Proactiveness'. My detailed break-up of each concept into subsidiary principles and actions builds hitherto unknown classifications and criteria that will benefit future researchers in related studies. The methodological tools bequeathed by this book will also benefit practitioners who wish to conduct independent evaluations of humanitarian IOs on the 'mainstreaming' question. The nuances and shades I have introduced in measurement of concepts also fills a lacuna in theoretical research on IOs in general.

The design of a 'three cornered fight' runs through this research and pits two opposing paradigmatic camps against each other by means of competitive theory testing. In doing so, this book corrects unsatisfactory theoretical renditions of IOs and draws attention to interaction effects among paradigms that are crucial to grasp humanitarianism in its fullness.

One intended contribution of my research is to criss-cross the International Relations-Comparative Politics divide and straddle across local, provincial, national and international levels of analysis. Barrier-breaking research can only materialise through interactions and intersections across space, time and intellectual constructs. The advantage of giving the capitalist world-system and patriarchy their due is that both these structures evade the simplistic spatio-temporal and mental divisions that populate political science as a discipline. If science is nothing but establishment of linkages, connections and correlations among diverse but related phenomena, this book chases that ideal.

My research has two principal theses. Firstly, it conveys that neither rationalism nor culturalism is in itself a sufficient explanation for the priorities of humanitarian IGOs and INGOs towards civilian protection. Rather, a combination of rational 'Power' and cultural 'Ideas' explains why some humanitarian organizations are more focussed on civilian protection than others. Secondly, my study offers a corrective to the 'Third Debate' of International Relations theory by reclaiming a special explanatory place for structuralist theories of Marxism and feminism.

In subsequent chapters, the case is made that 'Power' and 'Ideas' are not self-generated or self-sustained causes of humanitarian but offshoots of larger oppressive structures of patriarchy and the capitalist world-system. The 'Third Debate' has to shift beyond the current obsession with rationality and culture and explain political behaviour by tracing it to structures that are not rigid but changeable through human agency. One of the main contributions of this book to the discipline of political science is to harmonise structures with rationality and culture such that the latter two should not be treated as genuinely independent variables but rather as offshoots of larger systems. While building upon existing states of knowledge, the book transcends them by charting out a new track of theoretical endeavour that recognises the critical worth of structures.

It is only by looking at structures that one can logically reconcile variation in humanitarian IOs' emphases on civilian protection with a minimum common denominator or red line which the vast majority never trespasses. Civilians may be facing extreme violence and abuses from armed actors in wars, but humanitarians often turn their backs when approached by local activists to assist in protecting them. This regime-wide characteristic of sclerosis towards severe violations of civilian rights comes naturally to the humanitarian enterprise due to the rules and relationships set by patriarchy and the capitalist world-system. The endeavour of the following chapters is to shine light on the interconnections between humanitarianism as a liberal imperialist ideology and its violent structural roots.

This book locates humanitarian organizations within the fold of patriarchal militarism and develops the thesis that aspects of their behaviour are both a product of and a reproducer of patriarchy. As key actors in war zones, humanitarian IGOs and INGOs not only turn a blind eye to sexual violence on civilians but also sometimes take undue sexual advantage of the perilous circumstances in which civilians find themselves. For an IGO or INGO to preach 'gender-based programming' and to have expatriate and local personnel who exploit women and young girls in conflict-affected areas is not an oxymoron but consistent with humanitarian morals based on patriarchal militarism.

Patriarchal relationships and values, which are magnified during wars, get fortified by the bureaucracy and pathology of aid delivery mechanisms of humanitarian IOs. This militates against the anti-hierarchical forces struggling to obtain justice for survivors of violence. My book demonstrates through examples from both Sri Lanka and the Philippines that mainstreaming 'gender' into humanitarian IOs is an exercise laden with casuistry because many aid workers themselves engage in sexual opportunism and exploitation. Most IOs talk big about 'gender-based violence' (GBV) but do not follow up by participating in practical efforts to protect females from politically-motivated assaults. To understand why cases of women subjected to indignities by armed actors in war zones are often ignored by humanitarian IOs, one has to pierce the militaristic and patriarchal structures the IOs reproduce on a global scale.

Since the advent of the capitalist world-system in sixteenth century Western Europe and the Americas, patriarchy has been reinforced through commoditisation and sale of the female body. This book elaborates the numerous mechanisms through which financial oligarchs, multinational corporations, capitalist donor states and humanitarian IOs engage in systematic give-and-take and help to keep under wraps the central issues of impunity and abuses against civilians, especially women, in war. It generates a theoretical critique of 'developmentalism' and 'relief', which are the reference points of IOs in war zones and which purposely abet abuses and violence against civilians.

The empirical chapters from Sri Lanka and the Philippines show that the capitalist world-system is an entrenched impediment for humanitarian IGOs and INGOs to pursue justice in war-torn areas. I emphasize in this book the irony of how capitalist states which sustain the whole humanitarian aid edifice also stoke wars and abuses for resource extraction, market expansion, financial flows and geopolitical influence. Aid agencies enable donor states and their military industrial complexes to penetrate and weaken radical movements in countries like Sri Lanka and the Philippines, which in turn shrinks the local activists' capacity for civilian protection.

As one of the war theatres of this study is the Philippines, my research also sheds new light on the geopolitics and geo-economics of the global 'war on terrorism' that began in 2001. It shows how integrated humanitarian IGOs and INGOs are to the US-led military campaign in the Philippines to allegedly eradicate violent Islamic terrorism and how, in reality, this endeavour is aimed at strategic containment of China and continuation of mineral extraction in the Philippines by Western multinational corporations. This book reveals the utility of force and warfare for capitalistic and patriarchal exploitation and how humanitarians perform designated roles within this oppressive arrangement.

Schema of the Book

Chapter 1 sets the empirical stage that motivated this research, i.e. the totality of contemporary wars and the attendant erosion of immunity for non-combatants despite the accretion of international humanitarian and human rights laws. It broadly discusses the relevance of IOs in enhancing the climate of protection for civilians in internal wars, a theme that recurs throughout the book.

Chapter 2 states the assumed task of bringing the study of organizations 'back in' to IR after decades of neglect as a subject matter. It then provides the rationale for researching the behaviour of IOs in the context of the 'Third Debate' in International Relations theory. It unveils the empirical puzzle that sparked this research and the competing theoretical explanations for it, which accord with the four paradigmatic camps of political science elaborated previously in the Introduction.

Chapter 3 underlines the method of structured focussed qualitative comparison that guides the theory testing exercise throughout the book. It gives the methodological justifications for choosing humanitarian IO cases, geographical backdrops and measures for concepts and also elaborates the tenets of Marxism and feminism that are relevant to my quest of finding the determinants of humanitarian IOs' behaviour.

I have not used quantitative methodology in this book due to the small N-size of 5 cases per country. I do, however, employ a numeric measurement scale (described in Chapter 3) to rank the dependent variable (i.e. degree of proactiveness of each organization). If there were no numbered yardstick for this, it would be difficult to obtain a standard on which to compare the IO cases. Given the objective of testing whether different values of 'Power' and 'Ideas' cause different degrees of organizational proactiveness towards civilian protection, variation in the dependent variable must be shown. That is why a numeric table coded by expert observers is introduced in Chapter 3.

The theory testing in this book does not match rigorous statistical standards, but sticking to structured focussed qualitative comparison has the classic methodological trade-off benefit of in-depth investigation of a limited number of key humanitarian IO cases and scanning them intensively from top to bottom.

Chapter 4 qualitatively tests competing rationalist and culturalist hypotheses about the behaviour of five humanitarian IOs in the war zones of Sri Lanka. Chapter 5 repeats the pattern by performing in-country qualitative comparisons of the behaviour of IOs in the war zones of the Philippines.

Chapter 6 introduces calibrated qualitative methods and measures for cross-country comparison of branches of the same humanitarian IO between Sri Lanka and the Philippines and again tests rationalist and culturalist hypotheses.

Chapter 7 draws together the theoretical learnings of the empirical chapters and ties them up with an empiricist-cum-positivist reconsideration of the 'Third Debate' of International Relations theory. It reflects on the complexity of causation of humanitarian behaviour and proposes ways in which rationality and culture can interact to produce outcomes in war zones. Based on an exhaustive evaluation of the competing explanations, it defends one of the main theses of the book, i.e. *international humanitarian organizations set priorities and act according to them in response to both 'Power' and 'Ideas' rather than exclusively one or the other.* They are forced to set their agenda as per the pressures or dictates of materially powerful actors— donor states, host states, sub-units of host states, rebel groups, and competing humanitarian organizations. At the same time, they are crippled by staff-professed bureaucratic pathologies and understandings that limit the scope of choices and actions in relation to the outstanding problem of protection of civilians in war.

Chapter 7 moves beyond the Third Debate by highlighting the merits of two structuralist theories — Marxism and feminism — as the proponents of 'conditions' which enable rationality and culture to be 'causes' of humanitarian behaviour. By giving Marxism and feminism their due in understanding the world of humanitarians, this book strives to identify and challenge the material and non-material structural bases of humanitarianism instead of trying to repair or marginally improve it through superficial reforms.

Until now, the Third Debate has wallowed in a blind alley dominated by a clash between rationality and culture as if these two were *suo motu* variables devoid of historical structural precedent. Where does the rational cost-benefit calculus of humanitarians come from? What is the provenance of the bureaucratic culture of humanitarian IOs? These are ill-answered theoretical questions which have wider relevance for the study of all forms of political behaviour. If an actor is being rationally self-interested or normatively guided in her behaviour, the roots of such behaviour will need to be traced back in order to gain a complete picture of causation.

Chapter 7 lends theoretical rigour to the second main thesis of the book, i.e. *the roots of humanitarian rationality and culture are inextricably bound to the needs of patriarchy and the capitalist world-system.* To talk about mainstreaming protection without reference to these antecedent conditions and their changing form and substance is to perpetuate a clueless science. Hence, this chapter serves a reminder that recommending a revamp of humanitarian practice without touching its structural mother lodes is to intellectually perpetuate the suffering of war-battered civilians.

Chapter 8 addresses the ideological linkages between liberalism, humanitarian interventions and the values of humanitarian IOs. It raises policy-relevant concerns of whether humanitarian IOs can 'mainstream' protection in light of the iniquitous global structures that 'condition' them. It uses examples from the empirical chapters to recommend three concrete lessons for immediate change in praxis of IOs to meet the urgent challenges of impunity and unaccountability of armed actors in war zones. A key learning for pushing IOs towards the path of justice is to align them with local activists and organisers who strive to protect their communities from abuses.

Chapter 8 echoes the voices of civilians in wars who feel let down and betrayed by humanitarian IOs precisely because the latter distance themselves from proactive local groups of human rights defenders in whom the war-beaten repose great trust. This chapter ends by identifying radical alternatives to aid, development and humanitarianism in the tradition of peace with justice.

The Epilogue engages in theoretical musings about the nature and place of IOs in the violent global order that shades them. It envisages that discovering purposeful agency might help collective organizations break free of the structural chains which convert them into instruments for squashing popular aspirations.

1

INTERNATIONAL ORGANIZATIONS AND THE GLOBAL PROTECTION CRISIS

Civilian Victimisation in War

When the German military commander Erich Ludendorff coined the phrase 'total war' and implemented it in World War I, a revolution occurred to the detriment of civilians or non-combatants. Ludendorff's new strategy, which caught on in military practice around the world, spelt doom for the safety and protection of civilians in war zones (Ludendorff, 1943). The universalisation of 'total war' doctrines prompted French political scientist Raymond Aaron to award the twentieth century the lugubrious label, 'century of total war' where violence is unlimited (Aaron, 1954). Approximately 43 to 54 million civilians died as a result of wars during this brutal century, a tremendous increase in non-combatant casualties compared to all preceding eras (Downes, 2008). Given that the percentage figures of civilians in war deaths rose from 10 by the end of the nineteenth century to over 75 percent in the 1990s, the preceding century was truly 'the century in which non-combatant immunity virtually ceased to operate' (Blight and Lang, 2005: 233).

The reasons for parties to armed conflicts deliberately targeting civilians are manifold. The rationalist explanation is that when a state's military fortunes are dipping, it is desperate to reduce its own casualties or avoid defeat, and considers civilians 'legitimate' targets to coerce the enemy to give up, i.e. by raising the opponent's costs (Downes, 2008). Paralleling this logic is the calculation of rebel groups, 'insurgents', 'militants' or 'terrorists' who wage asymmetric internal wars against states. By intentionally harming civilians belonging to the 'other', violent non-state actors raise the costs of the enemy state and also invite repressive reactions from that state which help to unify the group whose 'self-determination' is the bone of contention (Hultman, 2007).

Culturalist explanations for the growing impunity against civilians in wars stress the dehumanisation of the enemy as barbaric or heinous, which normalises killing, maiming or torturing non-combatants of the other side. 'Dualistic thinking' is one of the main 'anti-civilian ideologies' permitting atrocities in war. It 'divides society into good people and evil people, worthy people and worthless people...leaving little room for overlapping categories of people like civilians' (Slim and Mancini-Griffoli, 2008: 10).

Progressive structuralists show how deformed masculinities that emanate from patriarchal relations condition brutality in contemporary wars (Enloe, 1998). They also point to the legacy of colonial wars of domination, which perfected anti-civilian methods of violence owing to racist beliefs that the subject population was unruly and needed to be 'pacified' (Ramsey, 2007). Abusive post-colonial states stepped into the footsteps of their former rulers and unleashed more violence on civilians.

Why did victimising civilians become *de rigueur* only in the last 100 years and not earlier? Technological advancements in armaments have broadened the scope and scale of risk to civilians in contemporary wars compared to previous eras. One must also take into account the changed structure of war from inter-state to internal once the de-colonisation of the 'Third World' was completed. Technically, the vast majority of ongoing wars occur within the boundaries of a state rather than across borders. Of the 116 armed conflicts in 78 locations since the end of the Cold War, 94 percent were intrastate wars (Eriksson and Wallensteen: 625-627).

The 'protection crisis' that looms over civilians in much of the world is thus playing out primarily in internal war settings. Since many internal wars are represented as conflicts of identity with in-group vs. out-group dynamics, dehumanisation of the 'other' becomes more psychologically feasible. The standard inter-state wars that realists obsess about are often conflicts of interest or power rather than 'blood wars', which are the staple forms of internal conflict (Ignatieff, 1995). At the same time, many internal identity-based wars are masquerades for plunder of resources or neo-colonial conquest by military entrepreneurs (King, 2001). But the framing of these conflicts on the axis of group identity lends a particularly lethal sharpness to the disposition of armed actors towards civilians.

Being conventionally inferior to state armies, rebel groups militarise the civilians on whose behalf they claim to be struggling. Hit-and-run tactics by rebels thrive on ideologically indoctrinating or intimidating civilians into harbouring or joining them. The guerrilla mode of fighting preferred by rebels exposes civilians to state army retaliation and erodes the civilian-combatant differentiation which is canonical to humanitarian law. If 'total war' was the opening gambit in widening the impact of war on civilians at the inter-state level, Mao Zedong and Che Guevara-inspired 'people's war' has heightened the threat to civilians in internal conflicts.

Since identity-based internal war is considered an existential threat to the state's territorial unity and integrity, all means are taken as fair and justifiable in defeating this challenge. From this crucible of extenuating logic emerge phenomena like 'dirty wars', where no-holds-barred counter-insurgency methods take a heavy toll of civilian freedoms (Goti, 1996). Disproportionate use of force against civilians in the name of counter-insurgency has been passed on to states in the developing world from the example set by Britain's much-touted success in subduing Kenya's Mau Mau rebels and the Malayan communists during the 1950s (Elkins, 2005).

The relationship between human rights violations and armed conflict is mutually reinforcing. Perceived denial of justice and fair treatment provokes victims or their representatives to take up arms and seek recognition of their rights through violent means. In response, the authority against which the claims for recognition are being made could react with counterforce to suppress the armed revolt/rebellion/movement. This generates a cycle of action and reaction, with both sides committing grave atrocities in order to press home their advantage. The worst sufferers of this vicious cycle of violence (see Figure 3) are civilians, whose civil and political rights are abandoned by responsible authorities during the emergency of war.

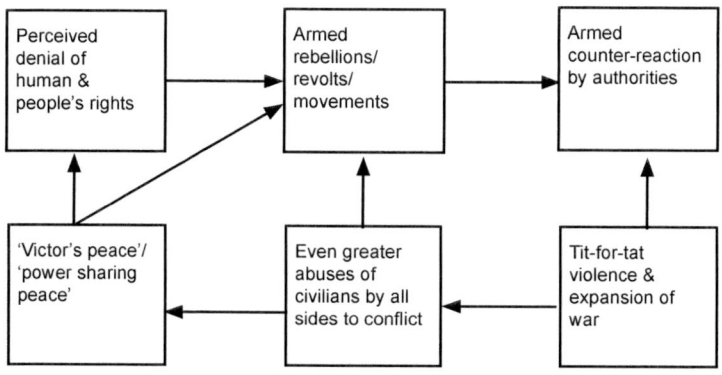

Figure 3. Vicious cycle of violence in internal wars.

Courtesy high statistical frequency of internal wars, the use of guerrilla tactics by rebels, and the excuse of extenuating circumstances by states, a global 'protection deficit' haunts civilians and begs for serious responses from national and international policymakers. The task of protecting lives in war has never been as urgent as in the present age, when state legitimacy is on fire from 'civil wars' that are 'breaking out at an all-time record rate' (Sarkees, 2003: 62).

International Organizations in Internal Wars: Searching for Relevance

The sheer weight of numbers of civilians victimised in internal wars has ignited international concern for ways and means to protect them, eliciting proposals like 'responsibility to protect' (IDRC, 2001) and 'duty to intervene' (Kouchner and Bettati, 1987). An articulate community of legal scholars, internationalists and human rights activists can take credit for unrelenting campaigns on behalf of sufferers of internal wars. By documenting and publicising the unspeakable acts of violence that accompany internal wars, they converted the plight of civilians trapped within state boundaries into an international problem.

The rise of an international human rights movement on the shoulders of a corpus of thematic human rights conventions after World War II is the lead force behind blurring boundaries between 'internal' and 'international' wars. For international opinion to accept that cruelty, genocide, crimes against humanity etc. are problems irrespective of whether a war is inter-state or intra-state, the credit goes to human rights organizations and transnational advocacy movements which universalised the previously narrowly-defined terrain of concern (Keck and Sikkink, 2002).

Yet, the climate of protection for civilians has progressively worsened in spite of the codification of numerous thematic human rights conventions applicable to internal wars. The yawning gap between law and practice is evident when one surveys the indiscriminate violence being showered upon civilians by armed actors in practically every internal war — from Colombia in the Western hemisphere to the Philippines in the East. The inability of laws alone to bring about a change in behaviour of violent actors is an instance of the larger policy dilemma of enforcing international law sans robust punitive tools (Barkun, 1968). As this book's chapters on Sri Lanka and the Philippines will demonstrate, the structure of political power — both domestic and international — works against implementation of well-intentioned laws.

Concrete suggestions on how international actors can respond to the worsening protection crisis in internal war zones have taken two forms. The more controversial scheme is of direct military interference by one state or a coalition of states in a violence-ridden country to 'save lives' if the concerned government is unable or unwilling to protect its own citizens. The second mode is to urge international humanitarian and development INGOs and IGOs to 'mainstream' protection into their projects and programmes and adopt a proactive stance in defending civilians and local activists in conflict areas. The definition of 'proactiveness' I employ in this book is *behaving in ways that directly attempt to deter armed actors from committing abuses and violence against civilians.*

A lot has been written by theoreticians of International Relations, international law and diplomacy on the first form of action — 'humanitarian intervention' — and its implications for the future of state sovereignty, North-South relations and human rights promotion. The term 'humanitarianism' has earned a black name from attempts to fulfil military motives of powerful states by riding piggyback on the internal human rights situations of developing countries (Kennedy, 2005; Chimni, 2000). This book goes further to prove that military humanitarianism is not separate but an integral aspect of the political economy of humanitarian IGOs and INGOs.

Little research exists in International Relations theory about the second form of action — the politics of transforming the behaviour of international humanitarian IGOs and INGOs toward civilian protection. Since these organizations enjoy unparalleled access to civilians affected by internal wars, they have been subjected to a global normative fillip by the office of the UN Secretary-General, some UN member states and human rights advocates to 'mainstream' protection in their emergency relief-cum-development mandates. The failure of humanitarian organizations to deter massive violence against civilians during and after the genocides in Rwanda and Yugoslavia came in for condemnation and intense criticism after 1995, leading to calls for a new 'protection culture' in the humanitarian sector (Annan, 2005: 15).

The explanation for the accumulation of a 'protection deficit'[1] in humanitarian IGOs and INGOs goes straight into the groove of Ideas vs. Power. Field-based humanitarian organizations face a different world compared to the human rights INGOs that operate from faraway capital cities and metropolitan environments. This book showcases empirical evidence about humanitarian IOs living in an uneasy zone of 'compromise' with local, national and international powers in order to have a foot in the door of internal wars.

As more and more humanitarian organizations dependent on the munificence of donors emerged in the 'marketplace', efficient delivery of material relief turned into a performance standard and overtook civilian protection as a priority. Since material relief distribution is quantifiable and technically measurable, it was attractive for donors who sought results for their money. Humanitarian organizations took the cue and saw an opportunity to grow financially secure and expand by concentrating more on relief delivery. Thus the monikers of 'aid agency' and 'aid workers' stuck to humanitarian organizations and their personnel. Through a mutual reinforcement loop between donor preferences and the culture of humanitarian IOs, organizational purpose and mandate were gradually confined to relief and distanced from civilian protection. One saw lip service being paid to 'international human rights' by the spokespersons of humanitarian organizations, but practice in the war zones turned in more conservative directions of 'business as usual' (Rieff, 1997; Maren, 1997).

Since 1995, advocates for humanitarian organizations to 'mainstream' civil and political rights have been harping that IO priorities must shift from 'biological needs' (material assistance) to physical protection of civilians from the planning stages of a field mission. The stock recommendation is that a 'security first' approach should be the basis of overall intervention strategy rather than an add-on or a public relations slogan (Jacobsen, 1999). However, as this book demonstrates, 'security' has a bureaucratised meaning for most humanitarians and trumps civilian protection as a priority.

In view of the domain overlap between human rights and humanitarian organizations, attempts have been made to build an 'interface' between the two so that they can combine to make international presence in internal wars more beneficial to civilian victims (Minear, 1999). The interface experience has thrown into relief internal divisions among humanitarian organizations between 'traditionalists' and 'muscularists'. The former are wedded to orthodox 'apolitical' relief delivery, while the latter wish to place protection at the centre of their activities in internal wars. This book shows that the divide does not stop at the organizational scale but percolates down to the individual programme managers or implementing staff members of each IGO or INGO. All the dynamics of Power vs. Ideas pan out in the arguments between these two sides, opening vistas into the deepest vulnerabilities and pathologies of the flesh and blood people that man the humanitarian enterprise.

'Mainstreaming' of protection is a touchstone for evaluating the utility of the humanitarian enterprise. Should humanitarian IGOs and INGOs fail the 'mainstreaming' test, it is doubtful whether they will survive too long as mediums that refract international agency and structure on to local stages. Civilian protection is not only a vital life-or-death matter for war-affected communities but also an existential litmus test for the unjust international structures that have captured collective organizations. This book probes why some IGOs and INGOs may have realised this moment of reckoning, while others are still doing 'business as usual'.

2

RATIONALITY AND CULTURE IN INTERNATIONAL ORGANIZATIONS

Bringing Organizations Back In

Though a heated internal debate rages on among 'traditionalist' and 'muscularist' humanitarian practitioners on whether and how to become more 'proactive' on civilian protection (Frohardt, 1999), International Relations scholars have bypassed this phenomenon's potential for re-evaluating existing theories on the determinants of IO behaviour in general. This is a manifestation of the neglect of formal organizations that has befallen International Relations theory since the 1980s due to framing of important questions under the encompassing concept of 'regimes/institutions' (Simmons and Martin, 2003). Asking important questions like what makes IOs set priorities or act upon them has been drowned out by the focus on whether institutions are explanatory, intervening or dependent variables.

The importance of researching IOs as actors in their own right and not merely executive servants of regimes cannot be overstated. International organizations deserve scholarly attention 'because they have agency, agenda-setting influence, and potentially important socialising influences' (Simmons and Martin, 2003: 193). Given their centrality to big issues of world politics like war and peace, income inequalities and development, IOs can be ignored by theorists only at the peril of systematic bias.

Without question, IOs are subsets of regimes. However, they are distinct from states and other non-state actors with effects of their own. This acknowledgement is necessary not only for theoretical clarity but for practical real world consequences. What was the role of the UN Department of Peacekeeping Operations and the UN Secretariat in the run-up to the genocide in Rwanda in 1994-95? Simply concluding with a shrug that there was not enough 'political will' among states to prevent the genocide is a half truth.

Without probing the inner dynamics of the IOs themselves, we would be left with a partial explanation of numerous happenings in world politics.

With the increasing independent impact of IOs on people's lives, especially in ungoverned or powerless spaces in the Global South, a chorus of questions is being raised about their accountability.[1] For theoreticians, assessing accountability requires bringing formal organizations 'back in' as significant research subjects. This book dovetails sentiments expressed in recent IR scholarship for the long due re-entry of IOs as actors whose behaviour needs to be problematised (Barnett and Finnemore, 2004).

Civilian Protection: Neutral Testing Ground

The purpose of this book is to underline the salience of formal organizations to International Relations theory and focus on fundamental questions of motivations for action in world politics. The broad research question guiding the book is as follows: '*Are IOs driven in their behaviour by material pressures and inducements of donor states, host states and violent non-state actors or by their own internal culture and bureaucratic understandings? Do they respond to Power or to Ideas?*'

I chose civilian protection as one arena of IO behaviour for testing the two competing explanations because the issue offers adequate chances for both rationalism and sociological culturalism to prove their explanatory strength. Civilian protection is politically very sensitive, as perpetrators of violence are agents of state and rebel groups, and these powerful actors exert pressure on IOs not to rake up controversial topics. The issue is also fertile for sociological culturalists because the meaning of what is 'humanitarian' is open for debate and serious internal discussion within the organizations. Civilian protection is neutral territory in which to test the relative explanatory tenets of all four paradigms listed in the Introduction, particularly the clashing propositions of rationalism and culturalism.

The empirical puzzle driving this book is that, over the last decade, some humanitarian organizations have adopted very proactive attitudes and behaviour towards civilian protection ('muscular humanitarianism'), while others have remained glued to their narrow specialised relief-and-development tasks ('traditional humanitarianism').[2] This disparity in behaviour in a single war zone has been observed in field evaluations of both IGOs (Kenny, 2000) and INGOs (Greenaway, 2000). Also, the same IO's branches have been found to display varied inclinations to protection in different countries (Slim, 2002). What explains the variation in organizational behaviour towards civilian protection within and across countries? To answer this, one has to first theoretically explain what factors determine these organizations' behaviour toward protection and then examine variation in those independent variables within and across countries.

My research is an instance of the larger argument about whether actors in international affairs behave under pressure and allure of material interests or due to 'social facts' like bureaucratic construction of meanings. If some humanitarian IOs are more proactive than others on civilian protection, does it mean that the proactive ones are not as bureaucratic as the conservative ones? If some IOs' branches in one country are more proactive than their counterparts in another country, does the former country setting impose less external political constraints than the latter? If the foreign policy role and preferences of great powers in one war-ridden country are different from that of the other, could it be impacting on the varied behaviour of branches of the same organization located in the two respective countries? Or is the difference in inter-branch behaviour across countries simply a manifestation of the different bureaucratic culture of each branch? In other words, does each country branch of an IO or INGO have a separate identity of its own?

Investigating these theory-generated questions in the contexts of field-based humanitarian organizations in internal wars allows a good test of competing hypotheses generated from the paradigms of political science.

Three-Cornered Fight

This book is problem-driven rather than theory-driven, in the sense that research aims to account for a specific political phenomenon (problematic attitudes and behaviour of humanitarian IGOs and INGOs toward protection), rather than being 'designed more to save or vindicate some (favourite or pet) theory' (Green and Shapiro, 1994: 7). The goal of research is not to grind an axe on behalf of one particular theory but to reach a satisfactory explanation of the determinants of humanitarian IGO-INGO thought and action toward civilian protection.

This segues into Imre Lakatos' contention that a sophisticated technique is to set up a 'three-cornered fight' between two alternative theories and factual evidence that will judge the propositions of the rivals (Lakatos, 1970). For my book, the scaffolding of a problem-driven three-cornered fight is provided by the so-called 'Third Debate' between rationalism and sociological approaches that duly or unduly preoccupies current International Relations (IR) theory (Fearon and Wendt, 2003).

Since the birth of IR as a distinct sub-field of political science, its contours have been motored by grand Manichaean narratives that last for decades and then get replaced by new debates. A theory-heavy sub-field like IR could not mature in the absence of these scholarly debates which set the academic context in which all research was conducted at a given time.

The advantage of having these theoretical bouts as backdrops was that they subsumed every research question asked during their heyday and generated healthy competition between two alternative hubs, each of which claimed to be better explaining real world events. The disadvantage was that they boxed in IR in a Kuhnian sense, making only certain 'known rules and procedures' thinkable and available in a particular epoch and deciding which were the right questions to ask at that point in time. Intellectual circumstances and possibilities were thus circumscribed in the scramble wherein two competing theories train the scholastic mind under the rubric of a great debate and 'force nature into the conceptual boxes supplied by professional education' (Kuhn, 1962: 5).

The First Debate of IR was launched by E.H.Carr's 1939 broadside against 'idealism' or 'utopianism' (Carr, 1939), loosely but incorrectly translated by some as liberalism. Carr's critique of idealism was refined and better theorised in the late 1940s by Hans Morgenthau, the founding father of 'realism' (Morgenthau, 1946). For the next couple of decades, the First Debate between realism and idealism was claimed to be the master narrative for scholarship which coloured the big question of the causes of war and peace. However, Brian Schmidt points out that it was in fact a non-debate due to the absence of a rigorously theorised and defended idealist corner (Schmidt, 2003).

The Second Debate in IR that broke out in the 1960s was epistemological and methodological. It was opened by American scholar Morton Kaplan's argument for more nomothetic, positivist and deductive approaches to research since the traditional content of historical examples and anecdotes had failed to improve IR's social scientific credentials. The orthodox idiographic side in the debate deemed deductive 'scientism' unfit to capture the moral complexities and realities of the social world (Knorr and Rosenau, 1969). A research design like this book's could not be conceivable if not for the Second Debate's 'scientism', which has friends and foes to this day (Lindlof, 2008).

In its early stages during the 1970s, the Third Debate was a reprise of the First Debate in a more coherent form. It was prompted by neoliberal institutionalism's contention that the world was 'interdependent' rather than conflictual, as neorealists claimed (Keohane and Nye, 1977). From the late 1980s to present time, the Third Debate has been locked in a second phase in which the 'neo-neo' script was overwritten by the rationalism vs. reflectivism/constructivism duality (Keohane, 1989: 161). What remained vague in the passage of the baton from 'neo-neo' to rationalism vs. reflectivism (later constructivism) was whether the division is merely methodological and epistemological or also ontological.[3]

If the ontological differences are kept aside as Fearon and Wendt propose, then the Third Debate's utility as a frame for research would vanish on grounds that it is unfair to comparatively test or contrast rationalist and constructivist hypotheses. However, scholars have distinguished between 'conventional constructivism' and 'critical constructivism', with the former understood to be interested in investigating 'possible causes of action' (Hopf, 1998 184) and not avoiding social scientific methods of showing variation in dependent and independent variables (Price and Reus-Smit, 1998). It is therefore not epistemologically inappropriate to contrast rationalist and culturalist explanations and put them to competitive empirical testing. This book does not agree with those constructivists who claim that theirs is not a theory per se and that their claims and those of rational theories 'cannot logically be opposed' (Finnemore, 1996: 27). Instead, it follows Alexander Wendt, one of the leading constructivists, who asserts that 'as if' normative (culturalist) accounts and 'as if' consequentialist (rationalist) accounts are both in need of 'more direct' empirical evidence to test their respective explanatory powers (Wendt, 2001: 1029).

Ontological disagreement between rationalism and culturalism keeps the Third Debate alive as a beneficial canvas for comparative theory testing. Should the rationalist vs. culturalist tussle lack philosophical divergence, research framed on its platform would not manage to extract more fundamental 'truths' about the essence of its cases (in our case, IOs). One of the principal ontological questions in political science is 'What drives political actors and what mental capacities do they possess?', a query that segues into 'the nature of the political subject and its behavioural motivations' (Hay, 2006: 81). Disregarding debates at this level of abstraction is to impoverish research.

This book will demur with Fearon and Wendt that synthesis between the two approaches is impossible if ontological divisions are accentuated (Fearon and Wendt, 2003). Rather, it will strive to establish that synthesis between rationalism and culturalism (or 'Power' and 'Ideas') is either feasible or infeasible depending on empirical evidence from the real world of war zones like Sri Lanka and the Philippines. This book evaluates not only stand-alone rationalist and culturalist hypotheses but also syncretic hypotheses that combine predictions of ontologically distinct paradigms and stand up for empirical validation or falsification.

The Rationality of IOs

There is sharp division on the question of what determines behaviour of IOs between rationalism and culturalism. The former's core theme is external political incentives and pressures on IGOs and INGOs which force them to think self-interestedly, while the latter's focus is on internal identity and culture of IGOs and INGOs, which make them see a problem and act upon it or just ignore the problem.

As mentioned in the Introduction, rationalism is a 'paradigm' or an abstract worldview that encompasses many lower level theories panning across the social sciences. Since this book adopts a political scientific approach to humanitarians, it is imperative to compile together all the rationalist theories (and respective mechanisms) obtaining in the discipline that offer explanations for IO behaviour.

Neorealism

Among the subsets of rationalism, the 'leading' theory of neorealism is outright dismissive of IOs (and the institutions they serve) as insignificant non-entities that do not matter in the tugs-of-war of great powers in the overarching systemic ambience of anarchy (Mearsheimer, 1994). However, the patriarch of neorealism — Kenneth Waltz — adjusted his systemic lenses after the end of the Cold War to say that devices like IOs can be helpful as instruments of powerful states in their diplomatic tussles and power politicking. His contention is that powerful democratic states of the twentieth century like Britain and the United States have been able to pursue 'peaceful means' of exerting control through IOs and institutions without having to formally invade or occupy states (Waltz, 2000). So, IOs can matter for neorealism, albeit only as implements.

Classical Realism

This older rationalist school did pay some attention to IOs, especially IGOs. To this branch, IGOs' behaviour is explained by great power national interests, direction, pressure and control. IGOs are seen as means or pawns of self-interested powerful states that place demands on these organizations to fulfil their strategic utilitarian ends. Hans Morgenthau, the founder of classical realism, saw foreign aid doled out by great powers (directly or through IGOs) as a non-military means of gaining control over weak states. Development and humanitarian aid thus 'perform a political function' for statecraft in the guise of charity (Morgenthau, 1962).

USAID, the donor arm of the US government, confirmed as much in 2004 by acknowledging that its charity plays a 'vital role in supporting US geo-strategic interests' (USAID, 2004). The controversial ascent of 'military humanitarianism', where IOs cooperate closely with armies, assist the military objectives of one of the parties to an armed conflict, or benefit from war by bagging new projects [4], is thus predicated on realist insights. To recall our observation from Chapter 1, there is a strong link between state-initiated 'military humanitarianism' and the 'rational' political economy of field-based IOs.

The second political function of IGOs that classical realism perceived is international socialisation to legitimise the dominant state-chiselled status quo in the eyes of dominated states (Schweller and Price, 1997). John Stoessinger, an early pioneer to explain IO behaviour, demonstrated that national-interests and preferences of large states overshadow the UN's agenda. His conclusion was that 'when the UN serves the superpowers' national interests, it is allowed to go forward. When it does not, its evolution is hindered' (Stoessinger, 1973: 189). Gil Loescher's study of the UN High Commissioner for Refugees, the premier humanitarian IGO, argues that its choices were dictated by American political stewardship since inception (Loescher, 2001). Eric Chester's expose of the International Rescue Committee, a giant humanitarian INGO, described the blatantly partisan use it was put to by the US government for its Cold War strategic objectives (Chester, 1995).

Practitioners of realpolitik have long found a use for NGOs as Trojan Horses in undermining and weakening rival states or coalitions.[5] Classical realists could visualise the foreign aid mechanisms by which powerful states' power translated into IGO or INGO power vis-à-vis weak states. For example, Volker Riehl explains the INGO domination of all walks of life in southern Sudan not only as a by-product of US foreign policy interests but also as 'an intended bid for political influence and direction on the part of the INGOs themselves' (Riehl, 2001: 4). Thus, the rational foreign policy pursuit of power by dominant states feeds off into the rational self-interests of IOs themselves.

Liberalism

Liberalism is a key rationalist theory which elevates 'non-state actors' as important agents in world affairs. Liberals conceive IOs as tools in the service of the foreign or economic interests of creator and donor states, but differ from realists by maintaining that the rational interests that IOs reflect in their behaviour are derived from domestic politics of powerful states and are not necessarily geopolitical or strategic in nature (Milner, 2006).

Neoliberal scholar Keohane posits IOs and INGOs as cost-saving devices that enable egoistic states to overcome collective action problems and pursue common interests under conditions of anarchy (Keohane, 1984). The implication of Keohane's take is that an egoistic state which wishes to end an internal war happening in some part of the world, but is uncertain about the sincerity of other states to share the burden, will fund humanitarian IOs as a cost-saving substitute for a more robust form of intervention and commitment.

David Rieff has shown humanitarian relief to be 'a sop to western conscience,' a cheap way for rational leaders and politicians to make people in rich countries to feel better about responses to disasters without really solving them (Rieff, 1995). There could also be rational states which do not wish to pressurise an aggressing party in an internal war for selfish strategic reasons. For them, demonstrating that they are offering humanitarian assistance is an alibi for political partiality.

Liberals expect non-state actors to have independent causal impacts and accept that IOs have a direct effect on states and other non-state actors via the mediums of multilateral regimes and institutions. For example, Xinyuan Dai argues that non-state actors have varied interests of their own and that these are explanatory variables for the degree to which they monitor state behaviour and compliance with an international regime (Dai, 2007: 26). Applying this to the humanitarian field, one can see that INGOs and IGOs in war zones have their own rational self-interests and the degree to which they will advocate and act for civilian protection and hold armed actors responsible will depend on these interests.

Political Economy

This subset of rationalism straddles the boundaries between International Relations and Comparative Politics. By virtue of looking deeper into the domestic realm of states, it simultaneously accords IOs agential potency and critiques their actions. IGOs and INGOs are seen by this theoretical lens as strategic actors operating in a highly competitive environment for donor funds and attention. Dependence on donors (states, foundations and individuals) as well as host states are considered to matter the most for IOs because they are the twin lifelines of finance and access to beneficiary populations.

Political economists especially attend to links between domestic politics of host countries and the behaviour of field-based IOs. For instance, Wafula Okumu paints humanitarian INGOs to be 'in a balancing act between the operational impartiality of the 'political eunuch' ('we are here to save our lives, politics is not our business') and the shrewd manoeuvring of the 'humanitarian prostitute' ('we are ready to compromise so that we can get through') (Okumu, 2003: 123). This book's empirical chapters on Sri Lanka and the Philippines will illuminate how and why '(international) agencies have to sell themselves to enter the theatre' (Donini and Niland, 1996).

The very language of selling and competition relates back to the functions of the capitalist world-system, because all humanitarian IOs agree that enjoying 'access' to the market of IDPs and the war-affected overrides every other objective. Pragmatic humanitarians argue that any concession to armed actors or to donor's whims is justified as long as it earns them 'access' to civilian beneficiaries in war zones. I will show in Chapter 5 how some IOs are complicit in the militarisation of parts of the Philippines by the US army, but condone this criminal collusion with the claim that they needed 'access' in war zones. That the same politics of 'access' prolongs war and endangers civilian lives is lost upon most humanitarians who propagate the impression that their material relief is desperately needed by IDPs and refugees.

Political economists advance the thesis that high financial insecurity makes material calculations, not normative motivations, the main determinants of IGO and INGO choices (Cooley and Ron, 2002). According to them, humanitarian emergencies are basically a business opportunity for IOs and INGOs and it is this facet which earns the sector the tag of an enterprise (Clifford, 2005; Maren, 1997). Roger Riddell estimates that the total flow of aid in this enterprise in 2004 was in excess of $15 billion, amounting to over 18 percent of Official Development Assistance by OECD countries (Riddell, 2007: 317). Mass displacement crises offer organizations the chance of getting their slice of this huge pie.

Such calculations were manifested in the humanitarian market principle of 'be there or die' after the Rwanda genocide, wherein IOs and INGOs overcame moral compunctions and set up shop in refugee camps that sheltered the killers out of anxiety that if they did not, some peer competitor will (Steering Committee, 1996). In this manner, humanitarians imbibe the exploitative ideology of the capitalist world-system and reproduce it on a micro-level in war zones across the world.

The Culture of IOs

To rewind to the Introduction, culturalism is a broad paradigm that includes many mid-level theories which populate different disciplines of the social sciences. Again, keeping in view the disciplinary bracketing of this book, it is apt to elaborate those culturalist theories which have currency in political science and which purport to explain the behaviour of IOs.

Constructivism

Among the subsets of culturalism, constructivism emerged in the 1990s as a main theory or approach in International Relations. For constructivists, IGOs and INGOs are norm-driven actors and they derive their sense of purpose, self-understanding and self-image from the prevailing normative climate within each organization (linked to norms of the host society in which it operates and to the norms of 'international society'). In the field of humanitarian relief, for example, constructivists see a transition between two competing sets of norms of international protection. The norms of sovereignty and non-intervention essentially protect borders. Human rights and humanitarians norms, by contrast, aim to protect individuals. Inconsistencies and mixed results in the record of IOs promoting civilian protection will be explained by the fact that 'traditional principles of sovereignty and non-intervention continue to operate, even if they no longer hold absolute primacy' (Weil, 2001: 82).

If an IO dilutes its proactiveness while working in a war zone, the constructivist explanation would revolve around how this is determined by the prevailing beliefs within the organization and among IOs as a community that state sovereignty should be respected or at least not transgressed beyond acceptable bounds. Should this IO become more proactive, the constructivist take on it would revolve around how an emerging norm (e.g. Responsibility to Protect or R2P) gains an upper hand over an existing norm (sanctity of state sovereignty).

The other constructivist take on IOs is that while they may be created or funded by states, they are 'constituted' by their identity as bureaucracies. Adam Roberts avows, for example, that the identity-derived penchant for 'neutrality' is a major constraint on humanitarian organizations when they confront protection crises in the field (Roberts, 1996). This book will elucidate how bureaucratic humanitarian IOs in Sri Lanka and the Philippines classify and categorise themselves on identity lines as 'needs-based' or 'rights-based', tags that shape their behaviour towards civilian protection.

Organizational Culture

Organizational culture theory contends that rationalist over-determinism in favour of objective material factors (power, market competition and stakeholder influence) misses an important determinant of IGO-INGO attitudes and behaviour — their *internal* culture (e.g. basic assumptions, values, norms, beliefs and formal knowledge). Culture defines what a problem is, whether it is an organizational priority or not and what the possible range of solutions for that problem is. Culture screens out some parts of the objective external reality while magnifying others. It establishes what is 'natural' and renders other patterns of behaviour inconceivable.

Though organizational culture theory was initially developed to understand behaviour of for-profit private corporations (Pettigrew, 1979; Schein, 1984; Trice and Beyer, 1984), researchers have adapted it for humanitarian IOs. Robert Walkup discerns a 'unique organizational culture type' in the overall humanitarian regime, characterised by conservatism, rigidity and delusion. He labels these traits the lesser known 'endogenous variables that affect humanitarian organizations' policy, decision-making and behaviour' (Walkup, 1997: 10).

Specific humanitarian IOs also develop 'socially constructed' organizational myths, rituals and symbols about 'presentation of self' in order to sustain their staff morale, internal coherence and loyalty (Walkup, 1997: 14). While there is a general normative culture permeating throughout the humanitarian regime, each individual IO falling under it is thus expected to have its own sub-culture which drives its programmatic priorities. This dovetails with sociologist Michel Crozier's point that each bureaucratic organization is a political sub-culture with spirals of smaller sub-cultures among different groups, bureaus, departments and desks within that organization (Crozier, 1964). The lower the level of analysis, the thicker the web of culture and norms one can discern in an IO. To conclude with Elizabeth Kier, a political scientist who applied organizational culture to militaries:

> Organizations differ in their culture and in their relation to their external environment — and failure to differentiate among them leads to an inability to account for differences in their behaviour (Kier, 1999: 19-20).

3

METHODS FOR RESEARCHING HUMANITARIAN BEHAVIOUR

A Strategy to Answer Questions

In choosing a methodology for research, the criteria should be to select one that 'helps you answer the question you are interested in, and that is feasible in your situation' (White, 1998:101). Choice of methodology is first and foremost tied to the type of question that is being asked. To recall, the broad research question of the book is '*Do IOs respond to Power or to Ideas?*' For answering it, one will need data that teases out the relationship between the behaviour of IOs, 'Power' and 'Ideas'.

The conceptual specification of this book's dependent variable is 'the degree of proactiveness towards civilian protection.' (Y) Power, in light of the rationalist sub-theories of political science, is taken to mean 'material pressures and inducements of donor states, host states and violent non-state actors.' (X1) Ideas, in light of the culturalist sub-theories of political science, mean 'internal organizational culture and bureaucratic understandings.' (X2)

Which techniques or instruments would best measure Y, X1 and X2? Y is measurable ONLY through qualitative observations. Proactiveness cannot be fully captured by monetary inputs (e.g. amount of money the organizations spent on protection projects or annual budgetary allocations in an IO for human rights programming) or head counts (e.g. number of individuals or groups that had protection problems and who were assisted by the IO). The agenda of 'mainstreaming' protection into humanitarian organizations, which forms the policy background for this book, has nothing to do with monetary spending or tallies. Rather, it is a push for qualitative improvement in humanitarian IOs and is thus measurable only through qualitative indicators gathered from close monitoring of a few cases over time. This book develops a numeric scale based on whether or not a particular case has acted in certain ways that would count as attempts towards enhancing the protection of civilians.

The coding for this scale was done by inferring from the following sources:

a) Proceedings of joint IO-INGO forum meetings held fortnightly or monthly in Sri Lanka and the Philippines in which information and views are shared about protection-related incidents and crises by representatives of attending humanitarian organizations. I personally jotted down comments from these meetings as an international civilian peacekeeper while working for Nonviolent Peaceforce, an international peace INGO, in both countries.

b) Inquiring from experienced IO-watchers in Sri Lanka and the Philippines about participation of each case in protection initiatives launched by local civil society activists.

c) Cross-checking a) and b) with views of local activists about each organization's perceived proactiveness. There are well informed local citizens groups that keep a critical watch on the activities of IGOs and INGOs in their areas. Wherever possible, I also personally spoke with civilians who faced protection threats and who had approached a specific IO. This helped me to better distinguish a proactive or 'muscular' IO from a 'traditional' one.

To measure the 'Power'-related rationalist independent variables, I used the following techniques:

a) Scouring 'gray literature' (official publications) of each IO case in both countries.

b) Securing donor states' literature about their objectives in aiding humanitarian-cum-development activities in Sri Lanka and the Philippines.

c) Interviewing local foreign policy analysts in universities and think tanks of Sri Lanka and the Philippines about the geo-economic and geopolitical motives of major donor states/great powers in their respective countries.

d) Conversing with headquarters-level and field-level staff members of each IO case in Sri Lanka and the Philippines about their relationship with donors, the host government (national, provincial and local) and the rebel group(s).

e) Collecting reports or anecdotes of all known incidents of pressure, harassment, threat, or inquiry conducted by the host government or rebels on any of the chosen IOs.

f) Analysing the specific institutions (ministries, forums, coordination committees or councils) that host governments and rebels use in each country to pressurise and shape the agendas of the chosen IOs.

To measure the 'Ideas'-related culturalist independent variables, I hewed to Kier's suggestion to avoid abstract concepts (Kier, 1999) and operationalised culture as internal organizational worldviews, beliefs, meanings, basic assumptions, values and norms. The main mode of enquiry I used for unpacking the thought systems that prevail within the chosen IOs was semi-structured conversations with programme managers or spokespersons familiar with the work of their respective organizations each country. In keeping with the method of structured focussed comparison (George, 1979), I asked all respondents questions which reflected the core research objective of unearthing the determinants of IO behaviour, and those which dealt only with certain aspects of IOs relevant to civilian protection. For instance, I could have included in the conversations with IO personnel details about the Byzantine principles and standards they employ in disbursing micro-finance loans or nutrient feeds to malnourished children. But they were left out in the interests of structure focussed comparison. I hewed religiously to civilian protection and related issues in all the conversations to avoid entrapment in the density of technical details that emanate from programme managers of multi-mandate IOs that cater to diverse sectoral portfolios.

While writing this book, I also dwelt extensively upon my own field recollections from two years of working for a peace INGO in both countries. The ethnographic 'participant observation' method is therefore, to some extent, reflected in my research.

Backgrounds and Cases

Suppose empirical observations about the behaviour of IOs and their determinants were drawn from just one internal war, they might not offer a fair chance to both alternative theories to prove themselves. Cross-country comparison is especially necessary for demonstrating variation in the rationalist independent variables, because external political pressures or 'Power' are unlikely to vary much within one country or conflict zone.

A research design in which the rationalist independent variables are constant will not be able to establish co-variance between them and the dependent variable. A single country/war zone background would rob research of theoretically fascinating queries about cross-country variations in macro-culture and their impact on sub-cultures of different branches of the same IO. Since the whole purpose of this book is to comparatively test rationalist and culturalist hypotheses, cross-country comparison is the best method for both to compete and unfurl the full range of their causal mechanisms.

Given the obvious benefits of analytical leverage from a comparative study, I chose two long-standing internal wars from south-western Philippines and north-eastern Sri Lanka as the war zone backgrounds for this book. The choice of these two specific countries was decided by two factors. Firstly, although they are both internal wars of secession/self-determination on ethnic identity basis, they are similar types of wars with dissimilar features that enable the researcher to carefully observe variation of the independent (particularly rationalist) variables.

In choosing war zone backgrounds for comparison, I kept in mind the methodological principle of unit homogeneity, which insists that cases or units of observation in research should be roughly comparable. South-western Philippines and north-eastern Sri Lanka are comparable despite contextual differences because they are both identity-based separatist conflicts that bloodily advertise the failures of nation-building in two post-colonial states that have shaky electoral democracies and roughly the same level of economic development.

At the same time, they are not identical war zone backgrounds and allow for healthy differences in state strength and institutions, relative value for great powers in global geopolitical stakes, nature of armies and guerrilla outfits, and Left-Right balance of social forces. A detailed comparison of the dissimilarities between these two country contexts is offered in Chapter 6 of this book, but we can safely assume that unit homogeneity is not being violated through my choice. Many of the generalised findings of this research are only likely to be vindicated more strongly had two even more dissimilar country backdrops been chosen.

A second and more practical reason for picking Sri Lanka and the Philippines owes to the fact that I have worked as a civilian peacekeeper in both countries and am familiar with the organizational cases as well as the protection problems faced by civilians in these two settings. Qualitative comparative research implies more detailed substantive knowledge of the cases, their peculiar traits and empirical processes as well as the socio-political environments in which they exist. Thanks to my choice of familiar wars of Sri Lanka and the Philippines rather than the unfamiliar wars of, say, Indonesia or the Democratic Republic of Congo, this book packs lesser-known empirical details that talk to theory and refine it.

Cases for this book were selected on the basis of which key humanitarian IGOs and INGOs with sizeable programmes on the ground have branches in both Sri Lanka and the Philippines, continuously for five years (2003-08). The size criterion was due to the highly representative character of big IOs in the humanitarian regime. Giant IGOs and INGOs dominate the funding channels from donors, have the maximum activities, and set the general discourse of humanitarian behaviour in war zones. Choice of big IOs as cases is also justified by the researcher's aim to improve the external validity of findings, as only the gigantic organizations have branches in other war zones elsewhere in the world. For the sake of inter-branch comparison, I left out some big organizations that are present in one country but not in the other (e.g. UNHCR or CARE in Sri Lanka and CHD in the Philippines).

The five-year-period rule was followed because organizations that began operations very recently in the field would not have accumulated enough learnings and reflections for the researcher to analyse changes in priorities over time. The policy context of mainstreaming is a temporal one, wherein IOs are being pushed by global and local activists to become progressively more participative in protection initiatives. If cases are chosen with a delimitation of five years of continuity in the field, it redounds to the richness of the theoretical enquiry about how rationality and culture vary in history.

The cases that survive all three exclusion criteria of size, place and time are the United Nations Development Programme (UNDP), United Nations Children's Fund (UNICEF), International Committee of the Red Cross (ICRC), Save the Children and OXFAM. The first two are IGOs and the last two are INGOs. The ICRC falls somewhere in between, with some characteristics of INGOs and some of IGOs.[1] In effect, this book has ten cases — the previously mentioned five organizations doubled into ten since I have two countries as the geographical backdrops.

Questions might be raised about combining IGOs and INGOs in the same bracket of cases, given their differences in origin and structures. But there is a single unifying umbrella of the humanitarian regime under which all these organizations exist, despite differences in style, ideology and specialisation (Walkup, 1997). In the issue areas of humanitarian and development aid, funding for field operations of INGOs originates to a large extent from public sources.[2] Just because INGOs lack Executive Boards with nation states as members does not mean they are any less prone to state pressures or inducements compared to IGOs. The gigantic INGO cases of this book, as shall be shown in the empirical chapters, are often meeker in advocacy on civilian protection than their IGO compatriots.

Since the ten cases share common features (all are field-based humanitarian IOs falling under the humanitarian regime), the comparative method used in this book is the Most Similar Systems Design. Had I chosen a set of dissimilar IOs coming from different regimes (human rights, development and humanitarian) operating at different levels (e.g. global headquarters-based, country headquarters-based and field-based), then it would be difficult to tell how much of their proactiveness is being caused by 'Power' and 'Ideas' as opposed to that being caused by their other dissimilar traits. The Most Similar Systems Design permits a focus on these two variables and controls for other extraneous causes, thereby reducing the likelihood of spurious correlations.

Establishing Causation and Accommodating Other Explanations

If the degree of donor state, host state or rebel pressure or inducement on the IGOs and INGOs in one country is greater than in the other, I expect to see cross-country difference in the proactiveness of the organizations in the direction suggested by rationalist theories. If the bureaucratic culture within IGOs and INGOs of a country varies, I expect to see cross-case difference in the proactiveness in the direction suggested by sociological-cultural theories. In other words, the basic method for showing causation and weighing causal strength of the two sets of theories is looking at correlations and covariance of independent and dependent variables.

Since the theory testing in this book limits itself to a small number of independent variables (only two — 'Power' and 'Ideas') so that they do not exceed the few selected cases (five), the methodological problems of control variables and omitted variable bias will remain. I hope to have minimised them through judicious field research in Sri Lanka and the Philippines which pointed to the relevance of other paradigms unutilised in the three-cornered fight design.

Of particular import here are Marxism and feminism. The former theorises that humanitarianism's objective is to restore and extend the reign of transnational capital and hegemonic states and convert Third World countries wracked by wars into neoliberal investor-friendly terrain (Chimni, 2000). By extension, the behaviour of humanitarian organizations will be dictated by capitalist donor states and neoliberal nostrums of post-war rebuilding in which capitalists of the donor states can corral, to the exclusion of competitors from other states, the market of war-recovering societies.

To illustrate, humanitarian IOs distribute food aid to refugees and internally displaced persons (IDPs) that is procured from Western corporate agro-businesses that aggressively aim to expand the market for their products. By a circular process, the aid that is transferred by USAID or ECHO to war zones in the Global South via humanitarian IOs eventually returns to the Global North in the form of earnings for Western corporations. Teresa Hayter's classic on the capitalist interests behind foreign aid in the name of 'economic development' shows how it is conditional on purchase of goods and services from the donor country (Hayter, 1971).

As brothers-in-arms of development IOs, the IMF and World Bank, humanitarians are willing accomplices in this market-capture manoeuvring.[3] It is a symptom of this alliance to see former World Bank or IMF top executives going on to serve as heads of humanitarian-cum-development IOs.[44]

The UNDP Administrator at the time of writing this book, Kemal Dervis, worked for 24 years at the World Bank.

Antonio Donini sketches globalisation of the market and Northern interventionism in the Global South to be historically parallel processes and maintains that 'it is in those countries where the market has reached the limits of expansion, where the structural obstacles to its penetration are strongest, that we find military and/or humanitarian interventions' (Donini, 2008: 32). Humanitarian IOs, by extrapolation, are sent to integrate societies that are on the 'borderlands' or 'fringes' of capitalist development. Samir Amin says in a similar vein that 'humanitarian organizations allow themselves to be made use of by the (capitalist) powers, just as in the past the missionaries — often armed with the best of subjective intentions — accompanied colonial conquest' (Amin, 1997: 73). Does the 'protection deficit' in humanitarian IOs and the corollary preference for delivering only material relief boil down to such capitalist commercial motivations? We will revisit this issue in Chapter 7, while evaluating 'conditions' for the behaviour of IOs.

As illustrated in Chapter 1, class interests had a profound influence on the early rise of humanitarian thought and they arguably still shape the behaviour and attitudes of expatriate humanitarian 'aid workers' in conflict zones. Naomi Klein speaks about the 'NGO wild life' in Sri Lanka consisting of high-end hotels, beachfront villas and brand new sport utility vehicles that generate anger and resentment among the local war-affected poor (Klein, 2007: 403). The up-market living styles of humanitarian expatriates and the utterly downtrodden civilians they pepper with aid offers a huge canvas of class privileges, dependence and destruction of local economies in war zones. It is incumbent upon us to ask to what extent IOs' proactiveness towards protection of civilians is a product of class prejudices and structures.

Feminism views unequal gender and power relations between humanitarian organizations and civilians as significant. Jennifer Hyndman stresses that the security and protection of civilians in war zones have been 'effaced by realist geopolitics and International Relations' which are gender-blind and which overwhelm humanitarian mindsets (Hyndman, 2004: 311). Helen Kinsella interprets the whole edifice of humanitarian law from the time of Hugo Grotius as built on gendered myths that women are paradigmatic non-combatants and victims of war who need male protection (Kinsella, 2005).

Charli Carpenter furthers the feminist line by citing the fundraising appeals and policy documents of UNICEF, ICRC and UNHCR to show how gender stereotypes that emanate from the patriarchal inter-state system are operationalised in war zones by these IOs. The consequence of this marketing strategy is creation of protection gaps by 'legitimising the neglect of civilian men and boys as deserving of protection and aid' (Carpenter, 2006: 92). Logically amplified, the hypothesis here is that institutionally and structurally-ordained patriarchal values correlate with behaviour of humanitarian IGOs and INGOs towards civilian protection. This structural explanation will be re-evaluated in Chapter 7.

Formal Hypotheses to Test 'Power' vs 'Ideas'

Competitive theory testing by examining empirical evidence can commence only after rival hypotheses are extracted from theories and formally stated in contrast to one another. The following rationalist hypotheses are tentative answers to the empirical puzzle of some IOs being more proactive than others:

R1: IOs that face greater material demands and inducements from powerful donors, host states and rebel groups are less proactive on civilian protection than IOs which face lesser pressures and inducements.

Auxiliary Hypothesis to R1: Powerful donors, host states and rebel groups oppose improvement in civilian protection owing to their respective vested interests in war.

R2: IOs that compete harder for scarce funds and political patronage will be less proactive on civilian protection than IOs which do not compete that much for funds and patronage.

Auxiliary Hypothesis 1 to R2: Donors and powerful political patrons have an inherent preference to marginalise civilian protection as a priority due to their respective vested interests in war.

Auxiliary Hypothesis 2 to R2: All IOs are 'strategic' actors that seek maximisation of organizational funding and political benefaction.

R3: The more the material demands and inducements from powerful donors, host states and rebel groups over time, the less proactive an IO becomes on civilian protection.

R4: The more the scarcity of funds and political patronage over time, the less proactive an IO becomes on civilian protection.

R1 is sourced from realism and liberalism, while R2 is taken from a distillation of political economy theories. Together, the two generate testable implications about the ways and means in which 'Power' enables or disables aspects of behaviour of humanitarians. R3 and R4 are corollaries that generate testable implications about temporal changes in 'Power' causing changes in aspects of behaviour of humanitarians.

Moving to the other side of the fence, the following culturalist hypotheses are a different brand of tentative answers to the empirical puzzle:

C1: IO's whose prevailing beliefs and norms privilege state sovereignty will be less proactive on civilian protection than IOs whose beliefs and norms do not give primacy to state sovereignty.

Auxiliary Hypothesis to C1: All IOs understand state sovereignty to be a norm that clashes with human rights norms.

C2: IOs whose bureaucratic culture and identity are less resistant to change will be more proactive on civilian protection than IOs whose bureaucratic culture and identity are more resistant to change.

Auxiliary Hypothesis to C2: All IOs are subject to the global normative fillip for change in the direction of proactiveness towards civilian protection.

C3: The more the strengthening of state sovereignty norms over time in national and international society, the less proactive an IO becomes on civilian protection.

C4: The more change-resistant an IO's bureaucratic culture grows over time, the less proactive it becomes on civilian protection.

C1 emanates from constructivist theory and C2 from organizational culture theory. Both these hypotheses dwell in the realm of 'Ideas' and generate testable implications about how they affect the behaviour of IOs. C3 and C4 generate testable implications about temporal changes in 'Ideas' causing changes in aspects of behaviour of humanitarians.

The theoretical eclecticism and empiricism touted in previous chapters requires us to state a syncretic hypothesis in which both 'Power' and 'Ideas' explain IO behaviour.

RC1: An IO that faces greater material demands and inducements from powerful actors *and* whose prevailing beliefs and norms are bureaucratic/ privilege state sovereignty will be less proactive on civilian protection than an IO that faces lesser material pressures *and* whose beliefs and norms are less bureaucratic and stress human rights.

There could be an IO which faces greater material pressures but has a culture of human rights. Will it be more or less proactive on civilian protection? Can it stretch the lines of 'compromise' further than an IO which faces a lesser amount of material pressures but which does not have a culture of human rights? These doubts can be clarified by adding a second syncretic hypothesis.

RC2: An IO that faces greater material pressures *and* has less bureaucratic/state sovereignty-affirming norms will be more proactive on civilian protection than an IO that faces lesser material pressures *and* has more bureaucratic/state sovereignty-affirming norms.

Is it not possible to assign clear primacy of rationalist over culturalist hypotheses or vice-versa and do we have to validate the hypothesis based on a mixture of the two? Could there be a larger set of structural conditions without which humanitarian rationality and culture lose meaning and impetus? These questions about interaction effects will be addressed in the empirical chapters that follow and the final stocktaking of the evidence in Chapters 7 and 8.

Here, it is worth deliberating on why I left out hypotheses derived from the two progressive structuralist theories of Marxism and feminism from the competitive testing research design? The problem with critical theories from a methodological standpoint is that they do not easily submit to social science techniques of formally stating hypotheses and then subjecting them to rigorous empirical testing. Moreover, had I thrown in hypotheses related to patriarchy and the capitalist world-system to the existing ones about rationality and culture, there would be a 'degrees of freedom' problem in testing because there are only five IO cases.

Also, one of the propositions of this book is that the structural 'conditions' of the capitalist world-system and patriarchy shape the immediate rational and cultural causes of humanitarian behaviour. 'Power' and 'Ideas' which determine humanitarian behaviour towards civilian protection are not alternatives to structures but rather their children (or intermediate variables). Including structural hypotheses in the mix of theory testing of the early chapters would have confounded the real causal weights of rationality and culture. To compensate for the omission of structural hypotheses at the early stages, I return to their indispensable worth in the later part of the book.

4

HUMANITARIANS IN SRI LANKA: HUNTING WITH THE HOUNDS AND RUNNING WITH THE HARES

An Abusive 'Civil War'

From 1983 to 2009, the South Asian island country of Sri Lanka was devastated by recurring cycles of war between the Sinhalese-dominated government and the Liberation Tigers of Tamil Eelam (LTTE), which claimed to be waging a self-determination struggle on behalf of the discriminated Tamil-speaking minorities inhabiting the North and East. The official government-calculated death toll of the conflict, which the international media uses, remained static for a long time at circa 70,000 people. However, Sri Lankan activists for peace and justice make the point that unreported atrocities against civilians increase the casualty totals to above 100,000 or even higher than that.[1] Millions more have been injured, forcibly displaced as IDPs and refugees or simply disappeared in the vast silences of undiscovered graves and massacre sites.[2]

Direct physical violence and psychological fear of violence are everyday realities throughout the length and breadth of the country, especially in the secessionist strongholds of the North and East where the Sri Lankan Army (SLA) engaged the LTTE in some of the world's fiercest battles.

The roots of the conflict in Sri Lanka lie in Sinhala Buddhist revivalism and nationalism. Historian Stanley Tambiah dates it to the late nineteenth and early twentieth centuries, although its mythology goes back to the Buddhist 'holy war' against Hindu Tamils from the second century BC (Tambiah, 1992). Following independence from British rule in 1948, Buddhist revivalism was married to the power of the post-colonial state and cynical manipulation of ethnicity for electoral gains. Discriminatory policies in education and employment against the Tamils were put in place by successive Sinhalese regimes in Colombo on the pretext of correcting colonial-era imbalances and redistributing the country's resources to the Buddhist majority.

The rise of militant rebel movements in the name of Tamil Eelam (separate homeland) occurred in the 1970s due to the inability of Gandhian Tamil leaders to ameliorate the harshness of the Sinhalese ethno-state through parliamentary and peaceful means (Balachandran, 2006). The collapse of the Gandhian mode of struggling for equality created a vacuum filled by India-trained Eelam guerrilla outfits, of which the LTTE emerged as the most lethal and resilient (Gunaratna, 1993). From 1983 to 2009, LTTE waged four high-intensity all-out 'Eelam Wars' against the SLA, with intermittent periods of medium-intensity war ('ceasefires' in diplomatese).

The absence of limits on the use of force by both parties in the Eelam wars made civilians, especially Tamils, the primary victims. Not a day passed in the North and East without harassment, abductions, torture, disappearances, massacres, bombings, extortion, forced displacement and threats to civilians. In highly intensified stages of the conflict, the terror also reached the remotest parts of the Sinhalese South and the capital, Colombo, where the LTTE 'hit back' through suicide bombings and assassinations as revenge for the SLA's routine abuses against the Tamil people.

Over the years, the jostling of the two warring parties engineered splits between Tamils and Muslims (after 1990) and between Northern and Eastern Tamils (after 2004). These schisms further eroded the respect for civilian lives and liberties, as a multiplicity of armed parties hunted with impunity in a war zone haze that complicated pinpointing of the real perpetrators of specific acts of violence. As in Colombia, the fragmentation of rebel groups and creation of multiple centres of violence aggravated the climate for civilian protection and exposed every woman, man and child in the North and East, irrespective of class and identity, to potential bodily and mental harm. Tamil civilians lived on the edge and died under this hazardous predicament of being trapped between both sides with no idea what to do (Nolen, 2009).

Being Humanitarian, Crisis after Crisis

IOs have been in humanitarian mode in the North and East of Sri Lanka from the early stages of Eelam War I. As a development organization, UNDP had operations in Sri Lanka since 1967 but added emergency relief components after the wars broke out (UNDP, 2008a). UNICEF, a multi-purpose IGO, had a presence in the country since 1969 but took on a specific role of catering to children in war once the violence escalated from the mid-1980s (UNICEF, 2007). The ICRC came to Sri Lanka in 1989 on the invitation of the government when a Sinhalese Marxist insurrection was raging in the

South, but it gradually became a prime humanitarian IO in the North and East (ICRC, 2008e). OXFAM-GB, another multi-mandate INGO, first arrived in Sri Lanka in 1968 as a development organization but added a humanitarian element in 1986 in response to the mass displacement caused by wars (OXFAM, 2006). Save the Children UK has been operational in Sri Lanka for more than 30 years and has all its present field offices, barring one, in the conflict theatres (Save, 2008a).

The typical actions of humanitarian IOs in the North and East up to the mid-1990s ranged from planning and running IDP and returnee camps to providing war-affected civilians with emergency rations of food, roofing equipment, essential medicines, water, sanitation and non-food items (Parakrama, 2001). The two IOs with explicit mandates for civilian protection — the ICRC and UNHCR — did try to address issues of human rights abuses with both warring parties, but their efforts hardly approximated what we define as 'proactive' in this book.

UNHCR, which is not one of our cases, experimented with an innovative plan to improve civilian protection in the North in the early 1990s. William Clarance, the then country head of UNHCR Sri Lanka, revealed that his organization could have been more proactive in spite of rationalist roadblocks, provided the culturalist ambiguities of identity, bureaucratic rigidity and debates over appropriateness were resolved (Clarance, 2006). Can the same conclusion that culture trumps rationality in determining IO priorities be applicable if one compared five organizations instead of Clarance's single-N analysis? The rest of this chapter is devoted to this query.

IOs, Conscientious to Sclerotic

As detailed in Chapter 3, the dependent variable in this book is measured by a numeric scale about the degree of proactiveness of the five IO cases. In Sri Lanka, I requested three groups to code a table listing seven actions that the five cases either performed or did not in the last five years.

The first group of coders is a grassroots-based human rights association which has been working discretely in the North and East for the causes of mothers and families of conscripted children as well as adults facing serious threats to life from armed actors. Its members are all local people — Sinhalese, Tamils and Muslims — united by common concern for the fate of persecuted civilians.[3]

Their coding of the scale, which was done in December 2008, is as follows:

Table 4.1. Group I's scale on the degree of proactiveness of five IGOs and INGOs towards civilian protection in Sri Lanka.

Action	UNDP	UNICEF	ICRC	OXFAM-GB	SCSL
Participates in or provides inputs to protection sector meetings of IGOs and INGOs falling under Humanitarian Coordination, convened by UNOCHA.	1	1	1	1	1
Intercedes for justice on behalf of relatives of abducted or harassed civilians with relevant armed actors or authorities.	0	1	1	0	0
Participates in or provides inputs to protection/human security meetings of IGOs and INGOs at district level in Batticaloa, Trincomalee and/or Jaffna.	1	1	1	1	1
Participated in temple festival vigils by IOs and INGOs to prevent violent incidents or forcible recruitment of children in Batticaloa, Trincomalee and/or Jaffna.	0	1	0	1	0
Makes field visits to areas known to be critical to show conscious international presence and deter civilian abuse.	0	0	0	1	0
Shares sensitive information on protection/ human rights and cooperates with relevant human rights defenders at the local, national or international levels.	0	0	0	0	0
Has signed civil society petitions and press releases opposing atrocities or calling for armed parties to respect civilians and pursue non-violent paths.	0	0	0	0	0
Total score for each organization	2	4	3	4	2

Note: Coding rule is 1 if Yes; 0 if No.

In this version, OXFAM-GB and UNICEF earn the distinction of most proactive, with a total score of 4, while Save the Children and UNDP jointly share the position of least proactive. ICRC comes in between, with an average score of 3 out of a maximum of 7.

The second group of coders is a set of international observers of IOs in Sri Lanka who are based in Colombo and also in the districts of the North and East. They include Africans, Asians, North Americans and Europeans who have lived and worked in the war-torn parts of Sri Lanka and closely interacted with the five IO cases.

In this version, UNICEF is the most proactive, followed by ICRC and OXFAM. Exactly matching the coding of Group I, UNDP and Save the Children are the least proactive, with identical scores of only 2 out of a maximum possible 7 points.

The third group which was requested to code the table is a low profile human rights organization based in Colombo which has point persons keeping a constant flow of communication about violent incidents and abuses of civilians in the North and East. While there is some overlap between this group and Group I, the former is more a researcher and publisher about the state of human rights in Sri Lanka, particularly in the war-affected areas.

Their coding of the scale, which was completed in January 2009, is as follows:

Table 4.2. Group II's scale on the degree of proactiveness of five IGOs and INGOs towards civilian protection in Sri Lanka.

Action	UNDP	UNICEF	ICRC	OXFAM-GB	SCSL
Participates in or provides inputs to protection sector meetings of IGOs and INGOs falling under Humanitarian Coordination, convened by UNOCHA.	0	1	1	1	1
Intercedes for justice on behalf of relatives of abducted or harassed civilians with relevant armed actors or authorities.	0	1	1	0	0
Participates in or provides inputs to protection/human security meetings of IGOs and INGOs at district level in Batticaloa, Trincomalee and/or Jaffna.	0	1	1	0	1
Participated in temple festival vigils by IOs and INGOs to prevent violent incidents or forcible recruitment of children in Batticaloa, Trincomalee and/or Jaffna.	0	1	0	1	0
Makes field visits to areas known to be critical to show conscious international presence and deter civilian abuse.	1	1	1	0	0
Shares sensitive information on protection/human rights and cooperates with relevant human rights defenders at the local, national or international levels.	1	1	1	1	0
Has signed civil society petitions and press releases opposing atrocities or calling for armed parties to respect civilians and pursue non-violent paths.	0	0	0	0	0
Total score for each organization	2	6	5	3	2

Note: Coding rule is 1 if Yes; 0 if No.

This group's coding of the scale, completed in November 2008, is as follows:

Table 4.3. Group III's scale on the degree of proactiveness of five IGOs and INGOs towards civilian protection in Sri Lanka.

Action	UNDP	UNICEF	ICRC	OXFAM-GB	SCSL
Participates in or provides inputs to protection sector meetings of IGOs and INGOs falling under Humanitarian Coordination, convened by UNOCHA.	0	1	1	1	1
Intercedes for justice on behalf of relatives of abducted or harassed civilians with relevant armed actors or authorities.	0	1	1	1	0
Participates in or provides inputs to protection/ human security meetings of IGOs and INGOs at district level in Batticaloa, Trincomalee and/ or Jaffna.	0	1	1	0	1
Participated in temple festival vigils by IOs and INGOs to prevent violent incidents or forcible recruitment of children in Batticaloa, Trincomalee and/or Jaffna.	0	1	0	0	0
Makes field visits to areas known to be critical to show conscious international presence and deter civilian abuse.	0	1	0	0	0
Shares sensitive information on protection/ human rights and cooperates with relevant human rights defenders at the local, national or international levels.	1	1	0	0	0
Has signed civil society petitions and press releases opposing atrocities or calling for armed parties to respect civilians and pursue non-violent paths.	0	0	1	0	0
Total score for each organization	1	6	4	2	2

Note: Coding rule is 1 if Yes; 0 if No.

In this version, UNICEF is the most proactive, followed by the ICRC. UNDP and Save the Children score the lowest, with 1 and 2 respectively, out of a maximum of 7 points. The low rankings of UNDP and Save the Children here coincide with their place at the bottom in the coding done by Groups I and II.

Differences in coding among the three groups are to be expected because the scale is a perceptual rather than an objectively measurable index. Except the first and the third action (participation in protection/human security meetings at the national capital and in the war-hit districts), all the other criteria are subjective and predicated on the perception and memory of the coding group about a particular IO in the last five years. However, all the coders I picked have expert knowledge of the conflicts and their judgements are far more reliable than those of non-specialists who have only surface-level inklings about field-based IOs.

Since there are differences among the three coding groups in Sri Lanka regarding the second and third most proactive IO, I took an average of the scores of UNICEF, ICRC and OXFAM-GB from the previously discussed three tables. UNICEF has a net score of 5.3, ICRC has 4.0 and OXFAM-GB has 2.25. Should we then conclude that, in the last five years, UNICEF is the most proactive IO, followed by ICRC and OXFAM-GB? A qualification is in order here. UNICEF and ICRC have some aspects of protection written into their constitutional mandates, while OXFAM-GB does not have such a specific written mandate for civilian protection in its overall organizational priorities.

What we need to control for mandated action are weighted scores for UNICEF and ICRC that reflect the true degree of their proactiveness (adjusted to their mandated protection briefs). Among the action criteria in the table, participation and providing inputs to protection meetings in Colombo and the war-affected districts are routine mandated functions for UNICEF and ICRC, because the former is chartered as a 'child rights' IO and the latter is chartered to be a 'protection' IO. Weighted average scores for these two organizations are needed to reflect their true level of proactiveness. Ergo, I deducted .5 from the first and third action criteria for UNICEF and ICRC. They still get .5 each for the first and third action criteria because they are fulfilling these mandated tasks instead of neglecting them altogether (in Chapter 5, we will see that even mandated functions can be neglected by ICRC and, to a lesser extent, UNICEF). Performing a mandated task deserves at least half recognition. Cutting half a point each is a technique I will consistently use throughout the book where it is warranted by my theoretical definition and conceptualisation of 'proactiveness'. Just because an organization attends a few meetings as a proforma fulfilment of its job description does not make it proactive in relative terms to other organizations that attend these meetings out of genuine interest in civilian protection. Weighted scores narrow (but do not negate) UNICEF's and ICRC's leads over OXFAM-GB and generate the more realistic final ranking given in Table 4.4. It must be clarified that the weighting strategy does not in any way reverse the rankings by changing the position of any organization or introducing systematic bias into the study.

Table 4.4. Final ranking of IO proactiveness in Sri Lanka.

Proactive IOs in descending order	Net weighted proactiveness score
UNICEF	4.3
ICRC	3.0
OXFAM-GB	2.25
SCSL	2.0
UNDP	1.66

What is obvious from this ranking is that UNICEF is more conscientious towards protection of civilians compared to UNDP, which lags far behind and is mired in a sclerotic stance towards the daily violence and abuses that happen in the communities where it implements its projects. It is also clear that ICRC is more conscientious about civilian protection than Save the Children by one full point. The comparative strategy to explain these differences will be to juxtapose pairs of IOs that are at opposite ends of the spectrum and to ask why one is so ahead or behind the other in mainstreaming protection. Since we have an odd number of cases, dyadic comparison will leave out the middle ranking IO of OXFAM-GB without a pairing. To make its medial position count, I will compare OXFAM-GB with IOs just above and below it as well as those that are far from it.

Pressures and Inducements: Global, National and Local
Why is there a world of difference between the proactiveness of UNICEF and UNDP in Sri Lanka, although they are both 'sub-IGOs' of the same UN family? Why is ICRC somewhat more proactive that Save the Children? From rationalist hypothesis R1, the first point of enquiry for us is to ascertain whether UNDP faces more political pressures and inducements than UNICEF and if that is also the case with SCSL (Save the Children in Sri Lanka, formerly Save the Children Fund or SCF) vis-à-vis ICRC.

Before entering into the UNICEF-UNDP or ICRC-SCSL comparisons on rationalist variables, one must differentiate the levels, viz. international, national and local, at which material pressures are exerted in Sri Lanka on all IOs to remain conservative on civilian protection. Internationally, member states at the UN General Assembly, the UN Human Rights Council (UNHRC) and in the Executive Boards influence the direction and priorities set by UN Programmes and Funds within specific countries. The Government of Sri Lanka (GSL) has diplomatic representatives in New York and Geneva who issue statements, participate in sessions and/or vote on proceedings of the UNGA, the UNHRC and Boards on deliberations relating to civilian protection in war.

GSL contested and won membership in UNHRC (earlier known as UN Commission on Human Rights) in the periods, 1957-59, 1985-90, 1992-2000, 2003-05 and 2006-08. It was particularly keen on being a member of UNHRC during the Eelam Wars to ensure that no policy initiatives are introduced at the global level which might be detrimental to the sovereignty and image of Sri Lanka. GSL's strategy at the UNHRC is to ensure that intrusive monitoring or reporting about abuses of civilians in Sri Lanka's war zones never materialises. Sri Lankan diplomats at the UNHRC have, *inter alia*, proposed candidates for appointment of mandate holders to the 'Working Group on Enforced or Involuntary Disappearances', a category of abuse which is omnipresent in the North and East of Sri Lanka.

The global lack of consistency of donor states in insisting on human rights conditionalities aids GSL's mission of foiling intrusive UN inspection of abuses on civilians in the North and East. In certain countries where donor states perceive strategic and economic gain, they press governments to make concessions on civilian protection. Where it suits their geopolitical interests and the market expansionist motives of their multinational corporations, they turn a blind eye.[4] Governments fighting internal wars make the best of this selectivity and defy donors that might wish to tag aid to improvement in civilian protection by arguing that human rights conditionalities are neo-colonial and Western conspiracies to weaken their national security.

At the UN General Assembly, GSL allies with blocs like the G-77 and OIC to religiously stonewall more robust UN monitoring and verification of human rights conditions in war-affected countries due to legitimate fears of 'humanitarianism' being used as a pretext for military invasions. When former US President George W Bush's 'war on terrorism' was at its peak, these blocs of states flooded the General Assembly with appeals that Guantanamo Bay and Abu Ghraib should be monitored first before the UN 'goes after' developing countries. The climate of impunity and selective application of human rights unleashed by Washington in the Bush era thus provided cover for states like Sri Lanka to enfeeble and dictate terms to UN country missions, of which UNDP and UNICEF are integral parts, as well as other IGOs and INGOs which represent the humanitarian regime.

GSL has also solidified clever diplomatic alliances with regional powers like China and Pakistan in the name of Asian solidarity. The presence of a supportive statist regional structure (reified through the South Asian Association for

Regional Cooperation or SAARC) gives GSL more leverage and bargaining power over UN agencies and their Western donor states. An official of the UN Office for Project Services, who knows both UNDP and UNICEF inside out, explained the mechanism for this process as follows:

> GSL can tell any IGO or INGO that is critical on human rights to 'go to hell', because it has alternative sources of affirmation from despotic neighbouring countries. In South Asia, as in Southeast Asia or Africa, regionalism can be turned into a weapon for states to assert their sovereignties and perpetuate a culture of impunity at home.[5]

Even democratic India, which has consistently called for a negotiated settlement to the conflict and expressed concern over lack of civilian protection in Sri Lanka, was forced to cooperate with GSL for fear of being outdone by China for influence in its own backyard, as was the case in Burma (Ramachandran, 2008). Thus, when the British High Commissioner or the American Ambassador in Colombo issued periodic critiques of the state's one-track military solution approach and attendant human rights abuses, GSL had fallback options in the form of India, Pakistan, China and Iran. A dissident Sinhalese intellectual further elaborated how these diplomatic manoeuvres bring unbearable pressure on all humanitarian IOs in Sri Lanka:

> I have heard from defence sources that Colombo has an agreement with Islamabad for offensive weapons to be supplied steadily every single week by ship. Japan is ready to offer unconditional economic aid without bothering about rights abuses. The result of these alternative statist supporters is to create a 'devil may care' attitude on the part of GSL about human rights concerns and great confidence in the state machinery to 'discipline' the UN agencies or INGOs to behave or else...[6]

By mid-2008, among the principal donors to Sri Lanka, only the European Union held some cards through a threat of withdrawing the Generalised System of Preferences (GSP+) tariff concessions to Sri Lanka if it did not improve its record on protection of civilians (Taylor, 2008). In December, when the trade benefits were accorded to Sri Lanka, Brussels added a caveat that they could be withdrawn if a 'pending investigation' of GSL's compliance with international human rights standards finds the state to be in breach (ATc, 2008). Sri Lankan diplomats were quick to retort that they rejected any kind of investigations and exuded confidence that they would be able to convince the EU to back down (ATc, 2008).

Why did capitalist donor states not withdraw trade privileges or IMF loans to the Sri Lankan state despite huffing and puffing about its worsening human rights record in the Eelam wars? What gave GSL the chutzpah to assume that the EU or the US will not punish it with economic sanctions or isolation in retaliation for its harsh counter-insurgency methods in the North and East?

To understand this, it is important to note that Sri Lanka has for decades been held up by the international financial institutions as the model free market economy in South Asia. Since 1977, when the United National Party — one of the mainstream Sinhalese political outfits — came to power on the platform of 'democratic capitalism' and expansion of private enterprise, Sri Lanka has been held up in neoliberal circles as a free market success with high growth rates despite the Eelam wars. Sri Lankan proponents of the Washington Consensus pointed out as early as in 1985 that the free market strategy will 'support US and multilateral foreign aid to build up the private sector', 'promote American investment' and keep 'US markets open to Sri Lankan exports' (Sabasinghe, 1985: 10).

So, even as GSL gravitated towards China, Pakistan and India for military and diplomatic backing to continue pursuing a violent conclusion of the Eelam wars, it remained a poster child for the Bretton Woods institutions. Implicit in this star status of Sri Lanka as a good pupil of the Washington Consensus was a staying hand that prevented the US or EU from forcing Colombo to halt its punitive wars in the North and East.

GSL was thus globally assured of indifference or, at worst, verbal criticism of its conduct in the Eelam wars. It translated this confidence into chauvinistic bellicosity against all domestic opponents including the LTTE and a bossy attitude towards humanitarian IOs. The integration of Sri Lanka into the capitalist world-system was thus a global-level blank cheque for it to act with impunity against civilians in the Eelam wars and to tick off IOs for advocating civilian protection.

In Chapters 7 and 8, I will return to the theme of the global permissiveness towards extreme violence in the context of the role designated for brute force in the structures of the capitalist world-system and patriarchy.

At the national level, GSL has *bureaucratic, communicative* and *direct strong-arm action* strategies to check the proactiveness of UN humanitarian agencies. When Eelam War IV escalated in 2006-07, Colombo introduced elaborate visa vetting procedures for staff of IOs in their home countries. For UN agencies to become proactive on protection, they need staff with intimate knowledge of 'the field' and good relations with local communities in the North and East. GSL knew this and began giving only short-term work visas of 6 months or 1 year to UN agency personnel so that they could never really get to know local civil society and human rights defenders properly.

GSL also commandeers the Sri Lankan English and Sinhalese news media to publish and air refutations and rebuttals of any outspoken press release or statement by a UN agency that implicates GSL for violations of international humanitarian law (IHL). A senior human rights activist explained the dynamics of the media war that GSL carries out to tame 'rebelliousness' in IOs:

> GSL is carrying out a smear campaign against INGOs and IGOs by alleging or insinuating that they are pro-LTTE forces or sympathisers of terrorists. What this does to the IOs is to further take them into a shell of risk-averseness and conservatism. Some IOs have stopped using the title of 'Protection Officer' because they now feel that it is a taboo with GSL. The effect is to further downplay human rights as a worthy pursuit within the organizations.[7]

To back up this relentless pressure on UN agencies, GSL also planted commentaries in local newspapers, radio and television channels by articulate proagandists like Rajiva Wijesinha, the former head of the government's 'Peace Secretariat', which claimed that the SLA was fighting a 'clean war' with exemplary coduct towards civilians in the North and East (Chaulia2, 2008) and that the LTE was using IOs to raise bogus allegations about government human rights in order to weaken the territorial integrity of Sri Lanka (Samath, 2008).

Vivifying the adage that 'all is fair in war', GSL also indulges in crude intimidation to cow down UN agencies that might go public about violations against civilians being committed by the SLA or its paramilitary allies. I learnt from a senior UN coordinating official that one tested tactic is to make personal phone calls from the government's Ministry of Human Rights expressing outrage and dismay at public advocacy actions by any IGO or INGO.[8]

The state's propaganda machinery is adept in turning around IGO or INGO accusations of abuses and launching *ad hominem* attacks on the plaintiffs. For instance, the INGO Action Contre La Faim (ACF) was hounded out of the country after a barrage of newspaper items appeared to depict the organization as irresponsible and guilty of not caring for its local personnel's safety and allowing the massacre of 17 of its Tamil staff members in the eastern town of Muthur in 2006. This was most ironic because all reliable evidence suggested that the massacre was carried out by agents of state with the connivance of the Naval Special Forces (Apps, 2008; UTHR, 2008).

According to the UN coordinating official I spoke to,

> There is a seething frustration and feeling of impotence in the IGO and INGO community at the lack of justice in the ACF case, which has

sent chills down the spine of the entire humanitarian endeavour in the country. Mild threats and reprimands are the staple for any UN agency which decries GSL involvement or complicity in rights abuses. GSL also pushes IGOs and INGOs to condemn LTTE's abuses as much as possible while whitewashing the state's infringements. The effect of these pressures is felt in the entire UN family. UN agencies which do take an open stand once will hesitate to advocate for rights in the future because of a) risk of expulsion from the country or victimisation; b) lack of sense of efficacy (even if they advocate or quietly take up a case of violations with GSL officials, there would be little change in policy or behaviour of the state). On the ground, field staffers of UN agencies hesitate to report violent incidents in which civilians are victims when they see that the state can go to any length to silence critics.[9]

During my 2008 field research, Colombo-based IO personnel rarely talked about pressures or inducements to tone down rhetoric or action on civilian protection from the LTTE, but these did exist for many years in the past. I personally observed in Batticaloa and Trincomalee districts between 2003 and 2005 how they used to add another fear factor to the already state-shaken IOs.

LTTE was one of the world's most paranoid and ruthless guerrilla movements which believed in tightly controlling local and international organizations in the North and East so that they did not spread 'wrong ideas' among Tamil civilians and weaken the cause of Tamil Eelam. When the organization was politically at its acme during the ceasefire agreement (CFA) period of 2002-06, M.R.Narayan Swamy writes, 'the LTTE and its founder leader Velupillai Prabhakaran looked like the masters of Sri Lanka's northeast after virtually bringing Colombo to its knees' (Swamy, 2009).

LTTE translated this virtual suzerainty over the North and East during the CFA into effective *de facto* state control over every aspect of social, economic and political life. It invented new festivals and prohibited some religious traditions that Tamils had been used to following for millennia. It extracted informal taxes from Tamils and Muslims in cash, kind and human labour. It designated area commanders and leaders for civilians and set up elaborate judicial, prison and police systems that maintained the ethos and loyalty for the organization and weeded out rival Eelam guerrilla factions. It also used its own political party, the Tamil National Alliance (TNA), and its own humanitarian wing, the Tamils Rehabilitation Organization (TRO), as institutions to represent LTTE's position in public forums like the national parliament in Colombo and among IGOs and INGOs in the districts.

LTTE had a particular interest in 'coordinating' and regulating local NGOs in the North and East, with the goal of suborning them to the organization's political and military interests. Since local NGOs could be sites for genuine non-violent alternatives to Eelam militarism, their every move was closely monitored by the LTTE's 'political wing' in district towns and smaller divisions. So enmeshed were these local NGOs in the LTTE's planning that their forums could be disbanded or appointed at will by the outfit's local area commander. Given the internally secretive and unpredictable politics of LTTE, whenever a commander was axed or killed, there would be a new man in charge who would promptly dissolve the old local NGO forum and form a new one with his loyalists as presidents or chairpersons.

From late 2002 onward, LTTE also began insisting that IOs operating in the North and East should become members of the puppet local NGO forums, since the internationals were funding and implementing humanitarian and relief projects through the locals. The supreme leader of the LTTE in the East, Karuna Amman, went further and demanded that INGOs and IGOs had to share their annual plans and accounts with him for prior approval. Karuna's mansion in Kokkadicholai (Batticaloa district) often hosted heads of IGOs and INGOs in sessions in which he would quiz them about their projects and offer unsolicited 'advice' about which villages or divisions are in need of most help and which local organizations must be taken as implementing partners.

In 2004, I sat through a long group meeting of IGO and INGO heads with LTTE area leaders in Trincomalee, when the guerrilla bigwigs harangued the expatriates about the history of the Eelam struggle and the need for internationals to 'act responsibly on Eelam soil.' A charge sheet of sorts was read out by the LTTE's 'political wing' head against specific IOs for being biased and pro-government in their project implementation. The refrain of this meeting was that IOs must appreciate the great struggles of the Tamil people for self-determination instead of criticising the LTTE for rights abuses. The allegation that stuck was that IOs were not taking the SLA to task for its atrocities on Tamil civilians and were unnecessarily raking up controversies over 'minor things' like conscription of children by the LTTE. The warning was that IOs were 'too consumed by Colombo's perspective' and should change their lenses to see the realities on the ground.

In times of high intensity war and heavy displacement, LTTE also insisted on TRO being the only legitimate partner through which international aid must be channelled into LTTE-controlled territories. The compulsion on IGOs and INGOs to take TRO as their sole implementing partner was so great that many succumbed to the pressure in return for accessing LTTE-controlled areas. Even in SLA-controlled ('cleared') areas, the eyes and ears of the LTTE were all pervasive and so was the pressure on IOs to toe the line on everything from choice of project and location to staffing and partners. INGOs like Mines Action Group (MAG) were under most pressure because their work was primarily inside LTTE-controlled areas.

Like the GSL, LTTE also had cruder violent forms of limiting the freedom of action of IOs. The most common form was to abduct and take local staff members of IOs for 'investigations' about alleged wrongdoing such as being an army informant or personal misconduct against fellow Tamils. The expatriate head of the relevant organization would have to use all her/his persuasion skills with the top LTTE district leaders to get the employees released, sometimes to no avail. Once an IGO or INGO was marked as 'pro-army' in the eyes of LTTE, its Tamil employees would be constantly tailed and harassed until they quit the job or became moles for LTTE inside the IO.

After Karuna's rebellion and split of the LTTE in the East in 2003, two centres of scrutiny and pressure on IOs arose — one from the official 'Wanni' LTTE and the other from the breakaway faction. The split not only increased the fratricidal tendencies of Eelam militancy but also broke down normal channels of communication and interaction between IOs and the LTTE. With authority changing hands rapidly back and forth between the Wanni and the Eastern faction, IOs had to bear the extra pressures of the political vacuum in which anyone with a gun could issue orders to their local staff members living and working in the interior areas.

Not to be left behind, the SLA's own 'Civil Affairs Offices' were embedded during the CFA period with every brigade and regiment in the North and East to mount the government's own surveillance of IOs. Over the years, as Eelam War IV raged, the army's intelligence operatives penetrated almost all humanitarian IOs through local aides and kept a tab on every step they took. If LTTE put 'pro-army' IOs on notice, then the army had its own hit-list of 'pro-Tiger' IOs to 'teach a lesson.' For instance, ZOA Refugee Care, the Dutch INGO, was often caught in the crosshairs of SLA investigation or harassment for alleged closeness to the LTTE (Gardner, 2007).

By 2009, the LTTE had its back to the wall in Eelam War IV. Forced to muster all its resources for the battlefronts, it lost its totalitarian control over Tamil society, local organizations and IOs. On the run against an increasingly confident SLA, its administrative and institutional mechanisms of rule were in tatters, opening up spaces of freedom for Tamils and Muslims and also letting IOs off the hook. If one were to ask IOs in 2009 if they feared interference and dictation from the LTTE, the answer would be a resounding 'No'. But historically, the pattern has been of high LTTE pressure on IOs whenever the organization enjoyed *de facto* rule in the North and East. This is explained by the fact that when a rebel movement has virtual statehood, it behaves like a state which uses violence and the threat of violence to enforce its laws and commands on society. LTTE's militaristic culture and cagey leadership style exaggerated its tendency towards the totalitarian impulse which does not tolerate dissent and penetrates every available inch of social space.[10]

From the foregoing discussion, we can summarise the material pressures and inducements applying on all IOs in Sri Lanka to set their priorities on protection in Summary Table 4.5.

Summary Table 4.5. Generic 'Power' pressures and inducements
on IOs in Sri Lanka.

a) Donor pressures to lower emphasis on civilian rights — Low.

b) Donor inducements to increase emphasis on civilian rights — Medium to high, especially when there are humanitarian crises and mass displacements.

c) State pressures to lower emphasis on civilian rights — Maximum, especially during wars.

d) Rebel pressures to lower emphasis on civilian rights — Medium to High, especially when LTTE was politically strong.

e) Provincial government pressures to hush up abuses of civilians by paramilitaries — Low to Medium, as TMVP's11 command over eastern Provincial Councils is still in its infancy.

If these five assessments convey the gist of the overall climate of 'Power' that impacts upon behaviour of all IOs, it is now moot to probe whether they vary in their application to specific IO cases.

The Unlike Cousins

Is UNDP subject to more material pressures and inducements than UNICEF in Sri Lanka? If the answer is yes, is the pressure differential big enough to be the only cause of the wide gap in proactiveness between these two UN agencies?

Table 4.6. Summary of UNDP programmes and donors in Sri Lanka.

Key UNDP Programme/ Project	Main Donor Countries
Access to Justice	Sweden (SIDA) in 2008 and Netherlands in 2007
Peace and Recovery	European Commission and Japan
Capacity Building of NHRC, Sri Lanka	Foreign and Commonwealth Office, UK
Local Governance	Germany and Norway

From Table 4.6, we can see that UNDP Sri Lanka has four key programmatic areas financed by European donors and Japan. Unlike in the Philippines, UNDP Sri Lanka's Western donors do not pressurise the organization to downsize civilian protection or earmark funds in a way that demotes human rights concerns. There was visible tension between GSL and some Western donor country diplomats in Colombo over the deteriorating climate for civilian protection and press freedoms in Eelam War IV.

GSL was peeved with what it saw as political interference in internal affairs of the country by European diplomatic missions that are UNDP's donors and were also critical of the worsening civilian protection environment during Eelam War IV (GN, 2009). GSL's Defence Secretary Gotabhaya Rajapaksa chastised some of them with the threat of 'dire consequences' for 'giving a second wind to the LTTE terrorists.' He bluntly warned that all these enemies of his nation would be 'chased away' (Patranobis, 2009).

With the exception of Japan, which 'expressed satisfaction at the efforts undertaken by the Government to safeguard the civilian population in the North' and praised GSL's 'war on terrorism' (GSL, 2009a), no other donor of UNDP has insisted on turning a blind eye to civilian protection. Concern over the dwindling safety of civilians in the North and East was one of the main reasons for reduction and closure of bilateral (ODA) aid to Sri Lanka from European donor countries in recent times (AFPress, 2009). However, IGO-INGO administered humanitarian aid has not been withheld by the West on the grounds that it 'saves lives' in emergencies. Is not continuation of emergency aid through humanitarian organizations a green signal to GSL that it can blithely abuse rights, knowing that the relief aid will be available anyway? In this indirect sense, one can speak of state-donor complicity in marginalising protection of civilians in Sri Lanka. Directly however, donor pressure to lower emphasis on civilian rights is low and not a determinant of UNDP's sclerosis.

The previous section has elaborated the ways in which the Sri Lankan state has successfully used sovereignty, non-intervention and counter-terrorism as stratagems to cow down UN agencies and prevent them from raising human rights concerns. UNDP, in particular, is subject to strict GSL control because it holds the special position of 'Resident Coordinator' for all the UN organizations in the country. As the representative of the UN Secretary-General, the Resident Coordinator is expected to 'act in conformity with the objectives and priorities of the (host) government' and 'coordinate the humanitarian assistance of the UN system at the country level' (UN, 1995: 4). Global-level pressures from states to ensure that multilateral development assistance is 'owned' by the recipient government underlines what one UN coordinating official in Colombo described as the 'structural dominance of UNDP by GSL.'[12]

Apart from the global structural limitations on UNDP, there are myriad pragmatic pressures that force the organization's priorities to be shaped by GSL. As Colombo grew progressively immune to world opinion during Eelam War IV, it demonstrated that it was under no obligation to grant UNDP continued access to Sri Lanka. The threat of expulsion always loomed like a hanging sword on UNDP officials and made them 'extremely cautious to know better than to enrage GSL.'[13]

In February 2008, Rajiva Wijesinha, the GSL's Peace Secretariat former head, released a list of local and international personalities for funding projects 'that were inimical to Sri Lanka's independence and integrity'. One of the names appearing on it was Omar Noman, the expatriate director of the UNDP regional centre in Colombo, who was accused of 'interfering in Sri Lankan affairs' (Samath, 2008). Noman was forced to quickly dissociate himself from an activist local organization's petition that called for establishment of a Global Centre for the Responsibility to Protect (GCR2P) in Colombo to monitor and report abuses of civilians in the ongoing war. His publicised dissociation asserted that 'I would never sign a petition that had any political issue involved' and that 'I only signed to expedite a regional project on the Millennium Development Goals' (UNDP, 2008b). The belief that development is apolitical while protection of civilians is political will be revisited when we test the culturalist variables.

Most interesting from the rationalist perspective here is that Noman's dissociation was printed on the UNDP letterhead but carried an approving seal of GSL's Peace Secretariat. It was an undeniable show of strength by the state under which UNDP buckled.

One of the most common refrains in conversations with UNDP officials is that 'we do not want to get kicked out by the government by taking undue risks' in advocacy or programming. The fact that as many as three heads of UN agencies had already been 'PNGed', i.e. declared *persona non grata*, in the last few years for ruffling the state's feathers is a constant reminder to UNDP personnel to keep their heads low. A senior UNDP representative in Colombo explained the effect of this fear in the organization's field work in following manner:

UNDP'S field staffers have security fears and pressures and tend to 'hear no evil' and 'see no evil' in order to keep the balance. Experienced UNDP staffers know their limits and are pragmatic to get along well with national and local authorities. Sometime ago, some United Nations Volunteers (UNV) staff members were deployed through UNDP in the North and we had to withdraw them because they were not 'experienced' enough in the UNDP tradition and were being presented by civilians with complaints about rights abuses. Army officials regularly demand that IGOs and INGOs implement shelter construction in a particular area, claiming openly that this is what is required for 'winning hearts and minds' of the newly 'liberated' (from LTTE rule) people of the East. We have to obviously pay heed.[14]

The locus of 'Power' that renders UNDP conservative on civilian protection is undeniably located in the various organs of the Sri Lankan state. UNDP's state-driven brief can be illustrated by investigating its 'Peace and Transition Recovery Programme', which began in Jaffna district in 2001 and spread to the entire North and East with a humungous budget of $10 million. What is striking about it is the usage of language. When the CFA was in operation from 2002, it was reasonable to think about a 'transition' to peace through negotiated settlement between the GSL and LTTE. By 2007, UNDP could have asked itself and the state, 'transition to what?' The ceasefire had been broken long ago and the transition, if any, was towards more and more war. Only if UNDP were totally under the thumb of the GSL's propaganda could the word 'transition' be justified.

The manager of the 'Transition' programme spoke to me about UNDP's fealty to GSL's political goals:

We are like the 'arms of the GA'[15] in 8 districts of the North and East. We closely 'coordinate' all our programme plans with the Gas, who are very enthusiastic in welcoming UNDP's work. Even the military GA of Trincomalee, who is hostile to IGOs and INGOs, happens to be extremely friendly with UNDP. Two weeks ago, the new Provincial Council authorities in the East requested to 'coordinate' our plans with them. Therefore, UNDP will have to take the wishes of the TMVP on board from now onward. Basically, UNDP cannot 'go against' GSL or do anything that would invite the state's displeasure. The 'line ministry' for our programme in GSL is the Ministry of Nation Building, which has regular consultations with UNDP about how the programme should evolve.[16]

When asked how it is that no protection component was added on by the suggestion of either UNDP or by the line ministry when the situation on the ground for civilian protection was worsening, the manager responded that human rights matters were handled by the 'Equal Access to Justice' (A2J) programme rather than the 'Peace and Transition' section. The A2J programme's line ministry in GSL is the Ministry of Constitutional Affairs, and its activities are limited to training prison officials and policemen about human rights and offering legal advice to the poor. Although it operates in the North and East, I never came across a single victim of violence by armed actors who had benefited from this programme in my two years of experiences with survivors.

GSL ensures that UNDP's definition of 'vulnerable' is defined by income classification rather than exposure to ethnic discrimination, targeted violence and war. This is why the UNDP chief described A2J on its launch as 'a project giving voice to the grievances and disputes of poor people throughout the total justice sector of this country' (Malalasekera, 2004).

The main modality for UNDP programme implementation in the North and East is 'Direct Execution' (DEX), with UNDP's own personnel delivering projects. Yet, even in DEX mode, 'in order to promote national ownership', UNDP has 'District Review Boards' for 'development planning, prioritisation and resource allocation' (UNDP, 2007B:6). These Boards are staffed by the GA and by UNDP's quietist local NGO partners which, needless to add, steer programming away from 'controversial' topics like civilian protection that risk the wrath of the SLA.

To prevent UNDP from even remotely venturing into civil and political rights domains in the North and East, the SLA keeps a constant vigil over its humanitarian-cum-development projects and releases titbits of accusatory reports alleging that its local staff members are in cahoots with the LTTE. In November 2008, for instance, the army excoriated the humanitarian projects of UNDP in the Wanni as a 'fraudulent scheme' to fund the LTTE. A right-wing watchdog on IOs that draws its information from the SLA pounced on the news and denounced UNDP as follows:

When UNDP initiates a project for development of Wanni civilians, the terrorist organization (LTTE) decides who works for the project, and these aid organizations are persuaded, or coerced, to do what the terrorists want. (LankaWeb, 2008).

Objectively assessed, the material pressures UNDP faces at the time of writing are primarily from GSL rather than LTTE. When the rebels were stronger, they did exert control on UNDP's projects, especially after the tsunami natural disaster of December 2004. UNDP and international financial institutions such as the Asian Development Bank and the World Bank had initially 'coordinated' with LTTE after the tsunami, but they later cut these linkages to avoid angering GSL.

As the default Resident Coordinator, UNDP has to play host to specialised UN human rights actors and mandate holders like rapporteurs. The UN Human Rights Adviser's post, based in Colombo, is therefore arranged in a way that it falls under 'care of' UNDP. It is worth mentioning that the visa-issuance for new appointees to this post is drawn out over several months by GSL, during which elaborate background checks are performed on the person in her/his home country. One Human Rights Adviser in Colombo was not allowed to have her independent office with monitoring capacity and simply placed into the conservative cubicles of UNDP. I learnt from reliable sources within the UN complex in Colombo that the 'Human Rights Adviser has been informed point blank by UNDP that highlighting civil and political rights problems would 'put off the government' and 'jeopardise our programmes.'[17]

Thus, from being a dependent variable that adjusts its priorities according to the will of the state, UNDP sometimes moves one step upward into comradeship with GSL to suppress attempts at pushing the profile of civilian protection to the fore of the UN country mission. To say that UNDP Sri Lanka sabotages the New York and Geneva-level normative push for mainstreaming protection in the humanitarian sector would not be an exaggeration.

How does this dossier of 'Power' pressures and inducements on UNDP compare to those which impinge upon UNICEF? R1 would lead us to believe that the pressures are relatively a lot milder on UNICEF. The main donors of UNICEF Sri Lanka's humanitarian programmes in the North and East are Western states — Australia, EU members and the USA — all of whom accord high priority to the cause célèbre problem of 'child soldiers'. At its peak, children are believed to have comprised 40 to 60 percent of the LTTE's fighting cadres (Singer, 2006:33), of whom 44 percent were girls (Reuters, 2007). Since the 2002 CFA, UNICEF grew to be the leading advocate and supporter of the rights of underage conscripts to be released from LTTE custody and an active participant in grassroots strategies to prevent future abductions of children for combat purposes. UNICEF's spearheading of the anti-'child soldiers' campaign in the North and East received wholesome support of its donors.

Apart from protection of children in armed conflict, UNICEF Sri Lanka is a vast production house of programmes in many sectors of humanitarian activity like water, sanitation and hygiene (WASH), nutrition, health and education. When I quizzed a senior UNICEF official whether the personnel of these other sectors mainstream protection when they are implementing their respective projects in the field, he replied as follows:

> It depends on the donor for a particular project. If the donor stipulates that money should only be used on 'WASH' for IDPs, then mainstreaming protection becomes difficult. Japan, for example often earmarks funds specifically for socio-economic issues and does not like recipient IGOs or INGOs to go beyond them. Yet, overall, we have good donor backing to pursue protection programmes.[18]

Thus, with respect to the donor community barring Japan, UNICEF enjoys the same amount of inducements that UNDP has to emphasise civilian protection. The real difference between the two organizations is in pressures from GSL and the LTTE. A member of UNICEF Sri Lanka's protection section explained to me that UNICEF has the unique advantage of enjoying state inducements (not pressures) to be proactive on child protection in the North and East:

> One of the reasons for children in armed conflict becoming a major issue in Sri Lanka for donors, international organizations and the media is that GSL has been very active in using it as a stick to paint the LTTE as a 'bad' terrorist organization. The state has highlighted this aspect of LTTE's organizational makeup in a bid to denigrate it in the eyes of the world. By raking up the issue, GSL can also lay claim that it is fighting not only for Sri Lanka's territorial integrity but also to liberate Tamil children who are abducted and conscripted by an evil ogre that snatches children, i.e. the LTTE.[19]

LTTE's proscription by most countries as a terrorist organization owed mainly to two extremist tactics of the organization— the perfection of suicide bombings and child conscription, both of which fall under the category of abhorrent practices in world opinion.[20] The global ban on LTTE hurt its military and financial supply lines and gave the SLA a decisive advantage in Eelam War IV. GSL instrumentally led on UNICEF and the international media to highlight the 'child soldiers' problem and embarrass the LTTE. The stronger the push from GSL and donors, the more UNICEF gained the courage to advise and confront the LTTE to release its child conscripts back to their families. That UNICEF, along with SCSL, UNDP, TRO and the International Labour Organization (ILO), could 'facilitate the development' of the Action Plan for Children Affected by War in 2003 (UNICEF, 2008) was only possible with the material inducements of powerful actors. Under the Action Plan that was signed with GSL, the LTTE promised on paper to stop using children as combatants, a verbal victory for UNICEF (though not a real one).

Are we to conclude that UNICEF is more proactive on civilian protection than UNDP because, unlike the highly pressured and dissuaded latter, the former has enviable material inducements to tackle protection problems? The complicating aspect here is that as the CFA broke down and gave way to Eelam War IV, a new set of material pressures on UNICEF to downplay child conscription emerged from within the GSL in eastern Sri Lanka.

The TMVP, which split from the LTTE in the name of the Tamils of the East who were marginalised by the 'Wanni elites', continued many of the impunities of LTTE in Batticaloa, Trincomalee and Amparai districts. Karuna Amman's cadres, although repudiating the leadership of Prabhakaran, were virtually indistinguishable from LTTE enforcers in the nature of their brutality on Tamils and Muslims on the ground. Being GSL's ally after March 2004 offered TMVP political and legal cover to carry on abuses of civilians, especially children, without being bothered by the state's media and intelligence arms.

When I asked the senior UNICEF official quoted earlier about pressure from the GSL and TMVP to conceal conscription of children done by pro-government militias in the East, he was reluctant to speak frankly but indirectly admitted that TMVP's child conscription was a challenge to UNICEF:

> The fact that the new Chief Minister, Pilleyan (a protégé of Karuna), is himself a former 'child soldier' might bring future pressures on UNICEF if it exposes or acts against conscription of children done by his men. Pilleyan denies he is encouraging fresh conscription of children, but it is happening in hundreds of villages across the East with his organization's imprint.[21]

I have since been able to confirm that GSL is indeed mounting severe pressure on UNICEF to stop advocating or acting against the TMVP's excesses on children and their resistant families. As with LTTE in 2003, UNICEF succeeded in persuading GSL and the TMVP to sign another Action Plan in December 2008 (ATa, 2008). My sources in the East have since informed me that this agreement on paper has not been realised in practice. UNICEF faces powerful political and paramilitary obstacles to bring the TMVP to book for its continued policy of conscripting children for training and combat. What kind of pressures has UNICEF faced from the main target of its proactiveness — the LTTE? Initially, it accused UNICEF of committing 'errors' and 'misunderstanding the reality' (TN, 2005) and even threatened local Tamil and Muslim personnel of UNICEF with consequences if they worked for an organization that was undermining the military capabilities of 'Eelam forces.' Since the issue of children in armed conflict kept growing in public gaze and was defaming the LTTE around the globe, the organization decided to change its policies. Instead of threatening or using force on UNICEF personnel, it began to:

cleverly wait until a child grows older than 18 years and then abduct her/him. Many households are marked in advance for children whose nineteenth birthday is around the corner. As soon as the day arrives, the knocks come on the doors to hand over the boy or girl since it is now 'legal' to conscript them. If UNICEF perchance raised the cases of abductions and other violations of persons older than 18 years with the LTTE (or even GSL), they would respond coolly by reminding the organization that 'it is not UNICEF's business' as it is only a children's organization.[22]

Mandate rigidity or flexibility in IOs (e.g. whether or not 'overage recruitment' falls within UNICEF's mission) can thus be a function of 'Power' pressures and not just of 'Ideas'. Overall, notwithstanding the TMVP factor, UNICEF faces lesser material pressure from GSL or LTTE to hinder its protection work than UNDP.

But the difference in 'Power' pressures faced by the two UN IGOs is not that large as to be causing the 2.64 point gap in proactiveness (see Table 4.4 earlier in this chapter). Like UNDP, UNICEF has been kept on its toes by GSL's IO-baiters. Sinhalese chauvinists have accused UNICEF of providing 'combat rations to terrorists' and campaigned for 'measures to expel LTTE–friendly UNICEF officers' (DN, 2007; Heendeniya, 2007).

In December 2007, UNICEF was censured in the state-run media for the high energy biscuits that it was supplying to civilians in the North. Noting that the biscuits were manufactured by a defence contractor in France and had military seals on them, GSL's agents planted numerous stories about UNICEF being hand-in-glove with the LTTE. This was timed by the government to deflect attention from its budget session in parliament, where the ruling party needed the numerical backing of MPs from the xenophobic Sinhalese party, JVP, which saw itself as the watchdog against 'pro-LTTE IOs'. The combat rations controversy also coincided with the SLA's bid to check UNICEF's advocacy against the TMVP's conscription of Tamil and Muslim children.

UNICEF's refusal to endorse the SLA's claims that an orphanage it bombed in the North in August 2006 housed LTTE fighters rather than scores of schoolgirls (Xinhua, 2006) irritated Sinhalese chauvinists in and out of the government, who believe that IOs are duty bound to notarise the state's 'war on terrorism.' UNICEF was also subjected to 'focussed criticism' in June 2007 for sending international and local staff members to attend a protest against the abduction and killing of two Sri Lankan Red Cross workers, suspected victims of a government hit squad (LST, 2008a). In January 2008, rightist Sinhalese Diaspora lobbies launched a petition urging the Sri Lankan president to expel the UNICEF Country Representative for meeting the LTTE's political wing, an action which allegedly 'threatened Sri Lankan sovereignty and territorial integrity' (ATb, 2008).

Fear of being shown the door or simply 'PNGed' by GSL existed in the minds of UNICEF staff members I spoke to in 2007 and 2008. Thus, even though UNDP is more co-opted and silenced by GSL than UNICEF, the gap in pressures and inducements is not that marked to be causing the two UN agencies to be at polar ends of the proactiveness scale. For the causes of the unexplained variation in the dependent variable, we need to examine the differences in 'Ideas' between the two organizations.

Is UNDP's low proactiveness vis-à-vis UNICEF an organizational culture problem as hypothesised by C1 and C2? From the starting blocks of hiring staff itself, UN agencies bring in employees who are specialists in different humanitarian sectors with zero or minimum awareness of the larger UN Charter goal of protecting civilians and preserving their rights. UNDP's field staffers are not known for sharing sensitive information gathered about abuses of civilians and possible remedies.

According to a UN human rights official who has dealt with UNDP's arcane bureaucracy for a long time,

> UNDP personnel sincerely believe that civilian protection is 'not their job.' They do not think in terms of 'rights'. They see themselves as catering to civilian 'needs'. Where they do stress 'rights', it is economic, social and cultural rights only rather than civil and political rights. They remind themselves and tell me often that they are state creations and should act as 'partners' of governments, not as foes or critics. Overall, protection consciousness and action has not permeated much into UNDP's labyrinthine bureaucracy, which sees its mission as supporting the state's capacity (read power) instead of eroding it.[23]

The UN coordinating official I cited earlier concurs that:

> Knowledge of IHL is weak or non-existent among staff of a number of
> UN agencies. UNDP, in particular, has supreme ignorance about civilian
> protection problems. There is a general system-wide UN understanding
> that protection cross-cuts narrow agency-specific mandates and sectoral
> priorities, but acting on this awareness is rare. Even though civilian
> protection is one of the three 'Strategic Priorities' of the humanitarian
> community's vision in Sri Lanka, it is far from becoming a second nature,
> especially not in UNDP, which believes that protection is not its cup of
> tea and can be passed on to the shoulders of UNHCR and UNICEF.[24]

This is supremely ironic because UNDP was one of the earliest IGOs
to initiate thinking about the interface between development and civilian
protection (UNDP, 1998).[25] Throughout this book, I will draw readers'
attention to a massive gap between rhetoric and reality among humanitarian
IOs. UNDP epitomises this hypocrisy.

For a snapshot of the sanctum sanctorum of UNDP's sclerotic culture, I
spoke to an ex-UNDP staffer who had moved on to another UN agency. His
observations deserve lengthy quotation:

> UNDP is an incredibly bureaucratic organization with an obsession
> for 'following procedures'. It views itself as a 'governance' organization
> rather than a protection or human rights actor. Its mandate is very broad,
> within which there is plenty of space to innovate in favour of civilian
> protection. However, that rarely happens because its internal politics are
> highly conservative and its thinking is outdated. For example, the Equal
> Access to Justice programme could have been much more meaningful
> than it actually is, but for some mouldy values. UNDP often pumps
> funds into various Sri Lankan government bodies which are notorious for
> corruption. That is why its relationship with the government is cosy and
> the former tends to see whatever the government does with appreciation
> rather than criticism. Conscientious UNDP personnel sense that their
> organization is an instrument of government policy, especially in the
> recently 'cleared areas' of the East, where it is assisting in reconstruction
> and 'transition recovery' that serve GSL's strategic objectives. Yet, this
> knowledge of being used as a tool does not bring about any change towards
> a more balanced approach because of the personal stakes — people do
> not wish to forsake their cushy UN jobs and status. Compromise for the
> sake of retaining personal benefits is very common trait of staff members

in UN agencies. UNDP is also notorious for passing the buck and not having anyone finally answerable for a project or activity. The absence of responsibility and accountability in its work culture make it a hub of opportunists and careerists who have little idealistic motivation to feel the plight of victims of violence in the war zones.[26]

These testimonies leave little doubt about the deeply state-subservient and opportunistic culture of UNDP officials, whose dehumanising traits match Hannah Arendt's definition of a bureaucrat to the hilt: 'Except for an extraordinary diligence in looking out for his personal advancement, he had no motives at all' (Arendt, 1963: 287).

My personal encounters with UNDP expatriates in Sri Lanka over the years confirm the previously stated views. A senior UNDP representative's thoughts on her organization's work shed light on bureaucratic 'pathology':

> The goal of UNDP is 'state capacity building'. So, we try to strengthen institutions in the government that could address human rights problems like the National Human Rights Commission project funded by the UK. Our task is to make the institutions functional rather than to directly participate in protection activities.[27]

When I questioned if some of the institutions being strengthened could not be biased and prejudiced in conflict areas, the response was:

> Yes, that is where UNDP has to think in terms of 'Do No Harm'. UNDP field offices perform very thorough social and economic analysis of an area before, during and after a project to avoid unintended harm.[28]

UNDP Sri Lanka's bureaucratic routine does not include political analysis as a preparatory tool to minimise its pro-GSL bias and the attendant discrimination and harm towards civilians who are punished for suspected loyalties to the LTTE. Humanitarian practitioners had written ten years ago about how ignoring political analysis and simply relying on socioeconomic mapping of recipient communities leads to inadequate attention to protection issues (Danida, 1999). To this day, humanitarians and development workers remain weak at political analysis and often miss protection in their conception of what might or might not be a problem or a 'need' of civilians in the field.

UNDP has national and district-level Steering Committees to administer Conflict Prevention and Recovery (CPR) projects. It claims that these Committees 'have proven effective in bridging civil society and government participation in the humanitarian response' (UNDP, 2007a: 11). In reality, the Community Based Organizations (CBOs) and Civil Society Organizations (CSOs) who are picked to these Committees are all money-minded local groups that are chosen on technical criteria like deliverables, payment, financial reporting procedures and capacity to implement projects in agreement with UNDP's own objectives. UNDP's criteria for selecting them includes questions like, 'Does the CSO share UNDP's principles of human development?' and 'Does the CSO have partnership with government/UN agencies/private sector/ foundations/others?' (UNDP4, 2007: 23-24).

The cultural need for conformity of local groups to UNDP's ideology of 'peace and development' is paramount in choosing docile partners that are known to steer clear of 'controversial' issues like human rights and civilian protection.

Clifford Bob has written that IOs approach and fund 'those who will listen' and frame their work in the idiom that the IOs like and wish to propagate in the field (Clifford, 2005: 21) The more radical and critical a local movement, the less is its likelihood of getting into the good books of IOs. This policy has obvious rationalist rationales of political correctness and 'playing it safe' with the authorities. For instance, UNDP never risks angering the district GA by taking on local partners that are proactive on civilian protection. But there is a deeper cultural factor behind this behaviour, which is the need to seek conformity among local organizations for the overall 'economic rights' ideology of UNDP in which civil and political rights of civilians have no value.

In Chapter 7, I will show how this ideology is intrinsic to the needs of the capitalist world-system and patriarchy, the two structural overheads under whose watch the humanitarian enterprise opens shop in war theatres.

Lacking proactive local partners, how do UNDP's expatriate bosses learn about the abuses and sufferings of civilians at the hands of armed actors? I asked the manager of the 'Transition' programme and received this response:

I get most of my information about sensitive rights abuses from our 80-odd field staff members in the North and East who are implementing this programme in 'Dex' (Direct Execution) mode. UNDP field staffers are conscious of protection problems in the areas they work and I am very proud of their knowledge and conscientious behaviour on this count. Often, when I visit the field, they tell me that something terrible happened in this village so that I am aware of the human rights background of the place. UNDP operates very closely with UNHCR in deciding beneficiaries (i.e. returnees for whom micro-credit is provided). Of course, the list of beneficiaries is also finalised on the basis of consultation with the Gas. Sometimes, if UNHCR finds that IDP returns are involuntary, UNDP would not build houses or provide loans to such communities because it would amount to being accomplices in abuse of IDP rights. This is one example of how UNDP has mainstreamed protection. But in general, you must understand that the Peace and Recovery programme is not about protection. The Peace and Recovery section's aim is to make IDP returns sustainable, not to advocate for human rights. Actually, human rights issues are handled by UNDP's Governance programme, not by the Peace and Recovery programme.[29]

A number of loopholes arise with regard to this defensive account. Firstly, as we have seen in the coded proactiveness scales, UNDP's field staff members hardly tell anyone else than their own programme managers about atrocities in the villages that they regularly visit. There is no conscious international presence involved in UNDP's visits to project sites. Secondly, since UNDP was heavily involved in assisting IDP returns in the East, how could it possibly 'mainstream' protection without participating in the UNHCR-led Protection Sector meetings at the district level? Thirdly, how can any return of IDPs be 'sustainable' without adequate protection and advocacy for it by the IO that is directly in charge of the repatriation process?

All these anomalies lead us to the main question of what kind of 'peace' UNDP is promoting in Sri Lanka by ignoring the core issues of impunity and lack of justice for civilians. Activist scholar Sumanasiri Liyanage has critiqued 'liberal peace' during the CFA period, whose main failure was the downplaying of civilian protection issues and overplaying of 'economic development' by the GSL, LTTE and IOs (Liyanage, 2008). Patricia Daley's book on Burundi also conceptualises 'liberal peace' as a favourite ideological recipe of humanitarian IOs which comes out of Western conflict resolution models that exclude the mass of civilians from political negotiations and politics itself (Daley, 2008). Humanitarians like UNDP internalise the culture of liberal peace and de-politicise civilians into 'beneficiaries' of loans or relief handouts who are required not to raise their voices against violence and abuses by armed actors.

Are UNICEF Sri Lanka's cultural 'Ideas' more progressive than UNDP's? My own experience of meeting and talking with UNICEF officials suggest that they think relatively more proactively about making interventions that will improve the protection environment for civilians. UNICEF's personnel visualise protection structures at the grassroots level that can be self-supporting deterrents against the crushing quotidian impositions and extractions of armed actors. One of the commonly repeated ideas within the organization is the notion that good leadership qualities have helped it face political pressures and avoid dilution of the identity of the organization as a 'rights-based IO'. According to a senior member of the Protection Section,

> The personality of UNICEF's leaders is a key factor in how its country mandate is interpreted and how political pressures are managed. If the head of a country office decides to 'keep a low profile' and not venture into advocacy or action for human rights, then the organization will pull back from 'stretching' its mission into sensitive domains. Leaders with vision and creativity can 'balance' pressures of getting rapped or 'PNG'-ed with commitment to universal moral standards that the UN represents.[30]

Liam Mahony, one of the pioneers in international civilian peacekeeping, has recommended that IOs should always be on the lookout for 'stretching' entry agreements with governments and rebels so that they have 'the flexibility for activities necessary to improve protection' (Mahony, 2006:144). UNICEF's current leadership reflects a consciousness in this direction. A UNICEF staffer concurs that leaders with the acumen to push the envelope on protection have taken the organization in a more proactive direction:

> Personalities of UNICEF leaders matter a lot in determining how proactive the organization is towards human rights. For instance, the present head of office in Killinochhi is taking a different approach from his predecessor on the issue of coercive recruitment of children. I can say that UNICEF's protection mandate is subjectively interpreted by individual personalities who have decision-making authority as there is no institutionalisation of protection culture per se.[31]

One important factor about the primacy of personalities in determining an IO's behaviour towards civilian protection is the level at which a leader is operating. Suppose we are looking at UN Secretary-General Ban Ki-Moon at the global headquarters in New York, he operates as a leader of the entire system and can hardly change much of the organization's culture compared to his predecessor Kofi Annan. But as one comes down to the level of a country headquarters of a UN agency, there is room for personality to make a greater difference. Even further down, at the level of a field office in the North and East, a leader of an IGO or INGO has even more leverage to mould the attitudes of her or his staff in favour of or against proactiveness towards protection. This is because the field office is a sub-unit of the whole system, with more concentrated power for the leader and less checks and balances which slow down reform of beliefs and values at the top of the system.

When I asked a UNICEF programme manager how worried the organization was about local staff members' physical security owing to the fact that they work on risky protection projects in the North and East, she gave a refreshingly different reply from UNDP:

> This is a bogey peddled to cover up conservatism, because I know of no IGO or INGO's local staff being persecuted or killed for assisting human rights survivors. Targeting of local staff of IGOs and INGOs is more due to armed groups having suspicions about their loyalties to this rebel or paramilitary faction or that.[32]

UNICEF has local Sri Lankan implementing partners involved in child protection in the North and East, but their identities are kept confidential due to the serious security threats they face. Like UNDP, UNICEF's local partners are chosen on the basis of a thorough vetting procedure for their capacity, accounting and financial practices, a process called 'NGO Profiling' by insiders. But unlike UNDP, partners for sensitive protection activities are chosen specifically on the criteria of their proactiveness and proven credentials in rescuing abductees or persecuted civilians.

Since UNICEF has multiple focus areas in the North and East, I enquired from the Protection Section whether there is any bureaucratic wrangling among the different units that might hinder the organization's proactiveness on protection. Their response was as follows:

> There is no competition per se among different Sections of UNICEF for funds, because unearmarked funds from UNICEF headquarters are divided to make sure each Section gets its due. Donors permitting, sometimes our Education Section staffers implement the Protection Section's work in the field. Protection is well understood to be a cross-cutting concern within the organization and it is not grudged by other Sections. UNICEF's self-image is that of a 'protector of children's rights' and, naturally, this helps in mainstreaming protection, no matter what we do as specialists. Fortunately, there is no bickering over the primacy of protection because all of us believe that protection is the intended end result of our respective Sections.[33]

Unlike UNDP, where one Section passes on the buck to the other saying that it is not 'in charge' of protection, UNICEF's recent leadership has been able to develop an ethic of protection that metastasizes into the entire organization.

In spite of these positives, as one of UNICEF's own aforementioned officials admitted, the organization has not institutionalised protection to the extent possible. To understand why this is so, we have to dissect the meanings and symbols that the organization attaches to the material 'Power' that stymies proactiveness of IOs in Sri Lanka. I asked a UNICEF manager what the organization can do when its face-to-face representations on behalf of abducted or disappeared children do not bring about their release by armed groups. The answer was:

> Well, that is where powerful actors have the final say. We can earnestly try to persuade the perpetrators to release the children, but it is not always successful. And then, if we are seen to be persistently enquiring after a case even after an armed group denies having abducted that group of children, it would be read as a sign of aggression on our part and cause friction with the authorities. At the end of the day, our courage stops when the other side is carrying a loaded gun.[34]

The 'persistence' that is referred to previously is a sign of institutionalisation. Another sign is to see if UNICEF has managed to break out of the mould of being a *child* rights organization by acting and advocating for adult civilians who are subject to abuses. I asked a UNICEF official if he felt a moral dilemma that because of his organization's forceful advocacy for prevention and release of abducted child conscripts, adults get rampantly coerced to join armed groups. His answer was more bureaucratic than I expected:

> The Convention on the Rights of the Child gives us the legal authority to convince armed actors to refrain from conscripting children. But there is no such covering law for conscription of adults. LTTE and TMVP exploit this gap very well. UNICEF is handcuffed from doing much for those civilians above the age of 18.[35]

While not denying the pressures for 'mandate' restriction on UNICEF by strategic armed actors, I also found a certain rigid strictness with which the organization's personnel interpreted their mission as primarily restricted to protection of children and their families. A UN coordinating official told me that UNICEF's participation in Protection Sector meetings is active, but limited to cases where children are involved. Any report on human rights in the war zones of Sri Lanka will reveal that children are not the only or even the most frequently targeted categories of civilians by armed actors. UNICEF's self-defined distance from protection of adult civilians remains a normative failure that is not adequately captured in its ranking as the most proactive IO in Sri Lanka.

Returning to the comparison with UNDP, we can conclude that the two culturalist hypotheses, C1 and C2 stand vindicated. The variation in 'Ideas' between the two organizations is wide enough to be causing the large gap in proactiveness towards civilian protection. This finding is clearer than the more ambiguous validation of R1, which was not conclusive due to the lack of cross-country comparison. Until we reach Chapters 6 and 7, no proper validation or falsification of R1, R2 and the combinatorial hypotheses (RC1 and RC2) will be in order.

Proactive Reincarnation

Up to now, we have not performed tests on the temporal rationalist and culturalist hypotheses, R3, C3, and C4. UNICEF Sri Lanka provides an excellent case for evaluating their respective explanatory powers.

UNICEF Sri Lanka had not always been highly proactive on civilian protection. Instead, it grew over time to become the most proactive IO from among our five cases. What explains UNICEF's change in a more progressive direction over a course of 5 years (2003-08)? Is it changes in 'Power' or 'Ideas' or a mixture of the two?

Had I asked the three groups of coders to fill in the proactiveness scale in 2002-03, UNICEF would have received a net score of 2.0 out of a maximum of 7 rather than the 4.3 that it got at the end of 2008. In the early days of the CFA, UNICEF was quite similar to UNDP in bureaucratic conservatism and over-cautiousness towards sensitive topics like civilian protection. In 2003, an incredulous UNICEF district head in the East asked me why Nonviolent Peaceforce (for whom I worked at that time) was associating with certain activist local individuals and groups if they were not our 'implementing partners' who received funding from us.

UNICEF's idea of 'local civil society' in 2003 was strictly one of sub-contractors who could be tasked to execute an IO's projects in a technically efficient and managerially sound way. When its district chief saw that Nonviolent Peaceforce was opening up a new model of linkages between international and local activism sans monetary give-and-take, it rattled her bureaucratic sense of what an IO should be doing in a dangerous war zone. In her routinised rule book, IGOs and INGOs had to be 'careful' about radical local human rights defenders, lest working with them would compromise the 'neutrality' of the IO. This suspicious approach to local activists and passive definition of 'neutrality' led to an underachievement of UNICEF's potential to make a difference to the grave civilian protection environment during the early years of the CFA.

UNICEF's standard operating procedure with regard to violence against children by armed actors before 2004 was to document grievances with full particulars of the victims and their relatives, and then to present these details at face-to-face weekly coordination meetings with the political representatives of the SLA and the LTTE. The standard reply of the accused armed party was that the cases brought up by UNICEF were malicious propaganda against it and that 'we are not responsible for any of these civilians you just listed.' As a token for UNICEF's representation efforts, the accused party would add that they promise to 'conduct a fair investigation' within their different regiments or battalions and find out the truth of what exactly happened to the civilians under discussion. After procrastinating for three to four weeks, the armed party would blandly inform UNICEF that a 'thorough internal inquiry' (read silencing of victims' relatives through threats or physical punishment) was conducted and that the person(s) reported missing were 'not in our custody.'

LTTE, and to a lesser extent the SLA, played this parrying game to perfection, leaving UNICEF frustrated but unable to find another way to get abductees released. Despite knowing that the goal of protecting children from conscription or harassment was not being achieved through the same old futile methods, the organization did not innovate.

The tide turned in early 2004, when thousands of children fled the captivity of the LTTE after Karuna's rebellion in the East and became vulnerable to recapture by the rebels or arbitrary arrests by the SLA or police. Nonviolent Peaceforce convinced UNICEF that the scale of the protection crisis with escapee children was too huge to be left to dry presentations of lists of complaints to manipulative spokespersons of armed parties. The former allied with grassroots-based mothers' self-help groups and launched successful direct action interventions in Batticaloa district, wherein Tamil and Muslim women could be accompanied by international civilian peacekeepers to the exact rebel detention camp where their children were being held against their will.

The surprise value of poor local women having credible international backers beside them forced commanders of the LTTE and the 'Karuna Group' (precursor of the TMVP) to release dozens of children to reunite with their families.

UNICEF realised from these successful interventions that it had to change its mode of functioning or become irrelevant as far as the victims' families were concerned. From late 2004, its Batticaloa office reinvented child protection by becoming more assertive and proactive instead of blithely documenting complaints and building databases. The credit for this transformation in UNICEF goes to Nonviolent Peaceforce and local women's activists who showed that they are worth 'partnering' with if the objective was to reverse two decades of subjugation of children for the sake of a violent 'self-determination' war.

Though UNICEF did not undergo overnight value transformation, it took a pause and looked self-critically at its own clogged standard operating procedures (SOPs). Slowly, it moved away from falling back on the excuse of power inequalities between UNICEF and armed groups for IO failures in child protection.

As has already been broached earlier in this chapter, 'Ideas' of personalities within IOs can make a difference in making them more proactive. One astute observer of UNICEF from a different UN agency shared the following observations in this regard:

> It all boils down to personalities and their beliefs when it comes to being proactive on human rights for UN agencies. Personalities affect how the Colombo office deals with field offices, i.e. whether the former keeps the latter on a tight leash or if it allows them autonomy to pursue proactive policies on the ground.[36]

From my experience with UNICEF in the East from 2003 to 2005, the Colombo office allowed the district heads to chalk out new strategies in cooperation with Nonviolent Peaceforce and radical local activists. The relative freedom and confidence granted by the national headquarters to the district bosses enabled some of the latter to steer the entire field orientation of the organization to a more proactive line. Had UNICEF Colombo or UNICEF New York stamped down their feet and occluded the reforms in the districts, as was the case with UNHCR in the early 1990s (Clarance, 2006), this IO would not have topped the proactiveness scale in this book.

Another culturalist variable that pushed UNICEF into breaking with its past SOPs is the wellspring of popular anger against child conscription in the North and East during the CFA period. Tamil communities spoke out boldly against the totalitarian structures of the LTTE and asked poignantly why the organization still needed the sacrifice of their children to fight when its stated goal was to reach a negotiated political settlement with GSL. UNICEF was emboldened to follow Nonviolent Peaceforce and radical local activists after realising that the pulse of popular opinion among the Tamil people had grown indignant to LTTE's endless demands. A UNICEF Protection Section official, who has worked long enough to note the shift towards proactiveness, revealed the following:

> The high level of legitimacy and backing from stakeholders in the communities during the CFA enabled UNICEF to more confidently

confront armed actors with evidence of child conscription. We reflected internally among ourselves that advocating on the basis of the CRC (Convention on the Rights of the Child) was easier if the civilians organise and demand the return of their children. Without the community's self-mobilisation, our advocacy on behalf of international law would ring hollow to armed actors who care two hoots about Conventions or Covenants.[37]

This account implies that UNICEF's proactiveness on protection depends on how rights-conscious the survivors' families themselves are. UNICEF's transformation from a typical bureaucracy into a proactive actor involved learning from the communities.

Having credited UNICEF Sri Lanka for jettisoning 'business as usual', one must add the caveat that there is still a lot more room for IGOs and INGOs to be involved in supporting local activists than the former can imagine owing to the blinkers of self-constructed myths about 'neutrality' and 'politicisation.' To cite one critical local activist,

As of now, a great gulf separates IGOs and INGOs with their lavish and stand-offish lifestyles and the local people. The distance between some IGOs and INGOs and civil society working on human rights needs to be melted for any fruitful cooperation to emerge on civilian protection.[38]

The comparison between UNICEF of 2002-03 and UNICEF of today validates C4 because the organization became less change-resistant in its bureaucratic culture over time. As to the constructivist hypothesis C3 about a strengthening of state sovereignty norms in 'international society', the timeframe of the temporal comparison coincides with the US-led 'war on terrorism', which elevated national security as a legitimate end for which any means are justifiable. I did not find any change in UNICEF's internal thinking about being more or less proactive as a result of the normative struggles unleashed by George W Bush's 'doctrine of pre-emption'. Had UNICEF been socialised by the reassertion of state sovereignty and national security after September 11, 2001, it would not have dared to issue critical statements from time to time about the worsening plight of children at the hands of the SLA's aerial bombardment or indiscriminate artillery shelling in the North and East. We have to conclude that, in the case of UNICEF, elevation of the norm of state sovereignty at the national and international levels did not stunt its shift towards a more proactive approach.

How does UNICEF's move in a progressive direction after 2002 relate to R3? All evidence suggests that material pressures and inducements on UNICEF to de-emphasise civilian protection increased once the CFA dissolved and Eelam War IV formally started in July 2006. LTTE stepped up its opposition to UNICEF's 'interference in Tamil affairs' when it needed every ounce of human capital (including children) to beat back the SLA's advances. The SLA pressured UNICEF to downplay TMVP's child conscriptions and its own violence against Tamil civilians. If R3 is valid, then UNICEF's proactiveness should have declined instead of increasing over time.

The confounding factor, however, is that GSL's encouragement to UNICEF to expose the LTTE's child conscription also increased in Eelam War IV. So, material inducements do seem to partially explain UNICEF's increase in proactiveness (at least to violations committed by LTTE) over time. A combination of R3 and C4 seems to have caused the temporal change in UNICEF's proactiveness. But as stated earlier, the rationalist variables may have clearer explanatory power once we perform cross-country comparisons in Chapter 6.

The Legalist and the 'Saviour'

Why is ICRC slightly more proactive than Save the Children? With a net score of 3.0 (see Table 4.4), the ICRC has a one point edge over SCSL. R1 would lead us to think that the reason for this lead is that ICRC faces lesser material pressures and inducements than SCSL, while C1 and C2 imply that the difference is caused by ICRC being less influenced by state sovereignty norms and less bureaucratically resistant to change than SCSL.

In the North and East of Sri Lanka, ICRC performs humanitarian functions such as training the SLA, the police and the Special Task Force (STF) on IHL, visiting detainees, supplying food, water, medicines, fishing and agricultural inputs for IDPs, arranging safe passage for civilians, transferring human remains across battle lines, and collecting complaints of disappearances and other IHL violations against civilians. The organization divides its priorities and resources into two primary categories — 'protection and assistance.'

Political pressures on ICRC emanated both from GSL and the LTTE, with the latter letting up some of the heat in Eelam War IV due to its military and political weakness. Each party to the conflict instinctively demanded that ICRC monitor and report abuses committed by its opponents instead of focussing on its own violations. In 2005, ICRC Sri Lanka's personnel argued that 'we work in a real war that is interwoven with a subsidiary propaganda war, and the dilemma of being and appearing neutral is a huge pressure on us.'[39]

To illustrate this pressure, it deserves mentioning that the ICRC had to issue a Press Release in March 2008 'strongly objecting to misleading public references' by Sri Lanka's Ministry of Foreign Affairs, which cited ICRC's reference to claim that disappearances and unexplained killings of civilians had undergone 'a downward trend' in 2007 (ICRC, 2008D).

Several security incidents have been orchestrated over the years with the aim of cowing down ICRC and dissuading it from pursuing cases of grave violations against civilians. In 2000 and 2001, the ICRC office in the government-controlled Eastern town of Muthur was attacked with stones and grenades by unidentified persons, damaging the building and the organization's vehicles. In 2006, the ICRC's vehicles were attacked by angry Sinhalese mobs in Trincomalee district for the organization's alleged sympathies for the LTTE amidst clashes between the rebels and the SLA. In the same year, ICRC's Jaffna office was attacked with grenades by unknown persons, causing material damage to the building. In June 2007, two Tamil Sri Lankan Red Cross (local partner of ICRC) workers hailing from Batticaloa were abducted in Colombo by Sinhalese speakers for 'questioning' and killed.

In December 2008, a Tamil driver of the ICRC was shot dead in Jaffna on his way to work. In February 2009, the ICRC country headquarters in Colombo was attacked in broad daylight by a 'mob of about 200 pro-government people' after rumours spread that the organization had ordered 35,000 body bags in anticipation of civilian deaths from fighting in the North (TT, 2009). Instead of condemning the attack, the GSL's spokesman repeated the canard about body bags and accused ICRC of 'wanting to create a fear psychosis in the eyes of the international community' to the detriment of the SLA's fierce military campaign in the North (TT, 2009).

All these examples were far from being mistaken or unintentional attacks, since they coincided with particularly tense situations and can only be considered deliberate warnings by the state or by armed non-state actors to the ICRC to limit its proactiveness.

However, the ICRC's officials admit that the pressures they face are not of the same degree as other IGOs and INGOs due to the following reasons:

a) We do not have Executive Boards or Committees with state members like UN agencies; b) Our funding is well assured and not usually earmarked; c) We have an independent legal personality derived from IHL and customary principles applying to internal armed conflict that states and guerrillas accept for their own self-interests; d) Our traditional style of making representations on behalf of survivors of violence to armed parties is like 'whispering in the ear', a soft action that does not embarrass any armed party.[40]

Thanks to the rationalist calculations evident from c) and d), ICRC was the only IO allowed by GSL to remain operative in the North once the fighting of Eelam War IV peaked. In September 2008, UN agencies and INGOs were ordered to leave the war zone by Colombo on grounds that their personnel's safety could no longer be guaranteed, but the ICRC was permitted to remain as an exception (Dissanayake, 2008).

Yet, being present on the ground when hundreds of thousands of civilians were fleeing aerial bombardment and civilian casualties mounted presented huge pressures for the ICRC. In late January 2009, the organization was compelled by the human catastrophe unfolding before its eyes to issue an unusually strong public statement that 'hundreds of people had been killed and scores wounded in the latest fighting' (Sengupta, 2009). Rajiva Wijesinha, the then head of the GSL's Peace Secretariat, quickly retorted in his usual propagandist tone that ICRC was displaying 'wilful ignorance or naïveté' and took a verbal swipe at its much-touted fairness:

> It is true that the ICRC code of operation demands neutrality. Neutrality, however, demands objectivity in analysis and reporting, not generalisations that portray the government in a negative light (Wijesinha, 2009).

Unlike UN agencies and INGOs, ICRC leaders in Sri Lanka have never been threatened by the state with the 'PNG' weapon. But the organization's public statements about the worsening civilian protection environment in the North and East have been constantly 'corrected' or disabused by GSL's hawkish representatives. In one well-publicised visit of ICRC's Deputy Head of Delegation to the Chief of the SLA, the latter countered the former's expression of concerns about civilian protection by lecturing him that allegations of abuses against civilians by his troops were exaggerated (TI, 2008). In February 2009, Wijesinha wrote openly that 'some changes are in order' for ICRC's behaviour and that GSL had to issue 'clear instructions to the ICRC as to the parameters within which they are expected to act' (Wijesinha2, 2009).

For the geopolitical reason of lacking strategic interests in Sri Lanka, the ICRC's key donors — the US and European states — have not hesitated to amply support its protection budget. However, ICRC came into GSLs' firing range over the modality of delivering humanitarian aid received from one donor state in the war-engulfed North. In November 2008, the government of India handed over to ICRC 1,700 tonnes of relief material meant for civilians displaced by war in the North. A top GSL bureaucrat immediately insisted on the condition that state agents alone would distribute this aid. Sri Lanka's Commissioner General of Essential Services publicly disputed the ICRC's country head by maintaining that 'no foreign organization can directly go and distribute food (to) anybody there, bypassing the government mechanisms.' The most GSL was willing to concede to ICRC was a 'facilitator' role in disbursing the Indian aid (IANS, 2008). The incident exposed the powerlessness of ICRC when its desire to be independent clashed with the absolutism of the host state. According to a local human rights defender based in Colombo, ICRC has been the most successful organization in getting unlawfully detained persons released in Sri Lanka. Its success record is 'superior to the national Human Rights Commission and the numerous activist networks like ours.'[41] Yet, I know from ICRC contacts in the districts of the North and East that the ratio of the organization's confidential representations to releases of abductees is despairingly low from the point of view of the relatives of the victims. ICRC's leaders explain this ratio in terms of power inequalities in Sri Lanka:

> We are powerless to demand change in behaviour of alleged perpetrators. Whether the 'whispering in the ear' brings about an improvement or, in ICRC jargon, 'corrective measures', is an open question, but at the least, this activity conveys the message that internationals are watching what is happening in the conflict zone. We propose and the armed actors dispose. It cannot be the other way around.[42]

R1 implies that, compared to ICRC, SCSL faces greater material pressures and inducements from powerful actors to de-emphasise civilian protection. This certainly appears to be true, given that SCSL has endured a torrid time with GSL in recent years.

SCSL was one of the first INGOs to be publicly humiliated by GSL as an accomplice of LTTE and its humanitarian wing, the TRO, which the state accused of being a rebel front for arms-related fundraising. The triggering incident was the SLA's discovery that some boats donated for fisheries livelihood programmes by SCSL were found in an LTTE camp after it was overrun by the army. This led to an uproar that SCSL was supporting the Sea Tigers (naval arm of the LTTE). So devastating were the insinuations and verbal attacks on SCSL as a 'terrorist ally' by Sri Lankan parliamentarians and the media that the organization had to issue a press release in November 2007 assuring that it 'would not work in any way to undermine national security' (Save, 2007).

Local activist organizations contend that the subsequent volley of investigations and witch hunts against SCSL by state agencies 'have led to a near paralysis' and 'demoralised the staff' of the organization (LST, 2008A). My own contacts inside the organization narrated the impact of relentless state pressure as follows:

> The effect of the massive state campaign against us is to cripple our work. Where we have Sinhalese employees, they face severe social pressure from

communities as to why they work for an organization that is 'pro-LTTE'. In Sri Lanka, I am frank to admit that Save has an image problem. The mud sticks from scurrilous allegations made in newspapers, but we have no means to defend our neutrality when there is the powerful state machinery behind the media slurs. The eyes of the army are always on us and we are definitely on their watch list. The state's strategy is to corner us into a self-conscious mode so that if we make one more 'mistake' as they deem it, it could augur our expulsion from the country.[43]

If there is one issue that unites the Sinhalese South, it is anti-foreigner sentiment tracing back to the heroic defence of Buddhism against Hindu invaders from southern India in medieval times. One of the reasons GSL ferociously attacks INGOs and IGOs is because it helps reap political dividends to the ruling party and emotes well with the so-called 'Sinhalese psyche', which is prone to blaming foreign interventions for all the ills facing their country.[44]

Why has GSL reserved so much bile against SCSL and relatively a lot less for ICRC? I asked this question from the horse's mouth, a member of SCSL's Child Protection Team, and received this response:

It is precisely because we are a rights organization and have rights-based approaches unlike INGOs like OXFAM.[45]

To confirm this correlation, one need only examine the content of a public statement made by SCSL prior to its ordeal with GSL in late 2007. In June 2006, SCSL issued a Media Release deploring the increasing violence against civilians and faulting 'cordon and search operations by the security forces' for increasing tension and fear among communities in the government-controlled parts of the East. While the statement also criticised the LTTE's fresh conscription of children, what stood out was SCSL's appeal to GSL 'to undertake an immediate investigation and take appropriate action' on the abuses being perpetrated by anonymous groups (Save, 2006). For a bellicose state like Sri Lanka's, such advocacy amounted to showing a red rag to the bull.

From time to time, the ICRC issued its own public statements when the Eelam wars peaked, but its tone was much more ambiguous and general, without entering specifics of which party was committing what kinds of crimes against civilians. Significantly, SCSL never repeated public criticism of GSL following the 'investigations' launched against it in 2007. The organization entered a shell that shifted it to become more conservative towards civilian protection than the ICRC.

In other words, if the coding to our proactiveness scales was done in 2005 or 2006, SCSL may well have scored higher than ICRC. SCSL is thus a perfect vindication of temporal hypothesis, R3, i.e. 'the more the material demands and inducements from powerful donors, host states and rebel groups over time, the less proactive an IO becomes on civilian protection.' There was no corresponding change in cultural values of SCSL, implying that R3 had a causal impact on the organization's proactiveness since C3 or C4 remained constant during this time.

In mid-2008, when I engaged in semi-structured conversations with SCSL personnel, they were willing to still talk freely about the excesses being committed by the SLA and its paramilitaries, but only in private. I asked a senior expatriate SCSL official if he could repeat these charges, based on his direct access to Killinochhi, openly and got this response:

> (Pause)...'We have to find a way of saying it. The intense pressure applied on us by GSL reduces room for advocacy.[46]

In the districts of the North and East, SCSL is required to share its annual plan with the GA and with concerned Divisional Secretariat (DS) heads. As of late 2008, it had not yet faced a demand from TMVP to disclose details of its work with the new Provincial Council layer of administration. However, the fact is that most of the Grama Sevakas (lowest state representatives at the village level) in the rural areas are TMVP cadres now and so, they are adding one more layer of scrutiny and coordination structures for SCSL to manage. An SCSL local staff member discussed the dilemmas of taking on the TMVP after it was anointed by GSL as the party to head the Eastern Provincial Council as follows:

> TMVP's conscription of children is going on and we find it difficult to handle this problem at the group and community level in the East due to a culture of silence. TMVP stalks youngsters and snatches them away in droves. No one speaks out in larger gatherings of families about the pressures being placed on them to donate fighters to TMVP. Our own personnel have to be cautious not to openly support resistance by families to conscription because of the purge being carried out by the SLA and TMVP against suspected LTTE agents in the communities.[47]

SCSL's child protection programmes receive support from European donor states and, of late, from the US (USAID, 2008). As with all other IOs in Sri Lanka, SCSL is not subject to donor pressures to neglect civilian protection. Nevertheless, it must be noted that SCSL faces budgetary constraints in a way that ICRC does not. For the CHAP appeals made by SCSL in 2007 for US$ 330,000, only 73 percent were met by donors (UNOCHA, 2008). The ICRC never has a shortage of funds for programmes since it does not compete with other IOs from the common donor pool and is financially much more secure than SCSL.

Rationalist hypothesis R2 posits that 'IOs that compete harder for funds and political patronage will be less proactive on civilian protection than IOs which do not compete that much for funds and patronage.' However, Auxiliary Hypothesis 1 to R2 assumes that donors have an inherent preference to marginalise civilian protection as a priority in IOs. Since this is not borne out by the Sri Lankan experience, we will leave our judgement on R2 to Chapter 5 on the Philippines.

Overall, R1 does seem to be partly explaining why ICRC is more proactive than SCSL. But can the 1.0 point gap in proactiveness between these two IOs be wholly attributed to the slight difference in material pressures that we just analysed? SCSL has indeed been specifically targeted through media smear by GSL more than ICRC, but the former has never lost a single employee to physical violence by armed actors unlike the latter. SCSL personnel in the field have not had to face anything close to the long list of security incidents that ICRC has endured. Besides, with ICRC remaining inside the Wanni as the sole IO as Eelam War IV climaxed, it was under greater state pressure to keep mum on civilian protection than SCSL, which was ordered to evacuate the battle zone a lot earlier (Save, 2008b).

The lack of a clear difference in material pressures leaves open the possibility that C1 and C2 have some relevance in explaining the ICRC-SCSL gap. We must examine if ICRC's bureaucratic culture and normative understandings about sovereignty are less conservative than SCSL's.

My contacts in the war theatres of the East recount examples of how beliefs of personalities vary among ICRC field representatives. ICRC Sri Lanka is a 'bottom up' kind of organization, wherein the Colombo office does not micromanage its field offices. One recent ICRC Protection Officer based in Batticaloa was given basic guidelines from Colombo and granted the autonomy to get local civil society involved in the organization's protection initiatives. This was a first for ICRC in Sri Lanka and worked according to plan as long as this Officer was in her field posting. This proactive individual's successors did not continue her grassroots-based protection strategies, but the example does show the flexibility that ICRC's organizational structures allow for experimentation, which is at the heart of proactiveness towards civilian protection.

The mainstream ICRC culture is to distrust local activists and organizations and keep a safe distance from them. Aloofness from local human rights defenders is the organization's Achilles Heel, but its Colombo-level bosses are rarely sensitised to this weakness. The following comments of a headquarters-based ICRC official describe the extent of the self-delusion within the organization:

> All our protection work is handled by expatriate staff members directly. We do not involve National Red Cross societies in protection because it is less safe for locals to engage in sensitive issues. Moreover, in civilian protection, it is better for expatriate IHL specialists to interact directly with survivors or victims, sans intermediaries or local implementing partners. Not having local NGO partners works to the advantage of our civilian protection mission.[48]

The problem with these notions is that if ICRC stays so aloof from local civil society, with the exception of that one officer in Batticaloa, who are its informants about the ground realities in remote war-hit areas? ICRC offices, usually located in main district towns, react to registered complaints and do ex post facto investigations that are superficial. ICRC expatriates often have no clue about atrocities and violations happening in the interior areas that are highly vulnerable.

In 2005, I personally conveyed information about some villagers being beaten and threatened by an armed group in an LTTE-controlled area to my ICRC contact in Batticaloa district. This European officer went along with his local translator to the nearest main road point where the incidents occurred, pulled down the shutters to his air-conditioned vehicle and asked passers-by in a casual tone whether 'something bad' had happened there last night.

Completely unaware of the delicacy of the issue and the culture of silence that prevails in a war zone, he accepted the instinctive answers of one or two individuals on the main road that 'nothing had happened' to be true and decided that my information was baseless. The imperious and patronising manner in which he made the inquiries revealed how cut off ICRC was from the grassroots realities in a war zone. The organization's faith in 'expatriate specialists' and rejection of genuine local activist connections is the main reason why ICRC is behind UNICEF in proactiveness.

There are hundreds of cases of IHL violations on whose behalf ICRC makes confidential representations but fails to get any redress for the victim's families. I asked an ICRC official what this does to the morale of staff members who would have worked hard to piece together all the information about 'cases' of violations. He responded as follows:

Impact and achievement are not personal milestones for us. I cannot be egoistic and say that my goal while serving in this position will be to get 50 conscripted children released or 100 disappeared persons traced. As an organization, we see ourselves as in it for the long run and do not grieve over lack of immediate rewards.[49]

Is this lack of milestones on civilian protection not a license for becoming sclerotic and complacent? ICRC's annual blueprint in each country is titled 'Planning for Results.' Ironically, the internal consensus in the organization is that protection activities cannot be measured for results and impact. One of the reasons for ICRC to trail UNICEF in proactiveness is such bureaucratic smugness about being 'in it for the long run.'

'Public Denunciation' is a tool that ICRC sparingly uses when it feels that the situation warrants it and when regular back-channel diplomacy and face-to-face engagement with accused parties fail to make any difference. For example, breaking out of the mould of its quiet diplomacy in January 2009, ICRC declared Israel to be in contravention of the laws of war during its 22-day-war on the Gaza Strip (Nebehay, 2009).

In Sri Lanka, from time to time, ICRC has released statements expressing concern over deteriorating protection of civilians but not in the denunciation mode. An ICRC official described the thinking within the organization that leads to these statements:

They are products of studied internal deliberation and weighing of costs and benefits of public advocacy. Our statements in Sri Lanka do not accuse any single party. There is total unanimity inside the organization that statements must steer safe of pointing fingers.[50]

ICRC Sri Lanka has never issued a 'Public Denunciation' of any party to the armed conflict even though both sides have, from time to time, committed very grave offences against civilians. If 'Power' pressures explain this reticence, so do cultural attitudes within the organization that predetermine orderly and 'safe' speech and acts.

One of the biggest drawbacks with ICRC is that it is reactive and slow off the blocks when there is no clearly definable war in an area but low-intensity violence involving threats, abduction, hostage-taking etc against civilians. The mandarins of the organization defend this attitude by referring to their identity and self-understanding:

Our legal mandate authorises us into action only in the context of armed clashes. We are not a human rights organization to interest ourselves in threats to civilians that are not directly related to armed hostilities between parties to the conflict.[51]

Legalism, which flows through the arteries of ICRC, curtails flexibility, creativity and ultimately the degree of proactiveness of its protection work. I have personally witnessed ICRC's disinterest towards the day-to-day atmosphere of intimidation of civilians and sub-surface violence in the East. On one occasion, I telephoned the ICRC in Batticaloa town to inform that I will be escorting a group of critically persecuted individuals facing imminent threat to lives to their district office for registering a complaint. The expatriate ICRC official at the other end of the line sounded cool to the idea and said that she was going to take a two hour lunch break and that the 'case' can wait. Perfunctory investigations and bureaucratic inertia among many ICRC field staff members defeat the unique legal advantage the organization possesses in the form of acceptance by armed actors of its role as a maker of representations on behalf of inflicted civilians.

Notwithstanding these flaws, ICRC Sri Lanka does not need to 'mainstream' protection unlike other IGOs and INGOs. One of its strengths is permeation of a protection culture that overrides all other legitimate pursuits. To quote my ICRC interlocutor,

Almost everything we do (e.g. health care, water and sanitation, detention centre visits etc) has protection as the top priority. All the other activities are mere add-ons to our core protection mandate. ICRC staff are all trained and socialised to think from protection lenses.[52]

SCSL, on the other hand, lacks a clear identity and value system centred on civilian protection. A member of its Child Protection Team pored over the split identity that tugs at SCSL in two directions:

There are some INGOs which are purely rights organizations and others which are service delivery organizations in emergency situations. In the former are Nonviolent Peaceforce, ICRC, Amnesty International and Human Rights Watch. In the latter category is OXFAM-GB. Save in Sri Lanka is a bit of both. We have to juggle with our self-perception as a rights-cum-relief organization.[53]

SCSL's protection programmes receive funding from donors like Britain, Norway, Sweden and the USA. The Child Protection Team therefore does not need to compete with other sections within the organization for internal funds that are un-earmarked and at the discretion of the Director. My interlocutor in the organization described the relations among the sections as follows:

Education is our flagship section. We 'get access' to a community through our soft Education programmes and add on protection staff to the field offices that are opened by Education or WatSan. So, there is cooperation among the different sections. We call this approach, 'unified programming', where each field visit and entry is made by representatives of all four of our sections (Education, WatSan, Protection, Child Rights). The other sections have successfully integrated protection into their actions and consciousness. We rarely have situations where one of the other sections grudges protection goals because that compromises or jeopardises its specific projects.[54]

Some of these comments of SCSL expatriates put a positive spin to the organization's much less proactive culture in the field. In 2004, I recall meeting a district head of SCSL in the East at the funeral of a geography lecturer from the local university who had been shot dead by the LTTE for refusing to resign his position and make way for an LTTE-favoured academic who would teach 'Eelam geography'. The SCSL representative told me that he did not feel sorry for the slain man as 'he should not have stuck his neck out foolishly, because it is better to keep quiet rather than irritate the authorities.'

In Batticaloa district, when local activists and their international allies initiated a temple festival vigil activity to deter mass abductions of children for conscription by the LTTE, SCSL opted out of the joint initiative. I asked them often why they were not participating even though this was right up their alley as a 'child rights organization'. They had the standard replies of 'needing clearance from Colombo' or that all their staff members were 'busy in the field' managing projects. ICRC's field delegates are more autonomous in deciding how to approach grassroots protection activities, but SCSL's personnel on the ground always feel constricted by the rule of permissions from higher-ups in Colombo.

A local rights defender analysed the culture of silence in SCSL and like organizations as follows:

The key strategy for any IGO or INGO that has access to sensitive war-affected areas is to establish low-key relationships with rights monitoring or direct protection implementing organizations and to relay sensitive information and get sufferers in touch with those who can help them. Unfortunately, not all of them do this. UNDP, OXFAM-GB and SCSL are not particularly good at it. They are narrowly focussed on their own specific projects and do not believe that it is their role to perform conscious presence in the most vulnerable areas.[55]

Another bureaucratic hurdle within SCSL that makes it relatively less proactive than ICRC is its structure as a Unified Country Mission that combines SCF UK, SCF Norway, SCF USA and SCF Sweden.[56] The UK branch is the overall guidance centre for SCSL. It interacts with the Colombo office and sets the basic parameters of SCSL's mandate and programmatic areas of emphasis. The Unified Mission structure poses unique challenges to the organization's ability to be proactive towards civilian protection. According to my contact in SCSL,

> SCF UK and SCF USA are less prone to emphasise protection of children in armed conflict because they have developed a specialisation in relief supplies. The Scandinavian branches of SCF, on the other hand, have a greater capacity to deliver protection. SCF USA gets most money from USAID, which is not that keen on protection as a priority. Even the European Commission's Humanitarian Aid Office is not interested in this issue,[57] but individual European states have their own funds that do take protection seriously.[58]

SCSL believes in the idea of protection as a specialised activity that only certain country branches and certain staff members are more capable of implementing. The notion of mainstreaming protection was intended to overcome this narrowly professionalised allocation of roles within IOs. As one prominent local rights activist maintains,

> All it takes for conscious international presence to work is for an IO to spend a little extra time and a negligible amount of money for vehicle fuel to ensure that you are seen with your insignia in a vulnerable area at the correct time. No separate protection projects are necessary. However, many IGOs and INGOs are bureaucratically conditioned to think in terms of projects and funds with specialised protection staff members. Many of them display a 'disconnect' between protection and relief as two separate arenas with their respective 'experts'.[59]

While there are similar 'disconnects' in the legalist ICRC's organizational culture, the extent to which they stifle proactiveness is much greater in the case of the 'saviour' of children. For all its pretensions of being a 'rights-based organization', there are internal cultural obstacles for SCSL to become more proactive. I find no difference between ICRC and SCSL on the normative beliefs about primacy of state sovereignty (hypothesis C1), but there is an observable difference between the two in their bureaucratic flexibility and openness to change (hypothesis C2). If R1 offers only a partial explanation for the 1.0 point gap in proactiveness between the two organizations, C2 fills in with the rest of the causal weight.

The Middle Ground

With a net proactiveness score of 2.25 (see Table 4.4), OXFAM-GB is slightly above SCSL and well above UNDP, but slightly below ICRC and far below UNICEF. Why is this organization stuck in the middle and what prevents it from going up on the scale towards UNICEF? R1 suggests that OXFAM-GB is superior to SCSL and UNDP on civilian protection because it faces lesser material threats and inducements from powerful actors compared to the latter two IOs. I enquired about this possibility from a former head of OXFAM-GB in Sri Lanka and received the following response:

> There are clear limits as to what an INGO can do in a country like Sri Lanka. The state and the LTTE (when they were stronger) set the boundaries and one cannot get away with activities that are seen as 'dangerous' for the interests of the two warring sides. For instance, if OXFAM were to do a poster campaign on billboards appealing to all parties to respect human rights of civilians in the North and East, it would be seen as an oblique criticism of GSL and invite stern responses and possibly expulsion. I recall several instances before the LTTE became militarily weakened when it would invite IGOs and INGOs to 'coordination meetings' where it had copies of each organization's projects and pointedly demanded, 'Why are you spending so much on this village or DS (Divisional Secretariat) area or this type of project? Our Tamil people do not need it in that area.' OXFAM can ignore such pressures only at its own peril.[60]

What about the fear factor for physical safety of employees that often gets bandied about as a big material pressure against proactiveness? My interlocutor agreed that this had a bearing on OXFAM-GB's approach to sensitive issues of civilian protection:

> The 'business as usual' mentality of field staffers who turn a blind eye to atrocities happening in the villages where they have projects is not only related to unfamiliarity with mainstreaming but also to security risks.

Nobody wants to disappear for reporting sensitive incidents or being seen to be assisting victims of targeted violence. I can understand the fear of OXFAM employees, especially the local Tamils and Muslims who have to also live in their communities with their families.[61]

The flaw in this formulation is that there are secure and confidential channels through which sensitive incidents of abuse of civilians occurring in remote places can be monitored and reported to concerned rights organizations. OXFAM's field personnel do not engage much in such actions and fall back on the alibi of risks to staff security. That said, there have been a few incidents of harassment of OXFAM personnel by armed actors and these weigh heavily on the minds of the organization's leaders. A senior representative of the organization recounted as follows:

The North and East are in an atmosphere of total intimidation of civilians and civil society by thugs who are in power. The more violent the SLA, LTTE or TMVP is, the greater the risks of operation for IGOs and INGOs. I fear more Muthurs (incidents like the massacre of 17 ACF staff members) because armed actors see IGOs and INGOs from their ethnic-tinted lenses. For instance, the fact that local staffers of INGOs or IGOs in Batticaloa or Jaffna do not include Sinhalese could be enough grounds for an organization being branded 'pro-LTTE.' As locals with relatives who live in the communities, almost all Tamil staff members of any IGO or INGO can be said to have some connection or the other with a militant group. That then becomes the lead to vicious persecution and intimidation by state agencies. There is no doubt that GSL is coming down hard on IGOs and INGOs. In 2006, two OXFAM water suppliers at the Vantharumoolai Eastern University campus in Batticaloa were unfairly accused of involvement in a bomb blast carried out by the LTTE. For one month, we could not even meet these employees and it took ages for them to get exonerated.[62]

This incident did not lead to a smear campaign against OXFAM-GB as a 'pro-LTTE foreign NGO' the way SCSL got branded, although some paranoid Sinhalese chauvinists made outlandish allegations against it. Akila Weerasekera of Lankaweb wrote in December 2008 that OXFAM is 'one of the most powerful and secretive British intelligence organizations acting under non-governmental organization cover' (Weerasekera, 2008). In 2007, a mainstream Sri Lankan newspaper published a picture of a water purification plant with the OXFAM-GB logo and the caption 'certain NGOs, in the guise of providing relief to civilians, spent millions of dollars only to provide purified water to Tiger bases.' The organization's Country Programme Representative had to issue a written clarification denying that it was assisting the LTTE. The newspaper stuck to its guns that 'Oxfam, for reasons restricted to them, installed this purification plant close to Tiger bases in Verugal rather than in a civilian populated area' (SO, 2007).

I further investigated whether OXFAM had been subjected to any special surveillance or intimidation by armed actors and heard the following account from my interlocutor in the organization:

All INGOs are generally seen as thorns in the flesh by the state. Even the LTTE used to order IGOs and INGOs to dance to its tunes when it was stronger. There were many international organizations at that time which would wait for the LTTE to order 'jump' and then jump to the decreed height. So, the entire humanitarian community has, at one time or the other, come under the scanner of armed actors. No organization is really immune and we are no exception.[63]

This generalisation of threats to all IOs is misleading because every observer I met while researching this book opined that OXFAM had been relatively spared from persecution compared to SCSL, UNICEF or ICRC. Except for the previously mentioned incident in 2006 and a stray grenade attack on its Colombo office in 2000 that was attributed to the LTTE (FIC, 2007:p.22), the organization has not faced lethal security threats from armed actors. Yet, citing the generalised climate of IO intimidation, OXFAM's officials extrapolate threats to the organization in this manner:

If UN representatives can get 'PNG'ed and INGOs can be subject to smear campaigns, then international monitors can simply be shown the door. What happened to the Eminent Persons Group that was constituted under Justice P.N.Bhagwati?[64]

It did not receive any cooperation from the state and had to quit the country. When Louise Arbour, the UN High Commissioner for Human Rights, visited and expressed concern about the worsening abuses of civilians in the conflict zone, GSL mocked at her findings and denied that the situation was deteriorating for protection of civilians. If such internationally influential figures have been unceremoniously ticked off for speaking their mind, how can we pull it off?[65]

The British government's Department for International Development (DFID) is the main donor of OXFAM-GB in Sri Lanka, followed by ECHO,

Norway and Sweden. Donors do not particularly set the agenda for whether or not OXFAM can be proactive on civilian protection. OXFAM internally decides priorities and then approaches donors to fund those specific areas. The organization does not really have to compete with other humanitarian organizations in the donor market because of DFID's solid commitment to it. In the budget year 2007, OXFAM-GB in Sri Lanka appealed for over US $ 2.7 million to donors and managed to attain 100 percent of this funding target (UNOCHA, 2008).

Hypothesis R2 is thus being mildly validated here because OXFAM-GB is more financially secure than SCSL and does not have to compete harder for funding. However, if R2 was accurate, then the phenomenally rich and well-funded UNDP should be more proactive than OXFAM-GB. What must be stressed here is that donor pressures and inducements, in OXFAM-GB and all the other four IO cases discussed thus far, have not played a major determinant role in the proactiveness of organizations in Sri Lanka.

In sum, OXFAM-GB has not faced as many 'Power' obstacles to proactiveness as other IO cases chosen for this book. If R1 is true, then OXFAM-GB should have been at the pinnacle of the proactiveness ranking. To explain why it is in the middle rather than at the top, we have to turn to a test of the culturalist hypotheses, C1 and C2. Is OXFAM-GB's organizational culture more rigidly bureaucratic and subservient to state sovereignty than UNICEF's and ICRC's organizational cultures?

I asked the former OXFAM-GB country head why, notwithstanding the rhetorical claim that the organization's field personnel perform 'community level advocacy work' for the protection of IDPs (OXFAM, 2006), they rarely incorporate civilian protection into their relief and 'development programmes' (water and sanitation, housing, immediate livelihood needs, disaster preparedness etc.) The reply opened vistas into the internal 'Ideas' that make up the organization's behavioural mindset in Sri Lanka:

> The key problem with mainstreaming protection into OXFAM's work in the North and East is that field staff members do not understand what mainstreaming means. They often think that protection is something extra and an *additional burden* on top of the regular socio-economic projects, not an integral element of them. When I headed OXFAM, we used to have workshops exhorting local staff to be more cognisant of human rights abuses. I tried convincing them to at least be conscious of the climate of impunity around you even if you cannot do anything about it. They would typically say that they got the message, but the end result was zilch in terms of actual emphasis and analysis of protection

problems in the field. Personalities of OXFAM leaders matter a lot in whether or not it has an inclination for civilian protection issues. When I was at the helm, I realised that OXFAM's local staffers did not know exactly where the boundaries of permissible behaviour lay in terms of supporting human rights causes.

If the outer hexagon (see Figure 4) is the actual red line beyond which one could get killed or abducted for participating in protection activities, our local personnel used to be located somewhere along the inner hexagon, with a large cushion space that may be the product of living in fear and in dangerous conflict environments.

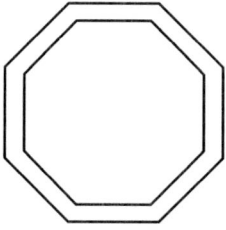

Figure 4. Hexagons of conservatism in OXFAM-GB Sri Lanka.

I tried to encourage my staff members to push themselves as far as possible to the outer perimeter so that they make a contribution to the acute sufferings of victims of violence. I had a principle that OXFAM will support local initiatives by civil society groups that will push the boundaries of Figure 4 without OXFAM's name coming out in public. This way, the political pressures of the LTTE and GSL could be somewhat circumvented. A different leader of the organization may not take this effort due to personal conservatism or plain timidity. In leadership's exercise of creativity, much depends on latching on to opportunities with an open mind. For instance, in 2006, the Sri Lankan president declared a 'Year of the Child'. I took this as an avenue that opened and helped launch a major programme to tackle violence and abuse of girl children. OXFAM under me also did a campaign against proliferation of light arms and it was appreciated by civians and activists in the North and East.[66]

The pinning of blame only on local staff members in this narrative is emblematic of many IOs' biased extolling of the virtues of expatriates. But it is instructive that the 'Ideas' that could push OXFAM-GB in a more proactive direction come from a factor identified earlier— the personal visions of leaders. An experienced UNICEF official confirmed the retrogressive direction that OXFAM-GB took towards protection after a change of guard in the Colombo office as follows:

> If personalities and their backgrounds matter a lot in UNICEF's proactiveness towards human rights, it applies even more intensely to OXFAM-GB. The current head of OXFAM-GB is a 'gender specialist' and she knows nothing about protection. The prism through which she sees the conditions in the North and East is that of gender inequalities and feminisation of poverty. So, she misses basic political rights as a value worth pursuing.[67]

What kind of 'gender' approach is it that can be viewed as inimical to civilian protection? We will return to the jaundiced and mechanical operationalisation of the concept of 'gender' in Chapter 7, while evaluating the structural condition of patriarchy that informs much of humanitarian behaviour. Here, it needs to be added that I learnt from a confidential source that this head of OXFAM-GB was appointed because the organization was receiving funds from certain donors that insisted on their own nominee heading the organization. Thus, 'Power' and 'Ideas' intermesh seamlessly and steer the organization away from proactiveness.

The former OXFAM-GB head I spoke to had also worked for SCSL and was therefore in a good position to compare the values and beliefs that drive the two organizations. According to him,

> Save is more conservative on civilian protection than OXFAM in general in terms of attitudes and sensitisation. This is because OXFAM is more involved in relief work and deals with emergencies relating to violent conflict. Save sees itself more as a development-oriented organization although its talks of rights-based programming in the North and East.[68]

This difference in self-identification is in spite of the fact that SCSL, unlike OXFAM, implements explicit 'child protection projects' for UNICEF and participates regularly in the Protection Sector meetings convened by UNOCHA in Colombo. The implication of this observation is that the more an IGO or INGO imagines itself as a 'developmental' entity, the farther it veers away from civilian protection concerns. We observe the same tendency in the case of UNDP. If mainstreaming protection is viewed as a continuum (see Figure 5), then 'developmental' IOs seem to be the least proactive. This speaks of the convoluted meanings of development that humanitarians construct.

Identity of IO

Developmental ....->
Humanitarian...........................->
Human Rights................................->

Proactiveness
towards protection

Figure 5. Identity and proactiveness of IOs.

To better understand OXFAM-GB's bureaucratic hurdles to proactiveness, I quizzed one of its expatriates about the failure of its field personnel to take interest in civilian protection despite the attempts of some activist officials at the Colombo level. His reply was as follows:

> Internally, mainstreaming protection in OXFAM faces hurdles. Field personnel just do not understand the concept of mainstreaming. They think it involves whistle blowing or advocacy, which is very risky. I am sorry to admit that field staffers' awareness about international civil and political rights is minimal. They prefer to stay out of 'trouble' even when all that I encourage them to do is to share sensitive information discreetly with relevant protection-oriented organizations. Many of OXFAM's field staffers think that 'doing' protection necessitates getting involved in a highly visible activity which would invite repercussions from armed actors. Sometimes, they unwitting perform protection tasks but do not realise its import. They think that it is a part of the SOPs of the organization while implementing, say, a public health programme. OXFAM staffers also choose not to see militarisation of IDP camps and related abuses of inmates by soldiers, believing that this is how 'order' in camps is supposed to be maintained by armed actors.[69]

The acquiescence of IOs to 'military humanitarianism' will emerge clearer in Chapter 5 on the Philippines, but here, the ideational pathologies of OXFAM-GB come out forcefully. A progressive OXFAM-GB staffer, who was frustrated with the organization's internal obstructionism to his ideas of mainstreaming protection, described the dilemma at length:

> The main drawback of IGOs and INGOs, including my own, is absence of will or determination to resist the shrinking space for protection of civilians. The state is regrouping Tamil civilians fleeing the fighting in the Wanni into what are basically detention centres in Vavuniya and Mannar and expecting IGOs and INGOs to provision these camps. Inmates of

these centres, which are akin to Nazi concentration camps, have highly restricted mobility, few freedoms and are subjected by the army and police to interrogations for their suspected loyalties with LTTE. IGOs and INGOs collectively need to debate if they want to be accomplices in ethnic cleansing of this sort or if it is better to just pack their bags and leave these camps. Usually, they do not think through this dilemma because it has high risks for job security and safety of staff members and for the organization's interests as a whole. They prefer the cosiness of received wisdom to the uncharted territory of courage. There is scope for IGOs and INGOs to bolster the spirits of human rights defenders, but it again comes down to the 'will' to bring about change in the human security situation on the ground. Courage and creativity emerge from unity and the only way forward is for IGOs and INGOs to come together with local activists and form broad coalitions of rights defenders. This is not impossible if IGOs and INGOs learn to play with the limits set by 'Power'. I am talking in a personal capacity here. Not everyone in my own organization shares my estimate that the envelope should be pushed more towards becoming proactive.[70]

Conformism to 'Power' is thus not purely a rational calculation of individuals and their IOs (as suggested by political economy theories) but also a socio-psychological one based on a conspiracy of silence in the entire IO community about the ugly realities of war. The INGO Medecins Sans Frontieres (MSF) popularised the idea of pulling out of conflict areas to avoid becoming an instrument of armed actors' strategies, an 'ethic of refusal' (Terry, 2002). But despite the regime-wide humanitarian rhetoric of 'Do No Harm' (Anderson, 1999), INGOs in Sri Lanka like OXFAM-GB and SCSL never hesitated to trade self-censorship and dilution of proactiveness for 'access' to beneficiaries of aid.

The existential necessity of 'access' to IDPs and the war-affected is frequently justified on grounds that humanitarians feed and clothe innocent civilians. But Chapter 7 will argue that the 'access' question is tied to the imperatives of patriarchy and the capitalist world-system.

Earlier in this chapter, we validated the temporal culturalist hypothesis C4 for UNICEF. The evidence of OXFAM-GB's variation in proactiveness over time is not that strong, since it tended to always stay around the same score, be it 2003 or 2008. However, an interesting insight into changes in leadership of OXFAM-GB's international office in the UK is worth examining. According to one of my OXFAM-GB interlocutors in Sri Lanka,

Leadership change is critical to how OXFAM's proactiveness towards civilian protection varies over time at the global level. We have a Protection Adviser for OXFAM worldwide in Oxford, whose mission is to push country programmes in a more rights-based direction. One previous occupant of this office had ideas of mainstreaming protection in a way which is different from the current occupant. One focussed on raising rights abuses issues of each country where OXFAM worked at the national level and in international forums at Geneva and New York. For Sri Lanka, this meant conveying concerns about civilian abuses to the GSL's Consultative Committee on Humanitarian Assistance (CCHA), which is chaired by the Minister for Disaster Management. Later, another occupant of the post of Protection Adviser wanted a more grassroots-level strategy of raising protection consciousness among OXFAM staff and allying with local activists in war zones. OXFAM Sri Lanka, which is not a 'protection organization' per se has thus been swayed from time to time in different strategic directions by the changes at the organization's global headquarters in Britain.[71]

To sum up, OXFAM-GB has significant bureaucratic complications that hold it back from being as proactive as UNICEF or ICRC in Sri Lanka. While the former is not relatively more subservient to state sovereignty than the latter two IOs (constructivist hypothesis C2 once again fails to be validated), it does have more inflexible and entrenched bureaucratic values that resist attempts at transformation towards greater proactiveness (affirming hypothesis C1). At the same time, OXFAM-GB's sclerotic identity and self-definition are not as retrogressive as the 'developmentalist' SCSL and UNDP. Absent any correlation along hypothesised lines between the material pressures that OXFAM-GB faces to downgrade protection and its proactiveness, we are left to conclude that the organization's median position on the scale can be explained by culturalist hypothesis C1.

Hunters and the Hunted

This chapter has revealed the Janus-faced nature of humanitarian IOs in an extremely violent internal war. On one hand, organizations like UNICEF have mainstreamed civilian protection against material odds after undergoing an ideational metamorphosis. On the other hand, there are organizations like UNDP which place themselves at the disposal of the state as it carries out bloody and prolonged violence in defence of national security and sovereignty. With little or zero consciousness of neutrality in the war, UNDP allies with the state and serves its military-political objectives in the North and East.

The pride with which UNDP advertises its intimacy and integration into the state's machinery for winning the war against the LTTE leaves no doubt about its partisanship and conservatism regarding protection of civilians. No serious internal debate has ever occurred in UNDP about whether it is being used as an instrument for promoting the state's militaristic solutions in the North and East by adding a developmental component to it. Neither has there been any deep thinking inside the organization about the problems of inequality and discrimination that persist in the state's majoritarian Sinhala vision of development in the North and East.

UNDP's enthusiastic backing of the state's agenda is most visible in its lead role in rehabilitation projects in the 'cleared areas' of the East ever since the LTTE was driven out of power by the SLA in 2006-07. Designed to change the ethnic demography of the East by settling Sinhalese from the South and eroding the majority of Tamils and Muslims, the state's ambitious *Nagenahira Navodaya* (Eastern Revival) programme costing $1.8 billion boasts of a panoply of development schemes being implemented by UNDP and other IOs under the jargon of 'post-conflict reconstruction.' Clear ethnic reengineering intent of the SLA and UNDP's 'line ministries' has heightened fears among many Tamils and Muslims 'that current government plans for the economic development of the Trincomalee district will be used to settle additional Sinhalese and strengthen centralised — and effectively Sinhala — control over the district' (ICG, 2008: 23).

UNDP unquestioningly acts as an instrument of the Sri Lankan state's majoritarian agenda, which is historically the root cause of the conflict. The complicity of UNDP in entrenching the cycle of violence and abuses of civilians during the Eelam Wars is second to none among the humanitarians in Sri Lanka. A mixture of rationalist and culturalist variables, with the latter weighing heavier, determine the totally compromised role of this organization. In Chapter 7, we shall see how lurking behind this mixture is the utilisation of UNDP as a pawn by capitalist donor states to expand the realm of liberal 'economic freedoms'.

This chapter critiqued the cultural conservatism of even the more proactive humanitarian IOs like UNICEF and ICRC. That they could do much more for civilians facing acute protection crises by transcending bureaucratic ideas, practices and procedures will be elaborated in Chapter 8. Here, it is sufficient to note that there are plenty of instances of inaction or unwitting collusion with perpetrators of violence in the work of UNICEF and ICRC. These failings have to be surmounted by the two IOs to win greater respect and confidence from local activists and communities which are struggling against the juggernaut of war and militarised peace.

Chapter 7 will argue that humanitarian culture can only change if IOs dissect holes in the violent structures of patriarchy and the capitalist world-system and unfetter themselves from their clutches. This chapter underlined the cultural limitations of 'rights-based' humanitarian IOs like SCSL which prevent them from being more attentive to civilian protection. The yawning gap between SCSL's verbal rhetoric and practical conservatism towards human rights is symbolic of the humanitarian fraternity's duplicity, wherein the talk is about 'empowerment' while the effects are to squelch local activism and people's spirits to resist war.

This chapter depicted a militaristic and strong Sri Lankan state that has the means to apply great material pressure on humanitarian IOs to toe the line on civilian protection. Unlike many internal wars in Africa, where state structures break down or fade and humanitarian IOs usurp power over societies in the governmental vacuum[72], Sri Lanka has a highly centralised state that keeps a tight lid on the freedoms of not only its citizens but also of IOs. Writing about Sri Lanka in 1997, one researcher pondered over the difficulties facing humanitarian IOs in the context of a strong government waging a war (Brabant, 1997).

Over the last decade, this state has grown in belligerence and self-confidence, hunting down dissent with an impunity that has been roundly criticised by human rights INGOs and even statist IGOs.[73] One of Sri Lanka's leading progressive political scientists explained how this criticism is linked to the state's imposition of a harsh regimen on IOs:

There is a schizophrenic aspect to the Sri Lankan state. While it appears to be cocking a snook at critics of its human rights record, it genuinely fears that its leaders may face war crimes charges at some international tribunal. That is why its agents are watching and harassing IGOs and INGOs at every step. Some of the eyewitnesses of the Muthur massacre of ACF employees got asylum overseas through the intercession of IOs based in Trincomalee. The state does not want eyewitnesses to escape the country and create a splash of embarrassment overseas. The regime has different types of intimidating means to control local civil society and international organizations. Threats can be nuanced but very effective when there are so many unsolved cases of disappearances and torture. Not everyone needs to be killed. The Sinhalese state is racist and discriminatory but keeps the violence from reaching genocidal proportions, since the latter would attract undue international censure.[74]

We saw in this chapter that the jingoism of the Sinhalese state and its ability to pressure IOs against trying to prevent abuses of civilians is the product of a pseudo 'Asian solidarity' construct that enables Colombo to gain military and diplomatic assistance from neighbouring great powers. At the same time, as a lodestar of neoliberal economic policies in South Asia, GSL gets away with brutality at home by riding on the permissiveness towards impunity that is reserved for 'successful' market economies in the capitalist world-system. As long as the Sri Lankan state remains within the confines of the neoliberal market economy, it is guaranteed freedom to exercise a militarised sovereignty over its citizens that involves extreme majoritarian rule.

To top it, Sri Lanka also had one of the world's most totalitarian guerrilla movements that finessed its own machinery to police and pressurise humanitarian IOs to be selective on civilian protection issues. LTTE's dimming military prospects and eventual collapse in Eelam War IV lifted this yoke on IOs, but its memory sticks in the minds of wary humanitarians who have worked in Sri Lanka for a longer span of time.

Together, a mighty state-cum-rebel pressure complex has exercised a stranglehold on the priorities of IOs in Sri Lanka. This chapter mainly validated some culturalist hypotheses but did not reject any of the rationalist hypotheses due to the methodological limitation of within-country comparison. Cross-country comparisons in Chapter 6 will better test the significance of donor, state and rebel 'Power' in determining proactiveness of IOs and remind readers of the puissance of the Sri Lankan pressure complex.

5

HUMANITARIANS IN THE PHILIPPINES: PROPS AND COUNTERS TO THE 'WAR ON TERRORISM'

Five Centuries of the 'Moro Problem'

Since 1565, south-western Philippines (henceforth, Mindanao) has been a theatre of waves of warfare between colonising Christian armies of the Spanish, the Americans and the Filipinos on one side and polities of the native Moro inhabitants who converted to Islam in the fourteenth century. The Sultanates of Sulu and Maguindanao resisted Spanish attempts to occupy their lands for approximately 333 years (1565-1898) in the 'Moro wars'.

When Spain was defeated by the USA in 1898, it ceded the Philippine archipelago to the Americans as a 'property' to be dealt with by the US Congress as it wished. The occupying US military in the Philippines faced a number of Moro uprisings in Mindanao and countered them with extremely brutal 'punitive expeditions', the equivalent of 'counter-insurgency' in contemporary military lexicons (Birtle, 1998). American colonialists inherited from Spanish Jesuits the 'Moro problem', i.e. 'stubborn Muslims who were not civilised and showed no interest in becoming so' (Amoroso, 2003: 122). As a solution, US administrators enacted a series of laws to dispossess Moros of their landholdings and, from 1913, began encouraging mass migration of Christian Filipinos from the North into 'public lands' in Mindanao. From 1920, American colonialists ended direct rule over Muslim Mindanao and transferred it to Christian Filipino hands.

The 'Filipinisation' of the governorships of Muslim Mindanao accelerated corporate Christian agricultural settlements and changed the demography of the region. From being the overwhelming majority of Mindanao, the Moros were stigmatised and reduced to the status of minorities within their ancestral lands. This process of internal colonisation in Mindanao sharpened after the Philippines became an independent state in 1946, when the state power of Manila was used to 'open up' more and more Moro territories to corporate farming and 'land reforms' (Rodil, 1994).

The earth-shaking impact of Manila's settlement policies on the demographic profile of Mindanao can be statistically comprehended by the fact that while in 1900, 76 percent of people in Mindanao were Moro, by the year 2000, only 18 percent remained Moro (see Figure 6).

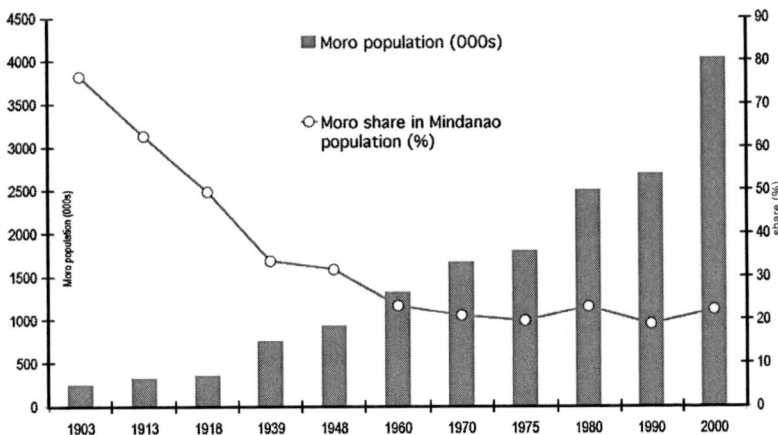

Figure 6. Moro population and share in Mindanao
population over 100 years.
Source: Philippine Human Development Report 2005. Quezon:
Human Development Network:29.

The rise of the Malaysian and Libyan-backed National Liberation (MNLF) and its offshoot, the Moro Islamic Liberation Front (MILF), as armed 'revolutionary movements' against central government rule in Mindanao was a product of the steady disenfranchisement and appropriation of Moro cultural, economic and political rights since the Philippines won freedom from the USA. The ideologues of MNLF and the MILF restated the Spanish-American 'Moro Problem' from their perspective as the systematic oppression and discrimination of Muslim Mindanawons by Manila (Asani, 1980).

The military conflicts between the MNLF and the Armed Forces of the Philippines (AFP) from 1972 to 1996, and between the MILF and AFP from 1997 onward, rage intermittently to this day, making Muslim Mindanao the venue of one of the world's longest internal wars. The human costs of the wars of the last 40 years are officially estimated to be more than 120,000 people killed and nearly 3 million persons displaced in iterative cycles (AI, 2008). The MNLF's claim is that the death toll of the last four decades of fighting is 'close to 300,000 precious lives' (Abadi, 2007).

Some of the wanton acts of impunity committed against civilians both by the AFP and the Moro guerrilla forces during 'hot' phases of wars in Mindanao include arbitrary arrest and detention, torture, humiliation and ill-treatment, threat, intimidation and harassment, kidnapping and extortion, forcible abduction and disappearance, extrajudicial killing, targeted assassination, looting and destruction of property, forced deprivation of livelihood means, forced displacement and eviction, indiscriminate firing, shelling and bombing, and occupation of schools and community centres for military ends.[1]

The excesses on civilians are especially scorching during 'all-out wars' such as the one launched by President Joseph Estrada on the MILF in April 2000 and the undeclared one that President Ferdinand Marcos waged on the MNLF under martial law in the 1970s. Limited wars or 'selective attacks' of the AFP against the MILF and MNLF or some of its 'rogue commanders' in the years 1997, 2001, 2003[2], 2007 and 2008 are microcosms of all-out wars and have the same patterns of victimisation of civilians, although in geographically confined patches.

Moro parts of Mindanao also suffer from feudal family hostilities (*rido*, *pagpauli* etc.), which sometimes imbricate with the larger GRP-MNLF-MILF wars. These clashes are even smaller in scale than the limited wars, but they involve shootouts and revenge killings of civilians and contribute to militarisation of society. There is also the daily dread of routine intimidation by armed actors which envelops Muslim and Christian Mindanawons in fear, irrespective of whether military clashes are occurring or not. The power of the gun, which is displayed and used openly in public spaces similar to Pakistan or Afghanistan, speaks in the precautions and preparations for flight that Mindanawons have devised with worst-case scenarios in mind.

Northern and eastern parts of Mindanao (Christian-populated) have witnessed a long-running armed communist challenge to GRP by the New People's Army (NPA), which generates its own forms of violence. But since the NPA's war is nationwide, based on Maoist ideology rather than ethnic identity, and thus not comparable to the Eelam struggle in Sri Lanka, this book will not deal with civilian protection issues produced by this other war. The geographical scope of this chapter, corollary to the North and East of Sri Lanka, are the Autonomous Region of Muslim Mindanao (ARMM) — an entity created after the GRP-MNLF peace agreement of 1996 as the first step towards devolution of power to the Moros — and adjoining areas where the 'Moro Problem' persists.

'Permanent War' and the Humanitarian Fraternity

After the 11 September 2001 terrorist attacks in the USA, Mindanao was integrated into the American global 'war on terrorism' through a mutual understanding between the George W Bush administration and the Gloria Macapagal Arroyo regime of the GRP. The presence of al-Qaeda affiliated terrorist organizations like Jemaah Islamiyah and Abu Sayyaf in Mindanao converted a hitherto nationally-circumscribed war into an international open-ended war. The Bush administration's war czar, Defence Secretary Donald Rumsfeld, wrote in an April 2006 memo how Mindanao was integral to his neo-conservative vision of permanent war:

> Talk about Somalia, the Philippines, etc. make the American people realise they are surrounded in the world by violent extremists. It is going to be a long war. Iraq is only one battleground (Wright, 2007).

The superimposition of the 'war on terrorism' on the five centuries' war between colonising Christian armies and Moro political entities made the conflict more hazardous for civilians. The naming of Mindanao as one of the 'second fronts' of the 'war on terrorism' (the first being Afghanistan) created forebodings of a war that will never end.

Many strategic analysts agree that the real motive of the US government in declaring Mindanao as one of the 'second fronts' is to encircle China and prevent it from expanding its influence in Southeast Asia, a region traditionally under the American thumb. The think tank, RAND Corporation, had great influence on foreign policy in the George W Bush administration. It argued in December 2001 that 'China's emergence as a major regional power required a robust security assistance especially to the Philippines to re-establish deterrence' (Rabasa, 2001: 10). The anti-China aspect of the 'war on terrorism' coalition of the US and the Philippines is furthered by territorial disputes between GRP and the government of China over the Spratly (Nansha) Islands in the South China Sea (Lohman, 2009).

Since emergencies are the norm in a permanent war horizon, IOs have been operating in humanitarian avatars in the region right from the violence of the early 1970s. UNDP opened its office in the Philippines in 1965 and is the Resident Coordinator of the UN system in the country (UNDP, 2008C).

After the 1996 peace agreement between the Government of Philippines (GRP) and the MNLF, UNDP was made the Coordinator for the UN Multi-Donor Assistance Programme (MDAP), which funded emergency relief, disarmament, demobilisation and reintegration (DDR) of MNLF cadres, development of agriculture, forestry and fishery, 'strengthening of peace communities' and 'promotion of peace culture' (Carames, 2007: 3). Since 2005, UNDP has been the co-chair of 'ACT for Peace', the multi-million dollar successor of MDAP that aims to improve livelihoods in war-affected parts of Mindanao.

UNICEF started working in the Philippines from 1948 and provided 'emergency response' services in Mindanao from the late 1970s onward. The ICRC arrived in the Philippines at the invitation of the GRP in 1982, 'assisting and protecting civilians displaced or otherwise affected by armed clashes, primarily on the southern island of Mindanao', and also organising distribution of relief supplies to IDPs (ICRC, 2005A). OXFAM-GB began functioning in the Philippines in 1987 and has been active in shelter, education, healthcare and livelihoods sectors for evacuees in central Mindanao since the all-out-war of 2000 (OXFAM, 2003). Save the Children USA (SCF) has had a Country Office in the Philippines since 1982 and is into 'emergency preparedness and response' and 'helping children made vulnerable by armed conflict' in Mindanao. Since 2003, it is also the organiser of 37 local NGOs under the banner of Mindanao Emergency Response Network (MERN) to coordinate relief operations.

Frequent outbreaks of wars in Mindanao have kept our five IO cases ever ready to get into humanitarian mode of action, although most of them also have inclinations for long-term development programming. Each time a war has broken out in the region, foreign donor governments express interest in giving emergency aid through IOs.[3] This pattern of spells of intensified violence engendering relief and rehabilitation projects has been the mainstay of the humanitarian side of IO programming for decades, especially since Mindanao was made a theatre in the 'war on terrorism'.

IOs, Radical to Hidebound
For measuring the dependent variable — the degree of proactiveness of the five IO cases in the Philippines — I requested three astute sets of observers of IOs to code a table listing seven actions that the five cases either performed or did not in five years (2003-08). This table was formulated on the basis of locally relevant criteria which are a little different from those used in the Sri Lankan context (see Chapter 4) because no two wars are identical.

The first set of coders of my scale for Mindanao are diplomats from two European missions in Manila who cooperate discretely with activists in Muslim Mindanao on concrete solutions to persecution of civilians by armed actors.

This group's coding scale, completed in October 2008, is as follows:

Table 5.1. Group I's scale on the degree of proactiveness of five IGOs and INGOs towards civilian protection in the Philippines (GRP-MNLF-MILF conflict).

Action	UNDP	UNICEF	ICRC	OXFAM-GB	SCSL
Participates in and provides inputs to protection/human rights advocacy on Moro wars at the Manila level.	1	0	0	1	1
Intercedes for justice on behalf of relatives of abducted or harassed civilians with relevant armed actors or authorities.	0	0	1	0	0
Participates in or provides inputs to protection/human rights meetings at the Mindanao level.	0	1	0	1	0
Makes field visits to areas known to be critical to show conscious international presence and deter violence/civilian abuse.	0	0	0	0	0
Shares sensitive information on protection/human rights and cooperates with relevant human rights defenders at the local, national and international levels.	0	0	0	1	1
Has signed civil society petitions and/or issued any press releases of its own that oppose atrocities or call on armed parties to respect civilians and pursue non-violent paths.	0	0	1	1	0
Has field staffers who are conscious about human rights, irrespective of their specialisations in implementing relief or development projects.	1	1	0	1	0
Total score for each organization	2	2	2	5	2

Note: Coding rule is 1 if Yes; 0 if No.

In this version, OXFAM-GB is the most proactive, with a total score of 5 out of a maximum of 7. UNICEF is a distant second, with a score of 2 out of 7. UNDP, ICRC and SCF are tied at the bottom with scores of only 2 out of 7.

The second group of coders I approached for the Mindanao proactiveness scale are Moro attorneys who have legally defended civilians accused of involvement in 'terrorist' activities by the state security agencies. They are part of a wider network of lawyers who handle human rights cases of illegal arrest, detention, abuse and intimidation of civilians.

This group's coding scale, completed in January 2009, is as follows:

Table 5.2. Group II's scale on the degree of proactiveness of five IGOs and INGOs towards civilian protection in the Philippines (GRP-MNLF-MILF conflict).

Action	UNDP	UNICEF	ICRC	OXFAM-GB	SCSL
Participates in and provides inputs to protection/human rights advocacy on Moro wars at the Manila level.	1	0	0	1	1
Intercedes for justice on behalf of relatives of abducted or harassed civilians with relevant armed actors or authorities.	0	0	1	0	0
Participates in or provides inputs to protection/human rights meetings at the Mindanao level.	0	1	0	1	0
Makes field visits to areas known to be critical to show conscious international presence and deter violence/civilian abuse.	0	0	0	0	0
Shares sensitive information on protection/human rights and cooperates with relevant human rights defenders at the local, national and international levels.	0	0	0	1	1
Has signed civil society petitions and/or issued any press releases of its own that oppose atrocities or call on armed parties to respect civilians and pursue non-violent paths.	0	0	1	0	0
Has field staffers who are conscious about human rights, irrespective of their specialisations in implementing relief or development projects.	1	1	0	1	0
Total score for each organization	2	2	2	4	2

Note: Coding rule is 1 if Yes; 0 if No.

In this version, OXFAM-GB again tops the list as the most proactive IO, with a score of 4 out of a maximum of 7. UNDP, UNICEF, ICRC and SCF share the second place with a joint abysmal score of 2 out of 7.

The third group of coders are three local civil society leaders whose entire lives have been spent in espousing the cause of civilian sufferers of the Moro wars. They belong to one grand consortium of peace and human rights advocates that is the most prominent network of activists in ARMM and surrounding provinces.

This group's coding scale, completed in February 2009, looks as follows:

Table 5.3. Group III's scale on the degree of proactiveness of five IGOs and INGOs towards civilian protection in the Philippines (GRP-MNLF-MILF conflict).

Action	UNDP	UNICEF	ICRC	OXFAM-GB	SCSL
Participates in and provides inputs to protection/human rights advocacy on Moro wars at the Manila level	0	0	0	1	1
Intercedes for justice on behalf of relatives of abducted or harassed civilians with relevant armed actors or authorities.	0	0	1	0	0
Participates in or provides inputs to protection/human rights meetings at the Mindanao level	0	1	0	1	0
Makes field visits to areas known to be critical to show conscious international presence and deter violence/civilian abuse	1	0	1	0	0
Shares sensitive information on protection/human rights and cooperates with relevant human rights defenders at the local, national and international levels	1	1	0	1	1
Has signed civil society petitions and/or issued any press releases of its own that oppose atrocities or call on armed parties to respect civilians and pursue non-violent paths.	0	0	1	1	0
Has field staffers who are conscious about human rights, irrespective of their specialisations in implementing relief or development projects.	0	1	0	1	1
Total score for each organization	2	3	3	5	3

Note: Coding rule is 1 if Yes; 0 if No.

This version reaffirms the status of OXFAM-GB as the most proactive IO in the ARMM and surrounding provinces, with a total score of 5 out of a maximum of 7. UNICEF, ICRC and SCF share second place, with a score of 3 each. UNDP comes last with only 2 points.

As in the case of Sri Lanka, I averaged the scores from the three groups and came up with composite scores which are as follows: UNDP — 2.0, UNICEF — 2.66, ICRC — 2.33, OXFAM-GB — 4.66, SCF — 2.33. As in Sri Lanka, unless calibrated, the composite scores of UNICEF and ICRC would be inflated by the mandate factor, which is not the case with the other three IOs that chose to be proactive or not through non-mandated reasoning.

UNICEF does participate and provide inputs to protection/human rights meetings at the Mindanao level. This has to be seen as one of its mandated activities rather than evidence of its proactiveness. At the same time, the fact that all three coding groups mark UNICEF with a point for participation means that the organization's local personnel's diligence in fulfilling their mandated function must be recognised. So, I awarded a .5 instead of 1.0 for the relevant indicator. The net weighted score of UNICEF by this method is 2.16.

In the case of ICRC, none of the coders thought that it participates in advocacy at the Manila level or in protection/human rights meetings at the Mindanao level. So, its score is not inflated by the mandate variable and need not be adusted any further. The 2.33 points I obtained from averaging the three groups' tables can be retained as ICRC's proactiveness score.

The reordering effect of weighting the composite scores is slight (see Table 5.4). It makes UNICEF less proactive by a few decimal points than ICRC and SCF. While the weighting diminishes UNICEF's standing in the final ranking, I will show that ICRC and SCF have numerous gaps in their own behaviour towards protection of civilians and that there is no reason to celebrate their higher ranking over UNICEF by a small decimal difference. The distance between the rhetoric and reality of ICRC, SCF and UNICEF will become evident in subsequent sections.

Table 5.4. Final ranking of IO proactiveness in the Philippines.

Proactive IOs in descending order	Net weighted proactiveness score
OXFAM-GB	4.66
ICRC and SCF	2.33
UNICEF	2.16
UNDP	2.0

In the ranking of Table 5.4, OXFAM-GB is the radical leader with an impressive score of proactiveness that is 2.33 points clear of its nearest competitor. The most interesting comparison to evaluate rationalist and culturalist variables will be between OXFAM-GB and UNDP, which is at the bottom as a hidebound organization just like in Sri Lanka. Since two IOs, ICRC and SCF, are tied at second place, there is merit in comparing them to ach other and asking why they are coequal. The other puzzle that needs an explanation is the difference in proactiveness between UNICEF and IOs placed immediately and far above it.

Three-Layered Pressure Cooker

Before embarking on any of the specific dyadic comparisons of IOs that diverge in proactiveness, one must elaborate the *global, national and local* complex of material pressures and inducements that make up the 'Power' structures and bear down upon the prioritisation of all five IO cases.

As the temporal scope of the coders and of this book is limited to five years (2003-08) of humanitarian IOs' behaviour in ARMM and surrounding provinces, the unmistakable shadow that looms over every other 'Power' variable is the US' 'war on terrorism'. Since American forces began arriving in the Philippines in early 2002 under the new flag of the 'war on terrorism', the dynamic of the Moro wars and of the five centuries of conflict has changed. The Mindanao of 2010 looks different from the Mindanao of 1999 or 2000 due to the overwhelming global intrusion of the 'war on terrorism'.

While civilians and activists who have been the worst sufferers of the Moro wars complain of basic continuity and permanence of violence and discrimination against them for five centuries, the last eight years in which Mindanao became the 'second front' of the global 'war on terrorism' qualitatively altered ground realities such as the balance of power between the state security forces and the rebels, the type of weaponry and tactics used in combat, and the ways in which the humanitarian aid enterprise was tweaked to serve the interests of the warring parties. To contend that the 'war on terrorism' inflicted a paradigm shift on the Moro wars would be an exaggeration, but it definitely changed its hues.

The George W Bush-era 'war on terrorism' in Mindanao has throwbacks to the violent past of American colonial rule in the Philippines. Because US 'counter-terrorism' deployments tend to become constant, the US ambassador to the Philippines admitted that the American military presence in the country is 'semi-continuous' (Arguilas, 2005), though it is mostly as an ancillary to the AFP rather than to dictate terms to it. The official American and Filipino government position is that the US forces do not actually fight in Mindanao, but evidence has piled up in the last few years to the contrary (Docena, 2007). Human rights activists allege that US forces are directly involved in bombings and massacres of civilians on the island of Sulu and have a hand in atrocities alongside the AFP (Remollino1, 2008; Remollino2, 2008).

The AFP, rather than the Americans, is the local lead in launching attacks and mini-wars in ARMM and surrounding provinces. The backslapping and diplomatic-cum-military endorsement that the AFP gets from the US emboldens the former's officer corps to order disproportionate force in the war theatres with the assurance that the 'Big Brother' is on their side and that no force in the world can stop them from committing abuses.[4] American weaponry and technical assistance have also tilted the balance of fighting power in favour of the state.

Between 2006 and 2009, I often heard from MILF circles in Mindanao that they 'do not want to antagonise' the US. The MILF is aware that the creeping American acquisition of informal bases in Mindanao means that it can no longer demand outright secession from the Philippines in peace negotiations with GRP. In August 2006, the MILF went to the extent of acknowledging the possibility of allowing US military bases in MILF-controlled territory as part of a final peace deal on the grounds that that it was 'facing reality' (Scarpello, 2006). The 'war on terrorism' thus buttressed Manila's national security objective of defending its territorial integrity in Mindanao.

The doctrine of combining military thrust with humanitarian balm is a cardinal lesson that American instructors impart with religious conviction to AFP officers. US military analysts credit successes in counter-insurgency in the Philippines between 1898 and 1913 to 'the correct balance between attraction and chastisement', where conciliatory policies were selectively used to 'win the support of the local inhabitants' (Andrews, 2002: 5-6). In contemporary parlance, the 'hearts and minds' of some civilians have to be won to achieve total military victory against the enemy.

Military humanitarianism is not new in Mindanao, but it became a central pillar of AFP policy after annual 'counter-terrorism' exercises began with US troops in January 2002. GRP habitually rebuts progressives' criticisms of clandestine American war games in the country with the excuse that *Balikatan*'s 'focus is on humanitarian assistance' (Carcamo, 2009). Washington too insists that 'the close US relationship with the AFP has resulted in an important component that emphasises civil-military operations and human rights' (DOS, 2007). The US ambassador to the Philippines added in 2007 that 'these humanitarian assistance and training activities enable our soldiers to get to know each other, train together, and provide assistance in communities where the need is greatest' (GRP, 2008B).

Some of the humanitarian tasks being executed by the AFP with American assistance in the war-ravaged ARMM and surrounding provinces include free medical, dental and veterinary care camps, construction and repair of schools and other physical infrastructure in communities that are said to be 'most in need.' In reality, the choice of locating camps for these activities is primarily strategic and not need-based, i.e. in an area where the AFP is vying for dominance over the MILF or trying to weed out suspected MILF spies or dormant cells. The US military also distributes school bags, sewing machines and all kinds of non-food items to civilians as baits to enter these communities and 'soften' the path for an AFP or government-allied paramilitary to establish watch posts.

Central to the psychological warfare of the AFP and its American allies carried out in the guise of humanitarian missions is SALAAM (Special Advocacy and Livelihood Assistance for the Advancement Among Muslims), a plan to implement 'medico-civic services' in ARMM and surrounding provinces 'so that Muslims in the armed-conflict areas will be able to understand what the government is doing to help improve their lives' (GRP, 2008C). The strategic aim of these 'civic action' projects of the US military and the AFP is to win Moros over to the GRP side and to demonstrate to Moros that they can have a much better material existence if they defected or relocated from MILF-controlled territory to GRP-controlled areas. 'Civic action' in Mindanao is identical to the US military's 'civilian development teams' and 'provincial reconstruction teams' in Iraq and Afghanistan, which use humanitarian smokescreens for strategic ends (Save, 2004).

That civic action is a ruse to militarise ARMM and surrounding provinces and sink them deeper into the quagmire of war becomes crystal clear if one contrasts the expenditures of the US government on military inputs into the Philippines against the humanitarian inputs. According to the GRP's Department of Foreign Affairs, annual US military assistance to the Philippines in grants alone is $30 million. On top of that, Washington had given $12 million and $16 million in 2007 and 2008 respectively to the Philippines for naval security. The US also shares the costs of a Joint Defence Assessment (DFA) worth $400 million over ten years with the Philippines. Juxtaposed to these large military outlays to the Philippines as a major non-NATO ally (MNNA), 'humanitarian mission ships, such as the USNS *Mercy*, which visited Mindanao, helped 32,981 patients and 4.468 animals under the MEDCAP (Medical Civic Action Programme), valued at $2.068 million' (ME, 2009). Military humanitarianism is thus purely window dressing behind which the real objective is to prolong and intensify war.

With American inputs in 2004, GRP developed the National Internal Security Plan (NISP), which tied military objectives in Mindanao to 'poverty 'alleviation' or 'social development' schemes, many of which were budgeted to Official Development Assistance (ODA). US economic aid to GRP grew by an average of 33 percent per annum since the September 11th terrorist attacks, partly to finance NISP.[5] NISP's origins lie in the Trilateral Senior Leader Strategic Planning Symposia between GRP and the governments of the US and Australia, the two top donor states in the Philippines, over a two year period. One product of these trilateral meetings is the concept of '3D' peace, i.e. the merger of diplomacy, defence and development by the donors and the GRP to defeat 'terrorists' in the Philippines.

A key ingredient of 3D is for Manila and its donor allies 'to work in partnership to expand a stable zone of peace and development, thereby denying domestic (Abu Sayyaf Group) and international (Jemaah Islamiyah) terrorists the physical and psychological space they require to survive' (USG, 2006). Using the mega caption of 'peace and development' in Mindanao, the US pioneered the multi-million dollar 'Basilan model' of humanitarian relief to 'generate popular support for the AFP, enhance their freedom of movement and control over the terrain, strengthen force protection, and improve information sharing' (USG, 2006).

President Arroyo's theory that 'terrorism breeds on poverty' (USG, 2003) was amalgamated into the US-Australia-Japan multi-donor 'peace and development' aid plans for Mindanao, to the complete detriment of the burning issues of religious discrimination, human rights abuses and violence against civilians in the Moro wars. In 2003, GRP declared a 'war on poverty' with $100 million World Bank funding as the complement to the 'war on terrorism', unleashing the 'social development component of the AFP's pacification campaign' in Mindanao (Padilla, 2006: 133).

Australia, New Zealand, Spain, Japan and the US joined hands to finance these wars on poverty and terrorism in Mindanao under the aegis of the Development Assistance Committee (DAC) of the OECD. The DAC is guided by a 'whole of government approach' to foreign aid. According to the framers of this approach, problems in conflict-affected states used to be 'perceived (by donors) primarily through a development and humanitarian lens.' This perception 'changed following 9/11, however' due to the 'broader strategic significance of fragile states' (OECD, 2006: 17). In response, donor powers had to ensure that 'security actors and objectives related to the security domain are increasingly included in the development debate', tying the humanitarian enterprise to geostrategic and geo-economic motives (OECD, 2006: 7). In Chapter 3, we mentioned Morgenthau envisaging aid performing a 'political function' for statecraft. The 'whole of government' approach in the 'war on terrorism' is based on this realist logic.

In Mindanao, all the major foreign aid institutions of donor states like USAID (American) , AusAID (Australia), JICA (Japan) and DFID (UK) complement the strategic, military and intelligence arms of their respective states in accord with the 'whole of government' reforms. They also consult with each other through their respective diplomatic embassies and secret service representatives in Manila and with GRP's ministries in deciding which thematic and geographical areas of Mindanao need 'peace and development' interventions.

USAID, which has instituted thorough 'civil-military cooperation' with the Pentagon, funds IOs and local NGOs in ARMM and surrounding provinces to exclusively implement 'peace and development' projects that complement the relief and development funds dished out by the US army and the AFP. USAID claims that its 'socio-economic interventions' in Mindanao 'inspired' INGOs funded by CIDA (Canada's donor arm), AusAID, Spain and the EU to similarly 'complement the peace process' (KPM, 2006:5).

Here, we must note a nuance about Canada and Australia with regard to their aid strategy towards Mindanao. While they are willing lieutenants of the US under the 'war on terrorism', they also pursue pure capitalistic interests in Mindanao governed by the requirements of their multinational mining corporations. CIDA and AusAID earmark their aid to IOs with the intention of softening the path for Canadian and Australian natural resource extraction firms in Mindanao. Since their mining majors are themselves guilty of raising private armies and abusing local civilians in Mindanao, it would be illogical for CIDA or AusAID to encourage IOs to pay serious attention to civilian protection in the Moro wars. The linkages among aid, plundering of Mindanao's resources, and the 'peace and development' formula for IOs illustrate that relations of coercion and force are essential for the capitalist world-system to thrive.

The absence of donor interest in civilian protection and human rights in Mindanao and the corollary eagerness to fund relief and development projects naturally filters down to IO programming and priorities. Through donor monetary power and the writ of the state, 'peace and development' became a hegemonic idea in Mindanao, adopted by conservative local NGOs and humanitarian IOs. Donors, the GRP and even the post-1996 MNLF, which gave up secessionism through integration into the Philippine 'mainstream', defined the problem space in ARMM and surrounding provinces as the lack of 'peace and development' rather than the permanence of war, violence and abuses. IOs in Mindanao fell in line with this overwhelming layer of global pressure to downplay civilian protection.

The donor-imposed conservatism on IOs not only impacts their priorities but also their choice of local implementing partners (Chaulia, 2007: 19). Most humanitarian IOs in Mindanao cold-shoulder 'radical' NGOs that struggle against impunity due to this conservative donor-driven consensus. With rare exceptions, the humanitarian IO fraternity in Mindanao associates with only those local NGOs which are subservient to the 'war on terrorism's ideology of 'peace and development', which devalues civilian protection and justice for the abused.

Moving down the ladder from the global to the national level of material pressures and inducements on IOs, one must decipher the ways in which the Philippine state strives to keep abuses of civilians by its agents in the Moro wars out of view of citizens and the rest of the world. Malacañang, the presidential palace in Manila and the seat of national power, has been customarily wary of 'internationalisation' of the Bangsamoro claims to self-determination, fearing that it would externalise a domestic problem, invite unwarranted global interference and erode state sovereignty.

In 1975, GRP accepted mediation of the Organization of Islamic Conference (OIC) in peace talks with the MNLF only after being threatened with an oil embargo by OPEC. In later years, GRP voluntarily allowed a continued role for OIC in settlement of the Moro wars because the Organization compelled the MNLF to lower its aspirations to autonomy within the framework of Philippine territorial integrity (Santos, 1999).

Likewise, GRP involved Malaysia from 2001 as a 'third-party facilitator' and ceasefire monitor with the MILF only after being fully assured that, as a fellow ASEAN member state and an OIC member, the latter would respect the territorial integrity and sovereignty of the Philippines (GRP, 2003). Thus, be it Indonesia, Malaysia, Libya or the US, the only form of 'internationalisation' that Malacañang prefers is one that will squelch Bangsamoro secessionism. The same rule applies to humanitarian IOs, which are expected by the Philippine state to be aides in its efforts to preserve its sovereignty over Mindanao.

While permitting international media coverage of the Moro wars, Malacañang and the AFP attempt to minimise reporting that paints the state's actions in a poor light and to maximise coverage of Islamic extremism and terrorism as the real plagues in Mindanao. One leading Moro strategic thinker reasons that GRP has succeeded in averting undesirable international interventions in Mindanao by ensuring 'distorted media coverage tending to validate the Philippine government's positions in the conflict (and) dominated by the 'war on terror' discourse' (Mastura, 2008:97). A bamboo curtain separating the news media from atrocities and sufferings of civilians in the Moro wars exists due to AFP's protectiveness about its turf in Mindanao. The censorship has been described by rights defenders as 'a virtual news blackout or 'under-reportage' of the situation' (Rasul, 2008).

The Anglo-American international media, which caters to Western foreign policy priorities, also ignores protection crises in the Moro wars and mainly proffers 'juicy' stories that sensationalise and exaggerate the terrorism of the Abu Sayyaf and Jemaah Islamiyah.[6] This strategy helps to disseminate propaganda that the 'war on terrorism' is proving to be a great success in the Philippines (Wiseman, 2007; Montlake, 2007), while sweeping under the carpet the unending agony of war for civilians. The news blackout on Mindanao is also honoured by humanitarian IOs that witness far starker realities of war than journalists.

GRP has numerous institutional channels to guide IO behaviour along tracks that serve its strategic interests in the Moro wars. Principal among them is the National Disaster Coordinating Council (NDCC), which determines the 'system' and rules for humanitarian operations in the country. Headed by the Secretary of National Defence and staffed *inter alia* by the Chief of Staff of the AFP, NDCC issue authoritative guidelines 'that all stakeholders and players in the humanitarian efforts related to disaster management shall follow' (NDCC, 2008: 2). The onus of the NDCC-steered humanitarian ship is on relief distribution of food and non-food commodities. Each IO and local NGO has to share its Assistance Distribution Plan (ADP) and Reports for clearance with Regional Disaster Coordinating Councils (RDCCs), sub-units of NDCC on the ground in war zones.

The RDCC for ARMM 'coordinates' with IOs in the Moro war theatres. When the Memorandum of Agreement (MOA-AD) between GRP and MILF broke down in August 2008 and led to forced displacement of more than half a million and killings of hundreds of civilians, all that the RDCC and IOs decided was to focus on 'clusters' like 'water, sanitation and hygiene (WASH), nutrition, health, food and emergency shelter' (GRP, 2008A). There was no protection/human rights cluster for obvious reasons — the AFP and the MILF were going on the rampage against civilians, with the latter killing scores of Christian Mindanawons and the former bombing and shelling Moro villages with full gusto.

An important member of the NDCC is the GRP's Secretary of the Department of Social Welfare and Development (DSWD), which takes the lead in the 'social protection' cluster during humanitarian crises. The 'social protection' that DSWD manages is defined as a 'targeting system for the poor' and includes 'livelihood' and 'hunger mitigation' programmes (PDF, 2008). It is a rehash of the 'war on poverty' referred to earlier and has no civil and political rights content that could protect civilians from abuses and violence of armed actors.

DSWD bureaucrats supervise 'evacuation centres' and relief distribution by IOs during wars in Mindanao. They play a partisan role by doing the bidding of GRP's local government units (LGUs), which aim to neutralise the MILF's power and sway over the Moros. The all-too-familiar story of humanitarian aid being diverted and misused by parties to a war for strategic ends is commonplace in the Moro wars thanks to DSWD's manipulation by the LGUs. Elsewhere, I have documented examples of how most IOs of MERN, with the exception of OXFAM-GB, acquiesced to this manipulation of aid without a murmur (Chaulia, 2007).

The Philippine state has powerful Muslim-dominated LGUs in Mindanao to assist the AFP's military objective of defeating secessionism. The ARMM Governorship was first won by the MNLF supremo Nur Misuari after the 1996 peace agreement but passed on to a leading pro-Malacañang Moro feudal clan known as the Ampatuans. The absolutist military and political control that the Ampatuans and their relatives had over government-controlled parts of ARMM for over a decade was akin to a fiefdom[7]. They possessed their own posse of private armies and enforcers, a horde of vassal *Datus* (Moro gentry), paramilitaries called CVOs and CAFGUs (technically under AFP command, but often leased to the LGUs to enforce 'peace and order'), and a claim over central government funds and welfare schemes at the regional and provincial levels. The abusive behaviour of LGUs in ARMM and surrounding provinces is folklore because it stretches from the office of the Governor down to the Barangay Captains (lowest government representatives at the village level) who owe their posts to the feudal benevolence of clans like the Ampatuans.

President Arroyo's victories in elections were dependent on the Ampatuan's feudal machine politics, which delivered clean sweeps to her 'Team Unity' candidates. Political scientist Paul Hutchcroft explained the indispensability of Andal Ampatuan, the former feudal patriarch of Muslim Mindanao, to Arroyo's political fortunes in this fashion:

'Whatever the president wants, he will follow, said a family friend to Newsbreak.' 12-0 is what Ma'am wants (Hutchcroft, 2008).

The feudalistic hold of LGUs on Moro societies outside MILF control and their inflated importance in the eyes of Malacañang demand respect from humanitarian IOs in Mindanao. For field-based personnel of IOs, the embodiment and symbol of the sovereign state are the LGUs. IOs can ill-afford to anger LGUs that happen to be major violators of civilian rights.

Broadly speaking, the MILF welcomes humanitarian IOs and does not threaten or try to co-opt them into its politico-military structures the way the state does. As a guerrilla movement organised for Bangsamoro self-determination, it nurses ambitions (sometimes cloaked for expediency) of an independent homeland that should be recognised by the UN and the major world powers. The MILF leadership always hankers for the 'internationalisation' of the 'Moro problem' so that it can build global sympathy and goodwill for its liberation struggle. Therefore, it wants more IOs to come to Mindanao and operate there so that the oppression of the Moros can break free of the news blackout of abuses that GRP and the Americans have instituted.

The MILF's Bangsamoro Development Agency (BDA) is mandated by the peace process 'to determine, lead and manage relief, rehabilitation and development programs in the conflict-affected areas in Mindanao.' Humanitarian IOs do not have to answer to the BDA or MILF in the same way as they do to the NDCC system of the state. As an Islamist revolutionary movement, hardcore fundamentalists within MILF warn IOs against harming the 'local culture' of Muslims in Mindanao by changing their values or faith. This limits IOs' programming on occasions but is not a big constraint since most of the IOs in Mindanao have local Muslim implementing partners.

Humanitarian IOs in the Philippines thus face a three-layered material pressure cooker, viz. a donor community that lionises the 'war on terrorism', a strong nation-state that has a grip over the institutional architecture of emergency response, and a panoply of LGUs that dominate provincial-level politics. Drawing upon the foregoing discussion, I have summarised the material pressures and inducements applying on all IOs in Mindanao to set their priorities on protection as follows:

Summary Table 5.5. Generic 'Power' pressures and inducements on IOs in the Philippines.

a) Donor pressures to lower emphasis on civilian rights — Maximum.

b) Donor inducements to increase emphasis on civilian rights — Low, even when there are humanitarian crises and mass displacements.

c) State pressures to lower emphasis on civilian rights — High, especially during wars.

d) Rebel pressures to lower emphasis on civilian rights — Low to medium, especially when MILF's 'child soldiers' issue is under the scanner.

e) Provincial government pressures to hush up abuses of civilians by paramilitaries — High.

If the ratings in Summary Table 5.5 express the eagle's eye view of the rational 'Power' structures that impact upon behaviour of all IOs in Mindanao, we must investigate whether the structures vary in their application to specific IO cases.

Radical versus Ultraconservative

What explains OXFAM-GB's 2.66 point lead over UNDP in the net weighted proactiveness ranking (see Table 5.4) for Mindanao? Why does OXFAM-GB appear so radical on civil and political rights compared to UNDP? R1's answer is that the former faces lesser material demands and inducements from powerful donors, the host state and rebel groups than the latter.

A recent episode in which OXFAM-GB faced GRP pressure helps test the ramifications of this hypothesis. In September 2008, when war escalated between the AFP and the MILF in central Mindanao, the Executive Secretary (highest ranking member of President Arroyo's cabinet) Eduardo Ermita denied that there was any humanitarian crisis due to the military campaign and described the situation as 'not that bad' (Avendaño, 2008). He added that GRP had enough resources to deal with more than half a million IDPs and that it 'did not need help from international aid agencies' (Avendaño, 2008).

OXFAM-GB'S Country Director reacted to this obfuscating depiction of a human tragedy by Malacañang with a strong statement saying 'the humanitarian needs in Mindanao are real' and that 'civilians live in fear for their safety and lives because of the presence of armed groups in their villages' (ABS, 2008). DSWD's national chief, the Social Welfare Secretary, took immediate exception to OXFAM-GB's outspokenness and said that reports of a crisis were 'exaggerated' (Fernandez, 2008). A day later, I learnt from confidential sources that Secretaries of GRP 'grilled' OXFAM-GB for its 'insolent behaviour' and insisted that it water down its language.

An OXFAM-GB employee in central Mindanao narrated the clash and its reverberations to me in this manner:

> By calling Ermita's bluff, our Manila office took a bold and daring step even by the normally proactive standards of OXFAM advocacy. In the field offices, all of us braced up for the worst, thinking that this step would make life difficult for us. But there are also countervailing forces that offer space for expressing concerns about civilian protection. The media is a major ally of OXFAM and we often utilise their broad outreach power in such a way that GRP cannot browbeat us into silence. There is a strong anti-establishment leftwing in the media at the national level which exposes the inadequacies and failings of the state and enjoys wide readership and viewers. Remember that our recent countering of Ermita

was carried by the popular breaking news channel, ABS CBN. OXFAM is also a beneficiary of the generally high state of civil society mobilisation in Mindanao, an advocacy space that enables us to join in and call a spade a spade and a massacre a massacre.[8]

True to these assertions, OXFAM-GB pre-empted every other IO in Mindanao to issue a Press Statement on the repercussions for civilian protection when the post-MOA-AD violence between AFP and MILF had just begun rearing its head. The Statement emphasised that 'the protection of civilians-whether Muslim, Christian or Lumad-should be a paramount concern' and that 'the safety of ALL (emphasis original) internally displaced people must be assured' (OXFAM, 2008).

OXFAM-GB has a separate Advocacy Department in Manila, led by an outspoken human rights activist. This Department plays a lead role as Chair of the forum of INGOs at the Manila level, known as Philippine INGO Network (PINGON), and is at the forefront of bringing issues of civilian protection in the Moro wars to the notice of other IOs.

While OXFAM-GB's national headquarters has shown a rare courage in advocating for civilian rights in the Moro wars, thanks to its closeness to progressive political forces in the Philippines like the Commission on Human Rights, the organization has not been able to evade the chokehold of feudal-dominated LGUs in the field. One of its local community organisers in Mindanao elaborated the fear that the Moro *Datus* engender:

> There is a culture of silence in ARMM which forces OXFAM to adopt a low profile approach when it gets involved in protection-related activities. If one were to openly criticise the LGUs, for instance, we would be killed. So, we try our level best to coordinate with the Provincial and Regional Governors' offices and engage with them so as not to fall foul of them. Even in our protection activities, care is taken to invite LGU representatives and make them feel important on their turfs.[9]

Thus, OXFAM-GB finds it relatively riskier to hold the LGUs and their paramilitaries accountable for violence against civilians than to criticise the federal government's agents. OXFAM-GB's field staffers witness the depredations of the LGU-directed CVOs and CAFGUs in central Mindanao but remain tight lipped about bringing it to wider notice due to this fear factor.

One advantage for OXFAM-GB to maintain autonomy in the Philippines is that it can fund itself from the financial support of the global headquarters in Oxford. Prior to 2006, it also received funding from ECHO, a donor that had an interest in seeing protection mainstreamed into IOs but which 'phased out' from Mindanao in 2006.[10] As a matter of principle, OXFAM-GB does not solicit from USAID for reasons elaborated to me by one of its officials:

Even if the Americans were willing to give us a million dollars, we decided as a matter of principle against taking it. This decision is important for the organization's neutrality and impartiality, since the US is a party to the conflict in Mindanao. Had we received funds from USAID, it would spell doom for OXFAM's strong social roots in Moro communities, who are highly critical of the American intervention in the conflict. It would also gag us and lead to downsizing of our human rights advocacy work and turn us into a clone of a fellow INGO, Save the Children-USA.[11]

The pressures of the 'war on terrorism' are thus somewhat relieved from OXFAM-GB's shoulders due to its donor composition. As a member of MERN, OXFAM worries about the misuse of humanitarian aid that happens routinely when government agencies are partners in relief missions in Mindanao. It therefore strives to forego intermediaries like DSWD and deploys its own field staffers who are trained in impartial means of aid delivery and civilian protection. In many ways, these dodging actions of OXFAM-GB reveal that there can be creative solutions to the avalanche of 'Power' pressures weighing on an IO.

UNDP in the Philippines, on the other hand, is an out-and-out ultraconservative IO that feels the heat and wilts under the load of material pressures from the global to the local levels. At every step, its work is compromised by cooptation into donor power and state structures, a burden that smothers any iota of proactiveness that might theoretically exist in an IO which rhetorically pays homage to 'human security' in its jargon and publicity.

UNDP's ACT for Peace is a government-sponsored programme with the explicit goal of contributing to the GRP's peace processes with the MILF (and the NPA in northern Mindanao). It is based on GRP's 'peace and development' strategy for resolving the armed conflicts in the country through a 'war on poverty'. Launched in 2005, ACT's first three phases were implemented through a mixture of DEX (Direct Execution by UNDP in the early stages) and NEX (National Execution in the later stages). NEX vests 'responsibility and accountability for the formulation, management and implementation of UNDP-supported programmes on the designated (government) Executive Agency in the programme's host country' (UNDP, 2006a).

The latest framework for Phase IV of ACT for Peace is called NIM (National Implementation Modality), which requires the programme to follow government priorities even more closely than under NEX. UNDP is only the 'managing agent' for the programme, while the reins of decision making and direction are in the hands of the LGU of the ARMM, which enjoys the status of 'lead implementing agency' (ACT, 2008).

I asked a UNDP hand in the field about how much direction and pressure he received from the LGUs, over and above those from the GRP. His response was as follows:

> Since the fighting has escalated in August 2008, UNDP is coordinating with the RDCC and the LGUs to distribute relief supplies to the IDPs. Often, LGUs recommend that we fund particular projects in particular Barangays or municipalities so that it suits their political games. We try to explain to them that projects will only be on as-per-need basis, but there is constant negotiation involved with the LGUs in which we have to defer to some of their wishes.[12]

ACT for Peace's budget is distributed among five components. The GRP's guidelines on which component should get how much percent of the budget share are clear. At least 60 percent is to be devoted to material services for livelihoods and socio-economic benefits (skill development, micro-credit, health, water etc.). A small portion is for 'peace-building', which is theoretically connected to civilian protection but not in practice. The allocations are decided by the GRP in agreement with the 'multi-donors' (Australia, New Zealand, Spain and Italy), close diplomatic allies of the US which subscribe to the '3D' peace formula of the 'war on terrorism'.

UNDP's eagerness to be the Coordinator of the Multi-Donor Assistance Programme (MDAP) means that it cannot ignore or sidestep the conservative ideology that attenuates civilian protection in the 'war on terrorism'. The organization has never faced funding shortages in Mindanao, but its desire to acquire more funds and be in the good books of the principal donor states in the Philippines leave it with little choice but to lobby to be the IO face of the MDAP.

Political economy hypothesis R2 suggests that IOs which compete harder for scarce funds and political patronage will be less proactive than those which do not compete that much. UNDP competes hard with other UN agencies to be the main beneficiary and shepherd of the MDAP and stay as close as possible to the Philippine state, the antithesis of OXFAM-GB, which distances itself from the USAID-dominated donor circuit. R2's explanatory potential is thus confirmed in this comparison.

Elsewhere, I have elaborated exactly how UNDP became a prop in the 'war on terrorism's' effort to conceal atrocities against civilians in the Moro wars

(Chaulia, 2007). Blissfully unconcerned about neutrality in a war zone, UNDP conspicuously throws in its weight behind the state and the donor agenda.

Does it not face any pressures and demands from the MILF due to its state-driven politicisation? An ACT official responded with some vignettes:

> Our 'Peace and Development Advocates' (PDAs) are ex-MNLF combatants who laid down arms after the 1996 peace agreement and joined the national mainstream. They have relatives in the MILF now and this makes it easy to gain acceptance for the programme with the MILF. Moreover, we involve the BDA (development arm of the MILF) in our implementation and that assuages the rebel movement. Recently, the MILF objected to Barangay Development Plans being decided by PDAs and asked that it be consulted in drafting them. Sometimes, the AFP does not heed our requests and even blocks our relief supplies from going into certain remote areas owing to suspicion that they may be siphoned off by the MILF. Sections of the army keep an eye on us because they know that many of our PDAs happen to be close to the MILF local commanders in the Barangays. These are samples of the kind of complex demands placed on us by armed actors.[13]

To sum up, the pressures and demands on UNDP to neglect civilian protection exceed those handled by OXFAM-GB. Yet, we have noted that OXFAM-GB faces lesser pressures precisely because its staff members used creativity and ingenuity to work around the three-layered pressure complex. The question arises as to why UNDP's personnel are happily status quoist and do not even attempt to innovate despite coming across cases of serious IHL violations against civilians. In other words, is there explanatory room for 'Ideas' in decoding the puzzle of the large 2.66-point-gap in proactiveness between OXFAM-GB and UNDP?

Hypotheses C1 and C2 propose that OXFAM-GB has a less bureaucratic culture and identity and a belief system that is not obeisant to state sovereignty in comparison to UNDP. This certainly appears to be true at the outset, but the proof lies in the specifics.

OXFAM-GB's personnel have a progressive worldview laced with fairly radical views of justice and human rights. Unlike any other IO, Ideological convictions within the organization have a definite contribution to making civilian protection an essential component of its work. The typical humanitarian IO in Mindanao has strictly lived by the rules and constraints set by donors, the host state and, to a lesser extent, by the guerrillas. The supremacy of state sovereignty (hypothesis C1) has never been in doubt for most humanitarians.

A leading Filipino intellectual, Benedicto Bacani, has accurately articulated this phenomenon as follows:

> Aid agencies and donor institutions respond only through Philippine government priorities, both national and local. They cannot impose their own agenda or priorities. They are taken in as partners of the government (Bacani, 2004: 100).

OXFAM-GB's leadership, however, thought outside the box of the state-dictated peace process and even criticised the DDR rush since 1996 to pander to the ex-MNLF combatants while neglecting the political and economic rights of ordinary civilians. One of the organization's officials expressed the disagreement thus:

> Such a militaristic approach to peace sends out the wrong signals that if you take up arms against the government, one day, you will be rewarded with a generous economic package. It conveys that it pays to be a warrior.[14]

The parameters set by the GRP-MNLF agreements downgraded civilian protection for humanitarian IOs who defined their mission and identity within the folds of this peace process. OXFAM-GB, however, did not allow itself to be subsumed by the ideational hegemony of 'peace and development' because it had activist local partner networks like Mindanao People's Caucus (MPC) and Consortium of Bangsamoro Civil Society (CBCS), which were pushing for greater popular say in the official peace processes between GRP and Bangsamoro militant groups.

Propulsion by radical local activists animates the internal thinking within OXFAM-GB. The organization's staffers often talk about civilian protection as a cross-cutting concern across all specialised programmes rather than in bureaucratic terms of creating a separate 'protection programme' with a budget. The method has worked well and led to mainstreaming protection in whatever OXFAM-GB does in Mindanao. I enquired if inter-sectoral tussles have ever intruded into this percolation of a protection culture and received the following response from an OXFAM-GB community organiser:

> Inter-departmental turf wars do exist, but thanks to the rigorous protection emphasis in staff nurturing, no one grudges the importance of protection. In fact, while budgeting, the Manila office makes sure that if there is a shortage of funds for protection and a surplus in, say 'WatSan', then it shifts resources to protection. Such an internal redistribution is

not gainsaid by 'WatSan' specialists, but understood. The reason for this is that all OXFAM staffers are made to memorise the key concept of VCD (Violence, Coercion and Deprivation) as the triple barriers to human security. This concept is biblical for OXFAM culture and is inculcated among incoming staff during orientation itself. We even train local implementing partner NGOs in the basics of protection consciousness and sharing of sensitive information.[15]

Identity-wise, the individuals at the helm and at the grassroots in OXFAM-GB Philippines see themselves as working for a 'rights-based organization.' Its staff members tend to be highly motivated by progressive values such as opposition to oppression and solidarity for the victimised. Proactive hiring practices buttress this identity.

UNDP Philippines' organizational culture, identity and beliefs are the obverse of OXFAM-GB's. 'Ideas' distinguish the two IOs like chalk and cheese. The UN system's Development Assistance Framework in the Philippines (2005-09) asserts that one of the root causes for human insecurity in Mindanao is 'abuse of authority and violation of human rights' (UN, 2004: 16-18). UNDP has incorporated UNDAF's benchmarks into its own programmatic reporting literature and claims to have a 'Justice and Human Rights' sector. The organization even boasts that it is 'alone among UN agencies' in 'mainstreaming' human rights throughout United Nations country teams (UNDP, 2006B). But as we have seen throughout this book, the gap between rhetoric and reality speaks out loud here.

Two programmatic examples of how UNDP turns a blind eye to political rights of ordinary civilians on the ground in Mindanao illustrate how stubbornly subservient the organization's personnel are to state sovereignty and bureaucracy. The GRP-UNDP IDP Programme was a one and a half year-long €3 million effort to rehabilitate IDPs in ARMM and surrounding provinces. Its three-fold programmatic focus was placed on 1) relief, 2) rehabilitation and 3) culture of peace and access to justice. The third component involved activities such as declaring the communities under UNDP's ambit as 'peace sanctuaries' and building and repairing Sharia Courts and Halls of Justice. When asked why civilian protection was not considered part of the justice component, former programme officials shrugged and said, 'We did not receive any reports of abuse or violence against our beneficiaries.'[16]

In fact, threats and violence against IDPs in ARMM by the AFP and government paramilitaries were so widespread that they could not be missed, especially the fear generated by proximity of army camps to resettled villages. When the main perpetrators are agents of state, traditional justice infrastructure is helpless. Unfortunately, the UNDP mandarins believed otherwise. One critic of this UNDP programme said:

> IDPs have political rights, including the right to return to their homes and lands. Instead of defending these rights, what international organizations do is act as pacifiers to take the sting out of civilians who have suffered great indignities and quieten them to the point that they no longer demand humane treatment from the army and settle for handouts and doles.[17]

Declaration of villages as 'peace and development communities' is a favourite theme in UNDP programmes. In Sulu, I met a local NGO partner implementing 'ACT for Peace' and learnt that five Barangays had been adopted and declared by its staff members as 'peace and development communities.' The criteria for choosing villages for this status were that they had to be in 'non-problematic areas where violence does not occur so that donors who want quantifiable results would be pleased.' [18]

This NGO claimed to be 'very close' to the Provincial Governor of Sulu and mentioned that whatever it implements goes through the approval procedures and 'blessings' of the LGUs. At that time, a fierce AFP and American military operation against the Abu Sayyaf was happening a few miles from these 'peace and development communities' with mortar shelling, aerial bombing and mass displacement. Local activists were agitated by the fact that the Provincial Governor was out of station and was either unwilling or unable to halt the violence. Avoidance of 'critical areas', thanks to the partnership with the executive arms of the Philippine state, renders UNDP impervious to political rights problems faced by the Moros. The policy that only 'non-problematic areas' should receive development aid furthers the economic imbalances between GRP-controlled 'safe' areas and the MILF or Abu Sayyaf-controlled 'dangerous' Barangays.

I specifically enquired from ACT personnel why, despite peppering their programme design literature with the phrase 'Human Security', they never advocate or act for human rights and civilian protection in the war zones. Their revealing response was as follows:

> The programme is government-driven and implemented and so, one should not expect that we will take any radical position. Instead of talking about violations and abuses, we make sure that all the socio-economic components are implemented on a 'peace-based approach'. By stressing capacity building and community empowerment, we adopt an indirect approach to addressing IHL and human rights problems.[19]

While one or two examples crop up about the success of UNDP's PDAs keeping their villages safe from attacks, 'Zones of Peace' in general have failed to protect their residents from armed conflict or militarisation because they lack the credible inputs of progressive local activists whose participation is discouraged by the top-heavy and LGU-friendly UNDP.

ACT personnel are impervious to civilian protection also because of their peculiar identities and self-understandings. The programme's staffers in the ARMM are neither fully UN employees nor GRP employees. One of them explained the ambiguity in the following terms:

> Our job contracts were signed by the former Secretary of the Office of the Presidential Adviser on the Peace Process (OPAPP). So, our identities and loyalties are somewhere in between the state and the UN. This has an effect on the way we visualise the needs of the communities and try to address them. ACT for Peace has a dual nature because it merges the political objectives of the GRP with the global mandate of UNDP.[20]

The entrapment of UNDP's identity with that of the state is so complete in Mindanao that it is not surprising that corruption and misuse of the millions of dollars of 'peace and development' aid is rampant in the organization. The brotherhood between ACT and LGUs is leavened by financial give-and-take on aid projects, an open secret in the local NGO circuit in Mindanao.

Corruption in the development and humanitarian fields is an ugly reality that has been widely observed. From financial fraud and embezzlement to misuse of agency assets, bribes and abusive/coercive practices of aid givers, the $15 billion per annum relief and aid industry has always contained within it the bureaucratic impulse for greed and accumulation (Barnaby and Harvey, 2005). Protection activities and programmes do no hold as much allure as relief and development because they are either legalistic in content or involve mainly human, not material, resources. The scope for black marketing and siphoning off is highest where tangible goods are being bought or disbursed, i.e. in relief and development.

Corruption through 'peace and development' rackets in Mindanao is at least one reason why 'despite almost a decade of mainly externally-funded development assistance, the ARMM has not shown any improvement. Instead, it has been pushed further into dismal levels of poverty' (Cagoco-Guiam, 2006:5). UNDP pumped millions of dollars into LGUs and local NGOs in Mindanao through the MDAP, but ARMM and surrounding provinces continued to languish where they have been for decades in national economic standings — right at the bottom.

Elsewhere, I have argued that the rent-seeking opportunities that the humanitarian-cum-development enterprise dangles are prime reasons why bureaucratic IOs like UNDP prefer to limit their interest to economic rights rather than civil and political rights of war-affected civilians (Chaulia, 2007). Even the economic rights pursued by UNDP and other humanitarians are constructed to stay 'soft', i.e. stressing livelihood, health and nutrition rather than 'hard' economic rights like return of army-occupied lands to their civilian owners or ending serf labour systems under the *Datus*. Bureaucratic organizations, to hark back to Crozier, have a pathological liking for orderliness. UNDP Philippines' culture perfectly matches this attitude since it accepts the existing feudal order of the *Datus* as immutable and cosies up to the LGUs as natural partners.

From the foregoing discussion, it is obvious that hypotheses C1 and C2 have explanatory power for the widely separable conservatism of UNDP and radicalism of OXFAM-GB. Since it appears that material pressure hypotheses R1 and R2 are also correlated to the difference in proactiveness of the two IOs, the only logical conclusion of this section would be to conclude that both 'Power' and 'Ideas' are accounting for the dependent variable. Chapter 7 will pick up the thread again from here by analysing the merits of syncretic hypotheses RC1 and RC2.

Progressive Reinvention

Was OXFAM-GB's organizational culture always this proactive or has it evolved over time? When the 'all-out war' campaign of 2000 began, OXFAM-GB launched water-sanitation, hygiene and non-food items distribution projects for the IDPs, following the menu card of all other humanitarian IOs. In 2004, a 'Mindanao-wide assessment' was conducted in the organization and a new protection-related component was added to the mandate. It was called 'Free and Informed Decision' and was placed under the 'Mindanao Rights and Governance' programme. This component involved IHL trainings and advocacy for the rights of IDPs and civilians caught in repeated cycles of warfare. It was easily integrated with regular programmes like Food Security and Livelihoods. The motivation of including protection in this manner, according to OXFAM leaders, was 'feedback from the local communities that they needed protection first and foremost.'[21]

The 'shift in thinking' actually happened inside the country office in Manila via feedback from field staffers, who were just a heartbeat away from civilians bearing harassments and insults on a daily basis from the nearest military camp. OXFAM-GB also benefited from radicalisation of local civil society activists who pushed the organization to reinvent itself in the face of continued atrocities by armed actors on civilians. A prominent community mobiliser from North Cotabato province told me how he exhorted OXFAM-GB to be bolder and more proactive:

> During President Estrada's all-out war, OXFAM used to avoid advocacy, especially open advocacy that might rankle the authorities. I often conveyed the wishes of the communities to them that relief or development alone will not solve the root causes of violence, which lie in religious intolerance, discrimination and corporate interests of some elites. Gradually, around 2003, OXFAM began increasing its subtle support to our protection and advocacy efforts in Mindanao and at the Manila level. They have gone further than any other mandate-driven IO because of the inputs they got from the Mindanawon peace constituency.[22]

In a different publication, I have elaborated the process of transformation in OXFAM-GB's 'Ideas' over time (Chaulia, 2007). Had I requested IO-observers to code the proactiveness scale for the Philippines in 2002 or 2003, OXFAM-GB would not have outdone the other four IOs with such a big margin of points. The turnaround towards proactiveness came gradually and through internal rethinking about the organization's appropriate role and values in the context of a ceasefire that showed no respite in abuses against civilians.

OXFAM-GB in the Philippines had never subscribed to a quietist acceptance of the supremacy of state sovereignty, leaving out the possibility that C3 explains the change. But what moved the wheels in 2003-04 in a more proactive direction was fresh and creative thinking emanating from the grassroots that broke the 'business as usual' regularity of bureaucracy. Since there was no corresponding decrease in material pressures and inducements on OXFAM-GB in 2003-04 (rationalist temporal hypothesis R3), the only plausible cause for the turnaround is offered by C4.

Equals in Apathy

In the net weighted proactiveness ranking for the Philippines (see Table 5.4), ICRC and SCF are tied at the common score of 2.33. The equality of these two IOs presents a unique scenario to test rationalist and culturalist hypotheses which were written with the relative language of 'greater', 'more' and 'less'.

A modified version of the 'Power' hypotheses R1 and R2 will answer the puzzle of ICRC and SCF's joint second position by postulating that both IOs face the *same* extent of material pressures and inducements, and the *same* extent of competition and rivalry for funding and political patronage.

The ICRC's work in the Philippines is predicated upon the organization's original agreement with the GRP in 1982. In late 2008, ICRC decided to 'scale up' its presence in ARMM and surrounding provinces in response to the breakdown of the MILF-GRP peace process and resumption of large-scale war. This necessitated a new set of legal permissions and agreements with GRP. An ICRC Philippines official explained as follows:

> The GRP is highly suspicious and wary of internationalisation of the Mindanao conflict. When we broached the subject of increasing the ICRC's role after the outbreak of violence in August 2008, GRP threw up its hands and was initially hesitant to allow more international presence in the conflict zone. However, we negotiated our expansion with them. GRP knows that we operate our protection mandate in confidential dialogue mode rather than shouting from the rooftops. This is the main reason why they are not blocking our expansion in ARMM and surrounding areas.[23]

ICRC had to assuage the state by promising to keep a low profile and to avoid pointing fingers directly at the abuses and violence being carried out by the AFP or LGU paramilitaries. This compromise was clearly a function of the 'Power' of the Philippine state and ICRC's rational decision to bargain with it. Since ICRC officials in the Philippines stress their confidentiality and non-confrontational protection mandate, I asked them what they made of OXFAM-GB's public spat with GRP about the existence of a 'humanitarian crisis' and got a revealing response:

> Making outspoken comments like this just does not improve anything. The state can simply chop us off if we exceed our brief. ICRC does not want to reach such a stage in its long-oiled relationship with the GRP.[24]

One institution through which GRP exercises control over the ICRC's humanitarian operations in war zones is the Philippine National Red Cross (PNRC). Constitutionally, ICRC can only partner with the PNRC, a heavily politicised body. In the Philippines, the spouse of the President of the Republic is often the head of the PNRC. When PNRC vans and jeeps go into buffer zones or anti-government strongholds to deliver humanitarian relief materials, accusations fly about its real motive. The dilemma for ICRC is that 'if our implementing partner is tagged as belonging to one side, how can we perform protection services?'[25]

The politicised leadership of PNRC and the fact that it gets AFP clearance and permission to deliver aid in 'critical areas' leads to questions about neutrality of the former, and by extension, of the ICRC. I heard numerous complaints of civilians and Bangsamoro activists in western Mindanao that PNRC often acts partially in aid distribution to further the AFP's vested interests during military campaigns.

The problem of reliance on PNRC is compounded for ICRC because of personal security threats to its foreign staff members from kidnap-for-ransom gangs in western Mindanao that are often associated with the Abu Sayyaf. As recently as January 2009, two ICRC expatriates of European nationalities were abducted in Sulu. In 1992, two ICRC staff members (including one expatriate) were killed in Lanao del Norte by armed assailants. The motives of these crimes could be purely financial or sometimes political. If an armed party does not want IOs to be present in a particular war theatre, it can instigate a kidnapping or a killing to deter foreigners from ever setting foot in that area. Due to these special security threats to foreigners, ICRC often deputes the local PNRC to deliver humanitarian aid on its behalf. The PNRC's inclination towards civilian protection, for the aforementioned political reasons, is practically zero.

Since ICRC's main donor is the US government, which shares the GRP's goal of not 'internationalising' human rights problems in the Moro war theatres, there are other donor-imposed limitations on how far the organization can go on civilian protection. One interlocutor admitted this was so in the context of ICRC's 'global relationship with the US government.'[26] As ICRC's style of functioning is pegged to be such that it would not embarrass the GRP, the US has no qualms in funding its expansion of protection programmes in ARMM and surrounding provinces.

IOs' silence about impunity and their feebleness in partaking of practical protection activities on the ground suit the credo of the 'war on terrorism's in the Philippines. It is a mode of operation that the 'rational' ICRC is happy to go along with, as long as the funding tap and the host state's political patronage keep flowing. What goes missing in this kowtowing to 'Power' is principle. For an organization obsessed with neutrality, ICRC does not ever bother to self-introspect that its principal donor, the US government, is a party to the conflict in Mindanao.

ICRC in the Philippines combines protection programming with relief distribution and developmental aid. Engaging in material relief and rehabilitation of IDPs and war-affected communities is a 'Power'-dictated necessity that ICRC has to conform to in order to ingratiate itself with armed actors who would otherwise not allow the organization to enter the war zones.

ICRC Philippines' literature insists that 'relief actions' are carried out by the organization 'if the civilian population is suffering excessive deprivation owing to a lack of supplies essential to its survival' (ICRC, 2005B: 17). But in the Moro war theatres, there are plenty of other IOs like the WFP which specialise in organising relief distribution. ICRC Philippines' material interventions to 'save lives' rarely reach civilians whose very survival is at stake. The real reason for the organization to peddle material relief has less to do with desperation of civilians and more with the pressures and demands of armed actors to deliver concrete material benefits to their constituents.

Here, once again, ICRC reveals itself to be a plaything in the 'war on terror' game of its top donor, the USA. The organization is acknowledging that the state and the guerrillas force a shift towards material aid distribution. Even the oral and written representations that ICRC makes to armed actors on IHL violations against civilians rarely yield success in Mindanao due to the power of armed actors.

In principle, Moro rebel movements welcome an increased role of the ICRC in civilian protection. However, I found that the ground reality in central Mindanao during the post- MOA-AD war in 2008 contradicted the ICRC's bogus claims in media reports that it enjoyed the confidence of both the AFP and the MILF. In late August 2008, nearly a thousand civilians of Datu Piang municipality in Maguindanao province were trapped amidst heavy fighting between the AFP and 'rogue' commanders of the MILF. ICRC, which wanted to impress donors and the Philippine state that it was doing stellar work in the area, claimed in its media publicity blitz that it was 'invited' by the MILF to come to the 'rescue' of the sandwiched civilians. The head of the ICRC delegation boasted that his expatriates acted in the nick of time and evacuated 900 civilians to safety, thanks to 'the trust gained among all those involved in the conflict, both the armed forces and the MILF' (AFPress, 2008).

Eyewitnesses present on the spot painted a totally different picture. ICRC was actually not invited by the MILF to come in and 'save' the civilians caught in a cleft stick. When ICRC officials began offering their evacuation service, the community members were mistrustful and refused to cooperate in the proposed exodus. All neutral observers who I spoke to later confirmed that no more than a handful of civilians were persuaded that they would be safe in ICRC's company. In the end, villagers trekked their way out of trouble spontaneously and with the support of some proactive local and international organizations. ICRC never 'rescued' 900 civilians as it subsequently tom-tommed for media consumption.

Worse still, the ICRC came prepared to the epicentre in Datu Piang to exploit the misery of the civilians by 'embedding' its own journalist crew to film some sequences and capture sound bytes as proof that the organization performed a superlative protection feat. I went to a gathering of IOs in Cotabato sometime after this episode and witnessed angry activists slamming ICRC for acting to jeopardise the protection of civilians and taking credit where it was never due. The ICRC representative kept mum with an embarrassed look.

This incident revealed how blatantly ICRC could lie in order to raise funds from its American and European donors for 'stepping up' its presence and opening new offices in central Mindanao. Shortly after publicising its 'rescue' act in Datu Piang, the organization appealed to donors for 'a budget extension of US$4 million, a 60 percent increase over its initial 2008 budget' (IRIN, 2008). The hypocrisy was not lost on the civilians themselves, who had nothing to thank ICRC for. Yet, 'heroic' incidents such as these got blown up by ICRC's publicity machine and were used as legends to garner more funding. I pieced together this hunger in ICRC for funding its expansion through hook or crook with another comment made by a leader in the organization about OXFAM-GB's tussle with Malacañang on whether or not there was a 'humanitarian crisis' in ARMM in late 2008. The ICRC official said,

It is a hasty step that will neither get OXFAM any extra funding nor change the government's political stance on continuing its offensive.[27]

That advocacy against the state's cover-up of civilian suffering could be weighed through the prism of monetary benefits became apparent to me as I interacted with ICRC personnel in the Philippines. Globally, the ICRC espouses seven 'Fundamental Principles', one of which is that it is 'a voluntary relief movement not prompted in any manner by desire for gain' (ICRC, 2002:9). How this rhetoric squares with the compromised realities of the organization's behaviour in the Philippines is a reminder of the pull of rational self-interest in the humanitarian business.

If R1 and R2 are true, then SCF must be facing more or less the same extent of material pressures and inducements, and competition for funding and political patronage as ICRC. As one of USAID's principal implementers in Mindanao, SCF is well assimilated into the 'peace and development' agenda of the 'war on terrorism'. USAID funds humanitarian-cum-development projects on livelihoods, health care, family planning, education etc. in Mindanao with an open acknowledgement that they 'directly support US foreign policy goals related to counterterrorism, regional stability, economic prosperity and democracy' (USAID, 2006: 3). It unsurprisingly praises SCF for its 'technical strengths in the health and education sector' (USAID, 2009).

To illustrate how SCF is party to military humanitarianism in Mindanao, it will be useful to narrate the episode of the US 'Navy Hospital Ship' *Mercy*, which was sent to Mindanao for 'medical missions' in June 2006 and May 2008. Apart from 'helping a lot of poor people', this mission brought American and Filipino military doctors together with their respective armies to conduct 'outreach programmes' in central Mindanao 'for the sake of humanity.'

The ARMM Governor, Zaldy Ampatuan, praised *Mercy* on behalf of LGUs 'and thanked President George Bush for sending American troops to help in various civic action programs in the provinces.' *Mercy*'s 'medical and surgical services' were delivered through the cooperation of SCF and the PNRC (ME, 2008). Neither of these two organizations thought twice before tagging along with the counter-terrorism bandwagon.

SCF's relationship with USAID is symbiotic rather than the classic patron-client equation between donor arm of a state and the recipient IO. A senior SCF Philippines official described it as follows:

> Donors have their own politically-determined agendas which place limitations on Save's protection capabilities. When the fighting broke out in August 2008 in ARMM and its environs after the collapse of the MOA-AD, USAID, our main donor, was insistent that it would not fund any emergency response activities. Save's field staff bombarded USAID with 'sitrep'[28] after 'sitrep' showing that the situation on the ground was very grave and that it warranted immediate attention. It took weeks of convincing before USAID relented and released funds for us to mount a relief operation. With USAID, I must say that they are on the GRP side through full military backing on one hand, but they also give out relief assistance with the other hand to save civilians impacted by the war. It is a strange dual policy and we have to work within this dynamic. Save also receives some funding from ECHO, rich individuals in the US, and corporations like Mattel, but USAID is our mainstay. We are trying to establish a mature relationship with USAID so that we do not have to run the rigmarole of round after round of appeals and pleas for funding every time fighting breaks out in Mindanao.[29]

SCF's leaders are well aware that the 'strange dual policy' is nothing but a manifestation of the oxymoronic but potent military humanitarianism of the 'war on terrorism'. Yet, SCF is so heavily under the donor state's thumb that it cannot extricate itself from the conservative programmatic blueprint that USAID imposes on recipient IOs.

When the latest war in central Mindanao broke out in August 2008, GRP and its local DSWD arms argued in unison that there was no humanitarian crisis and that enough supplies were on hand to meet the needs of all the IDPs. The WFP supported GRP's version by announcing that 'there is no crisis as yet' (Santos, 2008), much to the chagrin of SCF. Yet, SCF did not issue any statement contradicting the claims of the state. I asked an SCF official why the organization preferred silence when the lives of thousands of civilians were at high risk. His response revealed the 'Power' iniquities and perceived weaknesses of IOs vis-à-vis the host state:

> Since the August crisis broke out, Save has been trying to call all the international organizations working in ARMM for coordination. A lone voice cannot be helpful and there is a need for a unified international community to be able to withstand the state's backlash. Voices in the wilderness do not help the cause of suffering civilians. Instead, it gives the GRP an excuse to turn the screws on all of us.[30]

Continuing the theme of disunity among INGOs, SCF personnel say that even though they approached OXFAM-GB for joint implementation of projects, the latter has been cool to the proposals. SCF believes that this has to do with OXFAM-GB's 'ideological distaste for associating with INGOs that receive American funding.'[31] Elsewhere, I have shown how CSOs and local activist networks that oppose *Balikatan* get blacklisted by donors and distanced from IOs.[32] SCF's disagreements with OXFAM-GB and the general disarray in which INGOs find themselves on crucial questions that risk the state's backlash show how much deeper the divisive tendencies of the 'war on terrorism' have gone to the detriment of proactiveness in the humanitarian community.

More than ICRC, SCF feels the heat of LGU power in Mindanao because the latter is a specialised child rights IO and, theoretically, a threat to the 'Datuism' which thrives on under-aged serf labour and forced recruitment of children into feudal paramilitaries. My interlocutor at SCF explained how this material hurdle constrains the organization's proactiveness:

> There are limitations to what we can do on child protection problems, especially due to the political obstruction of LGUs. We have been trying to promote the idea of 'child friendly spaces' in evacuation centres in conflict-affected parts of Muslim Mindanao, but the efforts are being opposed by LGUs (some of whom are even pro-MILF) that wish to inflame passions and anger of young people instead of allowing them to play and be normal children. Their interest is in keeping the flow of recruits into fighting ranks. We are frustrated, but can do nothing except watch from the sidelines as the LGUs dictate the operational feasibility of our mandate.[33]

Needless to add, SCF has never dared to programmatically tackle LGU-sponsored conscription of children into CVOs, CAFGUs and private armies or that of the MILF, even though the IO's UK branch funded research documenting the extent of the problem in Moro areas (Quitoriano and Francisco, 2004).

Overall, SCF appears more vulnerable to donor, host state and sub-state pressures to keep civilian protection on the backburner than ICRC. But it has not displayed the rank opportunism and mendacity of ICRC to compete for funds or political patronage because it is less ambitious to expand and to be recognised as a messiah of civilians. Therefore, the implications of R1 are being neutralised by those of R2, roughly satisfying a modified hypothesis that the two organizations are equal in their degree of proactiveness because the sum total of material pressures and inducements applying on them are equal.

A test of the culturalist hypotheses C1 and C2 should buttress the equality of the two organizations' proactiveness scores through an equality of independent variables. ICRC has been dogged by cultural doubts about a more robust protective presence in Mindanao. According to one of its representatives, the thinness of ICRC coverage of the Moro war theatres had nothing to do with donor preference and was more an issue of 'our internal priorities.'[34] From 1982 to 1991, ICRC had a large and visible presence in the Philippines, with nearly 40 expatriate staff members, covering both the countrywide AFP-NPA war and the AFP-MNLF war in Mindanao.

However, when two ICRC staff members (including one expatriate) were killed in Lanao del Norte in 1992 by armed actors, a massive 'scale down' of operations and closure of field offices in Muslim parts of Mindanao occurred. Mindanao fell off the radar in the nineties as ICRC began concentrating on massive operations in Somalia, erstwhile Yugoslavia and the Great Lakes Region. Even though President Joseph Estrada's administration restarted the war in 2000 and drove ARMM and surrounding provinces into a very serious humanitarian crisis, the 'inside thinking' of ICRC was that it need not expand its protection functions on the ground. My ICRC interlocutor briefly hinted at the contours of this internal bureaucratic debate:

> We had this mindset that as long as we distributed relief supplies in the 2000-2003 war, it was enough. Now, fortunately, I can say that we have the right people at the right time in the organization and there are no internal hurdles to taking our core protection mandate seriously in Muslim Mindanao.[35]

In a dual-mandate IO like ICRC, there are bureaucratic tugs of war between the material relief specialists and the civilian protection specialists. In sectoral terms, ICRC's priorities for Mindanao are set by an annual 'Action for Results' meeting held in the Manila headquarters. At this meeting, decisions about how much of the budget should be allocated to which sector are made through 'open dialogue among staff members.' The 'dialogue' process still attracts a great deal of jockeying for funds by protection specialists and aid specialists, each of whom is bent on proving that their respective causes are imperative. Graham Allison's 'bureaucratic politics' model of decision-making (Allison, 1969) offers a theoretical lens to examine this internal churning in ICRC Philippines. The 'outcome' is a compromise arrived at not through rational choice but by 'the pulling and hauling that is politics' (Allison, 1969: 707).

Since ICRC continues to distribute material aid to IDPs in evacuation centres, I enquired whether it still suffered from turf wars, with relief delivery specialists resenting or turning a blind eye to civilian protection specialists. My ICRC interlocutor denied this was the case in the following manner:

> Infighting was an issue earlier on, but we have now sorted it out. Suppose we have a 'WatSan' engineer who goes into a conflict-affected Barangay to fix pipes and also notices something wrong in relation to threats or violence faced by the people, she immediately informs the protection point person in her team. We train all our non-protection staff with the protection perspective and try hard to have them incorporate it in their Plan of Relief Distribution.[36]

But the evidence from central Mindanao reveals that ICRC's relief distribution has been chaotic, uncoordinated and lacking in protection consciousness. The perception of local and international organizations in the field is that ICRC haphazardly distributes relief in the evacuation centres without doing anything concrete about threats to life and liberties of IDPs. Many activists told me bitterly that the ICRC expatriates in central Mindanao were unapproachable, haughty and disinterested in cooperating with peace and human rights groups. The personal traits of some ICRC expatriates in Mindanao have come in for criticism by rights defenders, adding to the perception that the organization is profiting from civilian suffering in war.

An episode from the July 2006 mini-war in central Mindanao between the MILF and the Ampatuans' CAFGU-CVO paramilitaries illustrates the gulf that ICRC has erected between itself and local activists. An emergency meeting of peace and human rights CSOs in Cotabato city proposed to form a 'neutral joint force' called *Tyakap Maguindanao* to interposition itself between the two warring parties and force the combatants to disengage. The CSOs asked the ICRC if it was willing to join hands because its mandate is promotion of IHL. I was present at the gathering where two activist spokespersons warned that in that hour of crisis, 'if ICRC opts out, we will isolate it.' Instead of creatively brainstorming if there was a way in which ICRC could back up this idea, its bureaucrats showed no interest at all in the proposal and came up with the usual alibi of 'mandate restrictions.'

Subsequent to that event, ICRC lost relevance as a protection organization and became a bystander as CSOs took the lead to bring the mini-war to a halt. The distance between ICRC and local activists naturally translated into a huge gap in communication between the organization and civilians living in interior areas where wars take the heaviest toll. Since ICRC Philippines publicises its centrality as the guardian of IHL, I asked one of its representatives whether and how civilian complainants residing in remote war-torn Barangays could reach the organization to report IHL violations. The following answer was befuddling even by normal standards of bureaucratic stolidity:

> They can come to our Manila headquarters, but it is quite impossible for those living in Mindanao to come that far to just lodge a complaint. Often, local Moro groups report violations on behalf of civilians to our field offices. But the problem with them is that they nearly always report abuses committed by the government side but not by the rebels. Thankfully, news coverage about abuses against civilians is quite extensive and we often conduct follow-up investigations in Mindanao on the basis of journalistic reports.[37]

If local activists' complaints are one-sided and biased, how could ICRC assume that newspaper reportage of abuses was fairer? To reiterate an earlier point from this chapter, the Moro wars are blanketed in a 'news blackout' and distorted as part and parcel of the psychological 'war on terrorism' by the GRP and the US. Lacking unbiased and authentic local connections in the field, ICRC's information sources are so limited that they cloud the minds of its personnel and render them insensitive to atrocities against civilians. Its grassroots information network about violent incidents and abuses of civilians is extremely poor or even non-existent.

One of the characteristics of bureaucracies is to paper over their inefficiencies and to put up a brave front that nothing is wrong or out of place. ICRC epitomises this tendency of remaining content with the status quo instead of reinventing organizational practices for the better.

Since ICRC is into the practice of entering into confidential dialogues with armed actors seeking redress for their indiscretions against civilians, I asked the organization's higher-ups whether staff members get demoralised when armed actors do not adopt 'corrective measures' even after they are confronted with evidence of culpability. The response was classically bureaucratic:

> No. We think that it is our mandate and keep on making representations on behalf of victims. Any IGO or INGO interested in civilian protection

is bound to face frustration, but we are *professional* (emphasis original) and have to keep trying through our time-tested best practices for greater respect of IHL by all parties to the conflict.[38]

ICRC's status quoism and excessive legalism induce a preference for the time-tested ways and occlude creative thinking of the sort that OXFAM-GB has successfully adopted. Another example of ICRC's failure to change its routines to become more proactive is provided by its inaction on targeted assassinations of civil society activists by hit squads in Mindanao (mainly against journalists and 'communist' sympathisers of the NPA but also against some Moro rights defenders). I asked ICRC Philippines why it does not treat these fear-drumming incidents as threats to civilian protection and received the following response in standard legalese:

> This is a highly sensitive topic. The ICRC was invited by the GRP to succour and protect IDPs in 1982. Unless governments allow it, the ICRC has no *locus standi* to address specific problems that are extensions of IHL. If there are extra-judicial killings in areas with no ongoing armed conflict, it is not within ICRC's remit as per our legal status.[39]

ICRC's understanding of where there is 'general armed conflict' and where it is not is so technical that if killings occur in ARMM and surrounding provinces during ceasefires, then they fall beyond its ambit of interest and action. Civilians in Mindanao who have been at the receiving end of endless cycles of violence describe their situation as 'permanent martial law.'[40] We have seen that the US 'war on terrorism' has also imposed 'permanent war' on Mindanawons. ICRC's book-bound technocrats are, however, blind to civilian understandings of what 'war' and 'armed conflict' entail.

ICRC Philippines asserts that it never publicises its protection activities and operates through its accredited status with the GRP and the MILF in 'in camera' settings. Therefore, its leaders argue, 'our protection activities may not be visible to the outside eye and could convey the sense that we are not doing much.'[41] Quite contrary to this defence, the Datu Piang incident of late August 2008 was a public relations splash celebrating ICRC's proactiveness. The entire INGO and IGO community in central Mindanao as well as the LGU officials witnessing the event repudiated ICRC's claims and criticised its false publicity stunts. Yet, as well-trained bureaucrats, ICRC officials keep parroting the defensive line that they are highly proactive but underrated by outsiders.

Are SCF's bureaucratic identity and cultural norms equally conservative as ICRC's? Although SCF made child protection a programmatic priority since 2002, protection of 'children in emergencies' is still an 'emerging area of work' because the onus is on less risky forms of protection like child abuse and exploitation, juvenile justice and training of school administrators. Entrenched bureaucratic interests within the organization which prefer traditional forms of child protection are quite influential when funding priorities are set in the organization.

Thanks to the research of SCF UK, SCF USA's Philippines branch personnel are aware that 'recruitment into fighting forces' is a major political rights problem in ARMM and surrounding provinces (SCF, 2004). The SCF UK study on child conscription in Mindanao recommends that INGOs take a new approach in humanitarian assistance in war-affected areas that would centralise protection and 'intensify information and education about child rights, humanitarian and human rights laws and conventions' (Quitoriano and Francisco, 2004: 71, 77, 109). SCF USA's Philippines branch has unfortunately not imbibed these lessons.

As mentioned earlier, SCF USA in the Philippines is the convener of MERN. In 2003, MERN organised a workshop on humanitarian standards for all field-based organizations working in Mindanao and adopted, *inter alia*, the following two protection-affirming 'Principles of Conduct':

> In our information, publicity and advocacy activities, we shall recognise disaster victims as dignified humans, not hopeless objects, whose rights must be upheld at all times.

> Our presence, work, and assistance shall in no way cause further harm to, or prolong suffering of the community we seek to serve (MERN, 2003).

Sadly, SCF has not lived up to these high universalistic ideals over the years. Its personnel emphasise other conservative sections of MERN's 'Principles' that unambiguously commit humanitarians to 'respect culture, tradition, custom and belief' of the Moros (MERN, 2003). For a development and relief-centred IO like SCF, even the minimal prospect of challenging certain egregious aspects of local culture is anathema as it risks enraging the communities in which it invests heavily for other sectoral projects.

Conscription of children gets sidelined in SCF priorities due to an internal organizational consensus that the practice is intrinsic to the Moro Islamic culture of *jihad* and that questioning it will jeopardise access to MILF-controlled territories. An SCF official described to me the logic behind the organization's overcautious attitude towards the critical issue of child conscription:

If one version of Islam claims that a boy aged 10 or above is a man, then we have to find more moderate versions and their practitioners and strengthen their hand in the Moro communities. Only such a gradualist approach will work. Teenage marriages and lack of family planning were other social obstacles to Save's work in the past in some provinces of Muslim Mindanao. But we have painstakingly built the awareness on these issues so that, now, there is more acceptability to the notions that Islam permits planning of one's family and does not endorse early marriages. The same can happen with 'child soldiers' as an issue and only after that can we plan a more direct protection programme.[42]

Switching from the obstacle of 'local culture', the SCF official went on to internal beliefs shared within the organization about the nature of the problem of child conscription:

> On protection of children, we mostly do indirect promotion that focuses on the root causes of abuses. Some people say that the root cause of children joining armed groups as fighters is injustice and violence on communities. But the real cause is lack of socio-economic opportunities. So, if we concentrate on health, poverty reduction and education, it is with the hope of minimising the fuel for violence and supporting the cause of peace in the long term. Save's school-based programmes for children integrate peace education, so that the basic principles of living harmoniously with other ethnic groups are ingrained into young minds. In this manner, since direct promotion of protection might rub the MILF and LGUs the wrong way, we are indirectly promoting protection. This approach is superior to direct advocacy because it develops local capacity for protection.[43]

Two incredulous claims in this statement deserve dissection. Firstly, MERN is a conservative local NGO forum with strictly socio-economic rights bearings. The forum is, at the time of writing, six-years-old and has not developed any 'local capacity' on conscription of children. In 2006, I personally witnessed MERN personnel in aid trucks delivering emergency rations close to the battlefronts in central Mindanao without batting an eyelid about the ubiquity of teenaged boys carrying weapons on both sides— the MILF and the CAFGUs. As far as MERN is concerned, the problem might well not exist. The other claim of SCF that child conscription can be 'indirectly' overcome through poverty alleviation is taken straight out of the 'war on terrorism's textbook paradigm of 'peace and development'. Contrary to SCF's assertions, this paradigm has hindered protection and human rights causes in Mindanao.

Very much like ICRC, SCF also indulges in technocratic temporising on the child conscription issue. One of its leaders told me the following:

> Save's inaction on recruitment of children as fighters is partly a result of the absence of concrete data. So far, we only have sporadic reports about this topic, but the question is 'How big is this problem?' If it is only incidental and geographically restricted, then the policy response from our side will have to be commensurately toned down.[44]

Dehumanised technocratic thinking among humanitarians typically treads the sequence of finding data, determining policy and then acting on it. All that IGOs and INGOs have done about child conscription in Mindanao for years is to document and gather more and more data. There has been no follow-up action at all. Data gathering seems to be an excuse for inaction and conservatism in organizations like SCF and UNICEF.

Another organizational bottleneck that hinders SCF's proactiveness is its mission structure. SCF is not yet a 'Unified Country Mission.' A leading SCF figure believes that a proposed merger with SCF Sweden in 2009 'will make us more proactive on child protection since the latter has a strong protection expertise.'[45] He is referring to the ambiguous identity of SCF USA which juggles multiple mandates. Given that SCF USA performs a number of different activities, ranging from development to emergency relief to child rights trainings, I enquired further about how the organization's leaders would characterise their identity as a whole and received this evasive bureaucratic reply:

> Are we a humanitarian INGO or a development INGO or a rights INGO? I cannot give primacy to one over the other. We are a bunch of things and so, naturally, our identity is also split into its components. I personally have never felt that we need to be typecast into one single mould. Since we have the capacities, we wear multiple hats.[46]

The 'split' personality syndrome has implications for any IO's proactiveness. SCF USA's global headquarters in Westport, Connecticut, designs a 'Strategic Direction' plan every five years. An annual review of this plan is held at the national headquarters level in Manila. My SCF interlocutor described the national review process as follows:

> Debates do happen during the reviews every year. As a leader, I try to propel a conscious effort to mainstream protection into those 'Priority Results' of our Global Framework which do not directly deal with

protection (Education, Health, Food Security and Livelihoods). One constraint in 'scaling up' our protection mandate is the shortage of funding which is dependent on the priorities of donors.[47]

What emerges from these contradictory comments is a cultural corpus of ideas within SCF that 'projectifies' civilian protection instead of treating it as a cross-cutting concern across other specialised sectors. SCF's bureaucrats, like their counterparts in ICRC, treat protection as a budgeted category of action that needs separate projects and funds. Needless to add, such a vision defeats the very notion of 'mainstreaming', which projects protection as an overarching activity that must congeal like a layer over each specialised sector.

One of the coding criteria for the proactiveness scales of IOs that I employed was whether or not the organization shared sensitive information about abuses on civilians with relevant organizations that could do something concrete to assist the victims. SCF scored a point on this criterion in the coding of all three groups. However, that criterion hid the nuance of age. SCF's field personnel are not known to share information on abuses of civilians if they are older than the age of 18. I enquired why the organization strictly restricts its field-based vision strictly to the mandate of being a 'child rights' entity. The reply from its managers again threw light upon the confused identity of the organization:

> Since our mandate is limited to children, we have to protect against the disease of spreading oneself too thinly by taking on extraneous concerns. We constantly remind ourselves that we are not a human rights organization.[48]

The perception that being 'humanitarian' is different from being a 'human rights' IO is based on division of labour and specialisation principles that have long stymied the normative fillip of 'mainstreaming' protection. SCF Philippines is thus blissfully divorced from the global attempt to forge an 'interface' between the two types of organizations (see Chapter 1). SCF prefers the safety and orderliness of being 'humanitarian' and 'developmentalist.'

From the foregoing comparison of ICRC and SCF, there is hardly any difference in the extent of bureaucratisation between the two IOs. Both organizations are almost equally resistant to change and have stifling identities and SOPs that pull them back from opening windows to fresh breezes.

On the variable of obeisance to state sovereignty, ICRC may be slightly more so that SCF because the former is a stickler for legalistic limits prescribed in its entry agreement with the GRP. Nonetheless, in practice in the field, SCF and its MERN allies are highly obsequious to the RDCC and LGUs and believe that they have to respect the writ of the state. With little dividing the two IOs in the realm of culture, it is appropriate to conclude that they are equals in apathy for victims of war due to approximately similar 'Power' pressures and 'Ideas' affecting both organizations.

The Toothless Champion

Why is UNICEF Philippines almost at the bottom of the net weighted proactiveness ranking, belying its global image as a champion of children's rights and a key protection IO? The combined answer of rationalist hypotheses R1 and R2 is that UNICEF faces greater material pressures and inducements and competes more for funding and political patronage than OXFAM-GB, ICRC and SCF.

Although mandated to tackle child conscription and other forms of violence committed against children in war, UNICEF's personnel admit that 'political difficulties' which are external to the organization limit their programme in Mindanao. In 2004, UNICEF and its partner organizations resolved to take a more pro-active stance on demobilisation of under-aged combatants by launching localised negotiations with armed groups, urging their provincial commands (whether military or rebel groups) to issue directives to their forces not to recruit children below 18 and to demobilize children in their ranks (Camacho, 2004).

However, this resolution remained aspirational, partly because UNICEF has little leverage over the MILF, the de facto state in many parts of ARMM and surrounding provinces and the main culprit in child conscription. As of 2005, approximately 13 percent of MILF's 10,000 fighters were below the age of 18 (CSUCS, 2008: 3). A UNICEF official explained how the organization has no option but to be deferential to the MILF's demands:

> Some in the MILF Central Committee are opposed to UNICEF's advocacy on child soldiers on the grounds that it is a GRP ploy to weaken the guerrilla movement. We have to factor this concern into our work. UNICEF is planning to expand its protection programme in Mindanao in the coming months, but bringing droves of protection officers might upset the MILF. They can make life difficult for us in the areas under their control. We cannot afford strained relations with them.[49]

In December 2008, MILF announced after meeting with the UN Special Representative for Children and Armed Conflict that it had 'agreed to stop recruiting child soldiers and return those in its ranks to civilian life' (MT, 2008). Noticeably, the Special Representative was accompanied by UNICEF personnel on her tour of ARMM that inveigled this promise from MILF. However, there was no genuine change in the rebel movement's policies on the ground. It had issued verbal assurances of this kind earlier in May 2006 that the general policy of the MILF is not to recruit children for combat (CSUCS, 2008), only to break the vows.

UNICEF Philippines lacks the power to enforce or at least hold MILF to its words because the movement qualifies its verbal commitments by citing the doctrine of military necessity as an extenuating circumstance. It speaks of the 'right of everybody, including children, to self-defence, especially when communities or villages are under indiscriminate military actions by the enemy' (ML, 2006).

The argumentative line that children should be going to school instead of fighting is also not a productive one for UNICEF, as under-aged MILF fighters continue to be in some form of schooling with absences during military operations. Those who do drop out 'do not really feel like they are out of school because they attend Arabic lessons in the camp' (Cagoco-Guiam, 2002: 28-29).

UNICEF's ability to negotiate a change in MILF's policy is compounded by the fact that its main partner in implementing health, education and protection programmes is the GRP. I asked a UNICEF official if being associated with the state hinders the proactiveness of the organization and received a candid reply:

> In the case of UNICEF personnel who are tight with the state, that impression is valid and might affect the human rights component of our mandate because MILF might believe that we are handmaidens of GRP. Of late, there has been talk that GRP will raise the issue of MILF's 'child soldiers' at the level of the UN General Assembly in an attempt to shame and ostracise the rebel movement. UNICEF has been wishing to increase the profile of this issue and, certainly, this can be enabled by a more conducive political climate.[50]

The sub-text of this 'climate' refers to the lack of consistent encouragement from the Philippine state for UNICEF to keep pegging at MILF's child conscription practices. The UN Secretary-General has described how the 'child soldiers' issue was sacrificed in the politics of GRP's peace negotiations with the MILF:

> The recruitment and use of children has been a controversial and sensitive issue for MILF and NDF, and attempts by Government peace panel members to place it on the agenda in peace negotiations have failed because it is perceived to cause tension among the parties. To date

there has been no mention of child recruitment in peace processes and negotiations (UN, 2008: 5).

GRP ratchets up the issue now and then in the media when peace talks with the MILF break down or enter a limbo. For instance, when the post-MOA-AD war started in late 2008, GRP's Executive Secretary Ermita threatened that President Arroyo 'will file a complaint before the United Nations (UN) against the Moro Islamic Liberation Front (MILF) for allegedly recruiting minors into their ranks' (Merueñas, 2008). In October 2008, I personally met AFP commanders in Maguindanao province who were tasked to photograph children fighting for the MILF and pass on the evidence to Malacañang so that it can be used as a bargaining chip to force the rebels to hand over its 'rogue commanders' wanted by the state.

GRP has also not been keen on UNICEF exposing the extent of child conscription throughout Mindanao because its own LGUs induct children into private armies, vigilante bodies and paramilitary auxiliaries for the AFP's counter-insurgency. A UNICEF official apprised me of the LGU dimension of 'Power' that drags back the organization's proactiveness:

> LGUs in ARMM and surrounding areas are also guilty of recruiting children as combatants. This is particularly the case with CVOs, which are controlled by Mayors and Governors. The objections and obstacles of LGUs are definitely a challenge for our protection advocacy work because all other UNICEF sectoral activities have to be coordinated with LGUs.[51]

UNICEF Philippines does not suffer from any donor pressure that could curtail the size and scope of its child protection mandate in Mindanao. In 2005, the organization appointed a Consultant on Child Protection through funding from ECHO. Later, when ECHO's funding ceased, UNICEF at the Manila level decided to continue having specialised child protection staffers for Mindanao. The financing was drawn from internal money raised at the Manila level by UNICEF's fundraising staff. Unsurprisingly, UNICEF does not receive any grants from USAID to support its child protection programmes. Neither the US embassy nor USAID has ever openly condemned the practice of child conscription, apparently upon GRP's request.

When a UNHCR official visited Mindanao during the post-MOA-AD war of 2008 and recommended that UNICEF take the lead role in a new 'Protection Cluster' for IOs, UNICEF headquarters in New York and in Manila excused themselves saying that they do not have the 'capacity' to work on civilian protection in general and that their mandate is limited to children and natural disasters. The UNHCR official interpreted this lukewarm response as a sign that 'UNICEF Manila is very cautious and conservative because they have to manage their larger relationship with the host government.'[52] This dovetails with my own experience of talking to senior UNICEF officials in Manila who frequently express anxiety about being 'asked to leave by the authorities' if they took on sensitive human rights monitoring.

Apart from child conscription, when AFP bombardment or shelling during wars kills or injures civilians, including children, UNICEF does not issue any condemnation or public statement of concern. I noticed that UNICEF was even quieter on violence committed against children by the AFP than on the MILF's child conscription.

That UNICEF Philippines is buffeted by strong material pressures from powerful actors to be passive is certain, but are these pressures greater than what OXFAM-GB, ICRC or SCF face? Unlike these three IOs, UNICEF has to grapple with the extra fear factor of the MILF, courtesy the latter's determination to continue child conscription for its *jihad* against the AFP. But what is equally interesting is that field staffers of UNICEF in Mindanao are not as afraid of being 'kicked out' or attacked by armed actors as their counterparts in ICRC and SCF. All three groups that coded our proactiveness scale awarded a full point to UNICEF on the criterion- 'Has field staffers who are conscious about human rights, irrespective of their specialisations in implementing relief or development projects.'

SCF and ICRC, on the other hand, do not score on this count. It is therefore not clear whether UNICEF's lower score in the ranking than SCF and ICRC is being explained solely by variation in material pressures.

Since a sharp difference in rationalist variables could not be established for the difference in proactiveness between UNICEF on one hand and OXFAM-GB, ICRC and SCF on the other, we need to test the culturalist hypotheses C1 and C2 for explaining why UNICEF lags being these three IOs. Is UNICEF more bureaucratic and more subservient to state sovereignty than OXFAM-GB, ICRC and SCF?

If UNICEF Philippines is scoring consistently on the proactiveness of its field staff while ICRC and SCF are not, it is ironic that UNICEF ranks below these two IOs in the net weighted ranking. It leads us to infer that UNICEF at the Manila level tempers down the activism of its field officials a lot more than the headquarters of SCF or ICRC do. The intra-organizational dynamics of UNICEF therefore need closer scrutiny.

On headquarters-field relationships in UNICEF, I heard the following testimony of an organizational insider:

Often, I have recommended to my superiors at the Manila level to be more active on advocacy efforts and condemn violations of human rights by various armed groups in ARMM and surrounding areas. But they have not followed my recommendations. The reasons are not clear to me. I often urge my superiors to issue press releases and statements condemning all armed parties for human rights abuses and even to call for resumption of peace talks between the GRP and MILF. So far, they have not done this. I often get frustrated with this hang up in the Manila office.[53]

The 'hang up' could be politically motivated (as shown while testing R1 and R2) or simply bureaucratic and procedural. My interlocutor went on to describe the gap between the headquarters and his own understandings of the organization's purpose:

I attended one Annual Management Retreat of UNICEF, where they set priorities for the following year and was at a loss to understand some of the goings on there. I think national headquarters of UNICEF has its own reasoning and logic that staffers on the ground are unaware of. I asked the Manila office to make a categorical condemnation of the recent violence since August that led to the death and injury of a number of children. Hopefully, my higher ups will take this advice. I am also arguing that it should press for a more active UN family role in civilian protection in Mindanao. Personally, I liked the European Union's statement on the deteriorating humanitarian situation[54] and wish that UNICEF could be as vocal as that to apply pressure on armed parties to respect their obligations under international law.[55]

Dashing these hopes, UNICEF Manila did not budge from its conservative silence even as the violence against civilians worsened in subsequent weeks. I learnt from an experienced local observer that the then Manila-level leadership of the organization believed that it must be 'respectful' to the host state's preferences and not tread on them. He added:

Leadership changes affect the emphasis given to child protection in UNICEF. The previous head of the country mission was very keen on expanding UNICEF's role in advocacy for children in armed conflict. When he left and was replaced by another person, who happened to be a 'WatSan' specialist, the onus shifted away from protection. Thus, protection has failed to become institutional culture in UNICEF Philippines. Its fortunes vacillate with changing leadership and their personal likes and dislikes.[56]

So, even as rationalist material pressures on UNICEF remained more or less constant over the last few years, the culture of the organization has become more 'developmentalist' due to leadership 'hang ups' and whims. These deductions validate temporal culturalist hypotheses C3 and C4 as capable of causing change in the organization's proactiveness by themselves (without rationalist support).

One of the culturalist hurdles that prevents UNICEF Manila from mirroring its activist field-based personnel is the former's orthodoxy that children join the MILF willingly due to their 'positive perception of the *mujahideen* or defenders of Islamic faith' (Legaspi, 2007). Between 2006 and 2008, I personally visited MILF area commanders in interior *Barangays* of Maguindanao, Shariff Kabunsuan and North Cotabato and saw scores of children receiving combat and Quranic training in their camps. On many occasions, I was told by local parents that the area commander, who usually doubles up as an Islamic *ustadz* (learned scholar), would threaten 'ostracism' or 'exile' from the community if they did not contribute their children for compulsory *jihad*.

When I asked UNICEF Manila's mandarins how such ideological coercion could be classified as 'voluntary', they replied that 'our definition' of coercion includes only acts of physically forcing a child to join combat ranks (i.e. either at gun point or by snatching him).

UNICEF Manila's restraining hand on its activist field personnel is thus partly ascribable to rigid textbook-style meanings accorded to concepts like 'force' and 'coercion'. SCF, for all its sheepishness towards armed actors, is spared of this type of bureaucratic 'hang up'. An SCF leader shared the following thoughts on the subject:

A commonly-held view in IO circles is that one cannot advocate against the phenomenon of 'child soldiers' because children join armed groups voluntarily. Save's opinion is that it does not matter whether the recruitments are voluntary or forced since they happen to be violations of the Convention of the Rights of the Child. As long as a practice is a violation of the CRC, we are duty bound to oppose it.[57]

Where SCF and UNICEF Manila concur, though, is on the messy stereotype of 'Moro culture' and the belief that Moro Islamic values condoning child conscription cannot be easily transcended by foreigners coming to preach universal human rights. Even UNICEF's field personnel opine that they must steer clear of intruding into Moro cultural rights for the sake of the organization's legitimacy. Whenever the topic is broached by UNICEF before the MILF, the rebel leaders retort that 'in Islamic society, we do not accept 18 as the age at which a person ceases being a child. For us, a boy or girl who attains majority age (puberty) is no longer a child and can be ready to serve the community's right to protect itself.'[58] The universality of human rights, which UNICEF is supposed to represent, is countered by the MILF's cultural relativism (Chaulia, 2007).

While monitoring and reporting on child protection in the Moro war theatres, some UNICEF local staff members also document and refer human rights abuses suffered by adults, even though the organization has the 'capacity' to only intervene on behalf of children. UNICEF Manila duly receives reports about sensitive incidents involving abuses of adult civilians but rarely includes them in any of its representations to armed actors about children's issues. Part of the tunnel vision of restricting the organization strictly to the mandate of children's rights has to do with the notions of inter-IO division of labour. UNICEF Manila believes that persecution of adults is not its bailiwick.

An episode from December 2008 reflects the organization's narrow understanding of humanitarian specialisation. The UN Special Representative for Children and Armed Conflict visited the war-hit parts of central Mindanao with UNICEF in tow (MTB, 2008). Although the majority of the victims of the latest war were adults, UNICEF and the visiting international dignitary decided to only touch on children's protection. Everything ranging from Malacañang's permission for the visit to self-understandings of UN bureaucrats of what issues they are entitled to raise contributed to this exclusive focus on children.

The rare situations in which UNICEF allows its name to feature in public advocacy for protection of all ages of civilians and for a halt to warfare is under the umbrella of the UN family's Inter Agency Standing Committee (CBN, 2008). In July 2006, UNICEF refused to sign a local activist petition in Maguindanao appealing to the warring parties for an immediate halt to fighting, humane treatment of civilians, and access to areas cut off by heavy artillery fire. In hindsight, the appeal of the IASC which UNICEF signed had little impact on stopping the post-MOA-AD war. UNICEF could have had a positive impact if it worked around bureaucratic routines and supported the other appeal of activists.

Like all other IO cases of this book, UNICEF Philippines is a multi-mandate organization that subcontracts relief and developmental delivery tasks to local NGOs. I enquired how sensitised UNICEF's local implementing partners were to civilian rights in ARMM and surrounding areas. The response from a UNICEF official was that 'only a few of our six local partners show inclination towards civilian protection.'[59]

Unlike OXFAM-GB, it never occurred to the smug bureaucrats in UNICEF that local implementing partners should be trained in civilian protection awareness and action. Lacking such orientations, the very spirit of 'mainstreaming' protection in humanitarian IOs gets defeated. Historically, relief and development budgets in UNICEF have been far bigger than those for protection. The assumption that Mindanawons need development much more than protection is cast in stone in the minds of UNICEF officials. It is no wonder then that they never bother to inculcate protection consciousness in their vast network of local implementing partners.

The foregoing comparisons indicate that UNICEF's bureaucratic culture and obeisance to state sovereignty are indeed far greater than those of OXFAM-GB's and somewhat greater than those of SCF. UNICEF may be forced by rationalist factors to be toothless, but its 'Ideas' reinforce a general conservatism and distaste for change. ICRC's 'Ideas', on the other hand, are more conservative than UNICEF's. The fact that ICRC has a slightly higher net weighted proactiveness score (.17 more) than UNICEF in spite of being culturally more bureaucratic means that there is merit in reconsidering the value of 'Power' in explaining proactiveness differentials among IOs. Chapter 6 of this book will reopen this thread of investigation.

Props and Counters

This chapter unveiled the principal humanitarian IOs in the Philippines navigating an endlessly violent conflict in Mindanao that has been exacerbated by the US-led 'war on terrorism'. At one end of the spectrum is OXFAM-GB, which prioritises civilian protection and steps in tandem with local activists who oppose the culture of impunity. Consistent with its progressive ethos, OXFAM-GB has campaigned not only for civilian protection and maintenance of ceasefires but also against patented medicines (PP, 2007), illegal logging and mining, and failed land reforms (Elusfa, 2008), all of which are integral to the political economy of war in Mindanao. In sum, OXFAM-GB is part of a stream of social consciousness and action that runs counter to the steady militarisation of Mindanao aggravated by the 'war on terrorism'.

This chapter also profiled humanitarian IOs that willingly submitted themselves to be used as props of the 'war on terrorism' in Mindanao. The readiness and eagerness of SCF and UNDP to unquestioningly serve the 'peace and development' mantra of the 'war on terrorism' makes them cogs in the soft power apparatus of the Philippine state and its American ally as they sweep 'the doormat for terrorism in Southeast Asia', Mindanao (Docena, 2006). The intricate weaving of donor preferences and host state interests with the prioritisation of humanitarian IOs within the cocoon of a geopolitical balance-of-power contest between the US and China has no better example than the cases of UNDP and SCF in the Philippines. These two IOs should have no qualms in accepting that they are politicised instruments rather than independent or neutral humanitarians. They reconfirm that humanitarianism is not apolitical by any stretch of imagination.

This chapter briefly raised the issue of Western capitalist interests in the abundant mineral wealth of Mindanao and how this has also coloured the aid priorities of donor states to IOs. In February 2007, the GRP's Environment and Natural Resources Secretary announced with pride that JP Morgan, the giant American investment bank, was going to finance international mining majors in the Philippines. To Reyes, 'the arrival of JPMorgan, the leading business banker, is a clear manifestation that the Philippine mining industry is back in business' (AFPress, 2007). The Philippine state is thus playing its designated role in the capitalist world-system by facilitating the looting of Mindanao's natural resources through international finance capital.

In the process, it has become beholden to 'oligarchs' based in Makati who were reluctant to allow the MOA-AD to come to fruition because of fear of losing their mining and logging rights if the MILF is granted its self-governing Bangsamoro Juridical Entity (BJE). To view donor state 'developmentalism' in the Moro war theatres as tied only to the geopolitical 'war on terrorism' would amount to reductionism. The extractive value that the capitalist world-system assigned to Mindanao is a central tenet informing donor pressure on IOs to go quiet on civilian protection in the Moro wars.

In the qualified classification of states as *core*, *semi-peripheral*, and *peripheral* within the global 'multicultural territorial division of labour' (see Introduction), the Philippines can be ranked as semi-peripheral. It is a supplier of raw materials to industrial MNCs that depend on Wall Street, but it also has its own indigenous commercial oligarchs who are local arms of global finance capitalists and who directly promote war in Mindanao.[60]

The link between capitalist structures and violence against civilians in war did not begin with the 'war on terrorism' and is systemically poised to outlast shifts in American foreign policy and military doctrines. Here, we are reminded of how humanitarian behaviour in a local war zone can eventually be traced back to global structures of exploitation and violence. Owing to our primary focus on the 'Third Debate', this insight from progressive structuralist theories could not be fully examined. But as the salience of the capitalist world-system and patriarchy to humanitarian behaviour is undeniable, I will return to their primacy as 'conditions' for IO priorities in war zones in Chapter 7.

This chapter dwelt at length on bureaucratic ideational traits which freeze creativity and accountability in humanitarian IOs like ICRC and UNICEF. Their cavilling over definitions, terminology, risk-averseness and legalism held back prospects for mainstreaming protection and trapped them in delusive routines that earned the ire of war-suffering civilians and local activists. The difference between their words and deeds separated two varied worlds — one, a bubble created through manipulation of the media, and two, the reality on the ground. ICRC, in particular, matched the psychological warfare tactics of the US-led 'war on terrorism' by claiming to be doing the obverse of what it really was.

This chapter briefly referred to unique personal security risks to expatriate humanitarians from kidnapping gangs in Mindanao. Depending on how they are interpreted, the physical safety threats can be added to the 'Power' variables as deterrents to proactiveness in IOs or simply ignored as financially motivated crimes. The Abu Sayyaf kidnappers of three ICRC expatriates in Sulu in early 2009, for instance, reportedly demanded 'the release of all detained Abu Sayyaf members in any detention cells in the country, total pull out of the military in the province, and $10-million in ransom' (Pareño, 2009).

Locals in western Mindanao often say that there are 'four different Abu Sayyafs', some phantom ones created by armed actors to scare away foreigners and some that fit the description of Islamist terrorists that kidnap and torture out of religious zeal. That there are several vested interests which wish to avoid 'internationalisation' of the protection crisis in Mindanao has already been suggested in this chapter. Notwithstanding the kidnapping menace, as of February 2009, some '100 foreign aid and peace workers are still operating in Sulu and Basilan, including American, Canadian, European and Japanese nationals' (Xinhua, 2009). To elevate the kidnapping risk to the level of another full-fledged fear factor that inhibits proactiveness of IOs would be a mistake. If at all it is a deterrent, then it affects all sectors of IO programming — relief, development and protection.

The empirical evidence of this chapter validated both static culturalist hypotheses (C1 and C2) and temporal culturalist hypotheses (C3 and C4). That 'Ideas' divide the lone 'counter' IO, OXFAM-GB, from the 'prop' IOs was established beyond doubt. At the same time, we saw that the entire humanitarian enterprise in the Philippines, barring OXFAM-GB, is consumed by the rational 'Power' of the 'war on terrorism'. Lacking the benefit of cross-country comparison, we could not do full justice to the explanatory potential of the static and temporal rationalist hypotheses, although their impact on IOs' proactiveness is definitive.

The next chapter will break the confines of single-country comparison and generate the opportunity for rationalist independent variables to prove their causal effect more comprehensively.

6

BETWEEN A ROCK AND A HARD PLACE: HUMANITARIANS ACROSS SRI LANKA AND THE PHILIPPINES

Similar Wars, Different Power Configurations

While justifying the choice of Sri Lanka and the Philippines as the two geographical backdrops in Chapter 3, I argued that these countries had 'similar wars with dissimilar features.' The Eelam wars of Sri Lanka and the Moro wars of the Philippines have much in common as examples of 'protracted social conflict' (Ramsbotham, 2005). They stand shoulder to shoulder in the annals of bloody internal armed conflicts.

Yet, war is the outcome of a specific constellation of political, economic and social forces that are so aligned as to generate cycles of violence. It is the specificity of these constellations which distinguish Sri Lanka from the Philippines or any other internal war. While most internal wars get externalised at some juncture (e.g. Indian intervention in Sri Lanka and Malaysian intervention in the Philippines), the fact that they are primarily internal means that the specificity of the internal array of forces within each nation state is bound to be different from that of another nation state. This owes to the historical evolutionary paths of different nation states and the attendant accumulation of national experiences which vary across space. The history and trajectory of the Eelam wars will be different from those of the Moro wars partly because Sri Lanka as a nation state has a different configuration of internal forces and dynamics compared to the Philippines.

The contrast in the strengths and interests of key powerful actors between the Eelam wars and the Moro wars is evident if we recall the difference between what I labelled as the 'mighty state-cum-rebel pressure complex' in Sri Lanka and the 'three-layered material pressure cooker' in the Philippines. Summary Table 4.5 from Sri Lanka (Chapter 4) looks quite different from Summary Table 5.5 from the Philippines (Chapter 5). Summary Table 6.1 in this chapter combines the gist of these two Tables and sharpens the contrast by juxtaposing each key actor's degree of pressure or inducement on humanitarian IOs in Sri Lanka against its counterpart's degree of pressure or inducement on IOs in the Philippines. On every single indicator of 'Power' in Summary Table 6.1, we find that the humanitarians in Sri Lanka face a different field of pressures and inducements compared to the humanitarians in the Philippines.

Summary Table 6.1 Generic 'Power' pressures and inducements on IOs in Sri Lanka vis-à-vis the Philippines.

Indicator of 'Power'	Sri Lanka	Philippines
a) Donor pressures to lower emphasis on civilian rights	Low	Maximum
b) Donor inducements to increase emphasis on civilian rights	Medium to High	Low
c) State pressures to lower emphasis on civilian rights	Maximum	High
d) Rebel pressures to lower emphasis on civilian rights	Medium to High	Low to Medium
e) Provincial government pressures to hush up abuses of civilians by paramilitaries	Low to Medium	High

The only conditional similarity between the two countries is on indicator d), where under certain circumstances of issue and time, rebel pressures might be equally 'Medium'. This nuance will be discussed later as we comparatively analyse each indicator between the Eelam wars and the Moro wars, keeping an eye on its theoretically expected impact on the proactiveness of humanitarian IOs.

Due to differences in geopolitical contexts, donor pressures to lower emphasis on civilian rights vary greatly between Sri Lanka and the Philippines. Sri Lanka is universally viewed as a South Asian sore spot that falls within India's sphere of influence. In the 1970s, New Delhi proclaimed the 'Indira Doctrine' wherein 'India would consider the presence or influence of an external power in the region as adverse to its interests, unless that power recognised Indian predominance' (Cohen, 2001:138). Keeping the USA, European powers, and China out of South Asia was and is a key foreign policy priority of New Delhi that has generally been honoured by the former two, although the third challenges it.

The approach of donor powers to the Sri Lankan conflict is therefore coloured by deference to India's lead role. It is customary for diplomats of donor countries involved in Sri Lanka to 'consult' with India before taking any position vis-à-vis the Eelam wars (GSL, 2000). GSL and the LTTE themselves recognised the primacy of India in ending the Eelam wars and each tried to have India on its side to be in a better bargaining position. Sri Lankan Presidents make beelines to India every year and strive to burnish the lustre of the bilateral closeness between the two countries following the LTTE's assassination of Rajiv Gandhi in 1991. GSL publicly 'promised' India of its intent of devolving power and autonomy to the Tamil-speaking people and protecting their safety in the Eelam wars (Reddy, 2009).

The LTTE too attempted to achieve a rapprochement with India after the assassination of Rajiv Gandhi, but to no avail. In 2002, Velupillai Prabhakaran appealed for a patch-up with New Delhi by commenting, 'our people love India and the people of India' and 'India is our fatherland' (Devraj, 2002). As Eelam War IV reached a crescendo in 2008-09, LTTE sympathisers in the Indian state of Tamil Nadu pulled out all stops to urge New Delhi to intervene and pressurise GSL to halt the SLA's military offensives. As LTTE grew isolated around the world with the tag of 'foreign terrorist organization', Prabhakaran fell back on requesting India to come to its aid (FE, 2008). Due to cultural linkages and the presence of a long-term refugee community across the Palk Straits, there is a widespread perception among Sri Lankan Tamils that only India can guarantee their rights as a minority in Sri Lanka (ANI, 2009).

For all its hegemony over Sri Lanka, India is not a major donor state that can impact upon the priorities of humanitarian IOs in the Eelam wars. The Indian state does not have a well developed foreign aid bureaucracy and has only occasionally stepped up to send relief aid to civilians during grave moments in the Eelam wars. India is not a member of the 'Donor Co-Chairs' comprising the US, the EU, Japan and Norway, which control the humanitarian purse strings in the Eelam wars.

In Chapter 4, I referred to an incident involving Indian aid to the war-affected civilians that was channelled through ICRC. New Delhi left it to ICRC and the GSL to sort out who would control the aid distribution instead of acting like a typical bossy donor which has clear rules about delivery channels for the aid it gives (Tighe and Shankar, 2009). New Delhi's advocacy for civilian protection goes through direct diplomatic channels from the government of India to GSL rather than encouraging the ICRC, a recipient of Indian aid, to be more proactive. Thus, the Morgenthau-theorised 'political function' of aid has relevance but does not extend to India using its cheque book to steer IOs in a desired direction.

Capitalist donor states have been satisfied with the Sri Lankan state's adherence to neoliberal free market policies since 1977 and have rarely attempted to twist Colombo by its arm for its bloody counter-insurgency in the North and East. The IMF and the EU have never used economic sanctions or denial of loans and trade preferences to the Sri Lankan state despite mounting criticism of state agents' abuses of civilians during the Eelam wars. Even the strategic-military closeness of Sri Lanka to China during Eelam War IV has not rattled the confidence of capitalist donor states that Colombo would turn to the IMF for a bailout, an eventuality that did transpire in early 2009.

Lacking any sustained economic or geopolitical interest in Sri Lanka, Western donors took a dual stand on the Eelam wars. On one hand, they expressed support for GSL's territorial integrity and sovereignty and condemned LTTE as a 'terrorist organization'. On the other hand, they criticised GSL's military solution to the conflict for prolonging the suffering of civilians and neglecting legitimate grievances of minorities.

The former line was dictated by inter-state solidarity oiled by GSL's foreign diplomatic missions and the need to keep the Sri Lankan state within the neoliberal fold, while the latter came from lobbying about the human costs of the wars by Sri Lankan Tamil refugees and international human rights organizations in Oslo, Washington, London, Brussels and Geneva. In the absence of a 'strategic embrace' type of alliance with the Sri Lankan state, the US and other Western donors have no qualms about criticising GSL on civilian protection in the war zones or financially goading humanitarian IOs to push the envelope on this issue.

Japan is the only exception to this rule because its relations with the Sri Lankan state are culturally imbued. Both GSL and the Japanese government toast the Buddhist angle of their closeness and refer to episodes that uphold the unity of the 'Buddhists of Asia' (Pandith, 2002). Tokyo sympathises with the constitutionally endorsed notion that Sri Lanka is a 'chosen land for Buddhism' (Thiruchandran, 2003). This is a key factor behind Japan's lavishing of praise on GSL for its 'war on terrorism' when thousands of civilians were being slaughtered by the SLA's offensive in Eelam War IV (see Chapter 4). However, Tokyo could never convince the other Donor Co-Chairs to drop insistence on protection of civilians in the Eelam wars. Japanese thoughts and ideas essentially lack the kind of hegemonic institutions that Western liberalism boasts of and they therefore cannot become ideologies that other states would want to mimic or internalise.

Summary Table 6.1 implies that the geopolitical stakes for donor states in the Philippines are at wide variance from those in Sri Lanka. Unlike in the Eelam wars, Australia, Spain, Japan, New Zealand and the USA have a completely different set of concerns about the Moro wars and their spill over in terms of regional security and balance of power in the Asia Pacific. To recall from Chapter 5, the big story about the Philippines that preceded (and will outlast) the 'war on terrorism' against Islamic fundamentalist outfits is its location in the context of the rise of China as a global great power.

How could the USA, Japan, Australia and European powers ensure that Asia is multipolar and not trampled by the Chinese behemoth? This is the mega-strategic problem which guides the attitude of donor states to humanitarian IOs in the Philippines. The Philippine archipelago is like China's Cuba. With the Philippine province of Palawan (claimed by MNLF as Moro land) barely 230 miles from the Spratly islands disputed by China, it should be no surprise that Palawan is one of the regular sites of the US-GRP *Balikatan* exercises dubbed as 'humanitarian missions to help residents' of a low 'socio-economic profile' (Tagacay, 2008).

The deliberate distancing of donor states' aid arms like USAID, DFID, AusAID and JICA from 'radical' activists and 'political' issues of abuses of civilians in the Moro wars is the necessary price to fine tune an alliance-like understanding between Washington, London, Canberra, Madrid, Tokyo, and Manila to jointly counter Chinese expansionism.

Military humanitarianism, of which the Philippines is an exemplary case, is necessarily an 'anti-civilian ideology' (see Chapter 1) because civilians need to be kept in a subdued condition so that the landed territory they inhabit can be taken over at will and used as a beachhead or springboard for geopolitical thrusts. The suffering of Mindanawons in wars is thus essential for the Philippines to become a convenient staging ground for the containment of China. For donor powers intent on utilising the Moro wars to meet grand strategic objectives, humanitarian IOs are the classic Trojan Horses which can be deployed to prepare the ground by mainstreaming 'peace and development' and hiding the violence and atrocities faced by civilians.

Since 2001, the US-led 'war on terrorism' was conflated with the China-containment logic because of the perception that Southeast Asian states like Indonesia, Thailand and the Philippines would become vulnerable to Chinese domination. While there certainly are violent fundamentalist Islamic currents in these three countries, the self-image of the USA as a 'resident power' in the region to counterbalance China (Koh, 2008) preceded them and absorbed them as rationales for rendering Western military presence permanent. Humanitarian IOs could not but be swept away by these great power winds that required a silencing of the victims of the Moro wars.

The only partial exception to the maximum degree of donor pressure on IOs to lower emphasis on civilian rights in the Moro wars is Canada (CIDA, 2006). Nonetheless, the bulk of CIDA's aid is given to 'peace and development' through the same Mindanao Trust Fund which also has the World Bank, Australia, New Zealand, Japan, Sweden and the US as members. That Canada is an ardent supporter of the GRP's 'war on terrorism' in Mindanao is clear from its ambassador's comments about how foreign aid is at the disposal of the Philippine state to conduct counter-insurgency:

> You have to build up a 'peace dividend'. When you push the insurgents out, you must come in with assistance. That way, when people see the improvements that can be theirs with peace, they themselves will want to preserve that peace (Jalbuena, 2007).

Canada and Australia use the 'war on terrorism' as a cover behind which they massage the political hurdles to their powerful mining MNCs which partner with Makati-based Filipino 'oligarchs' to jointly exploit Mindanao's mineral wealth. To the extent that neither Canada nor Australia has ever been threatened by credible Islamist extremist activity, their participation in the US-led wars in Afghanistan, Iraq and the Philippines should draw attention to other motives, including commercial, that have often escaped the geopolitically coloured portrayal of the global 'war on terrorism'.

State pressures on IOs to lower emphasis on civilian rights also vary between Sri Lanka and the Philippines due to the differences in state structures and ideologies in the two countries. Although both Sri Lanka and the Philippines are electoral democracies, the former has been described by Oren Yiftachel as an 'ethnocracy', i.e. a non-democratic system for and by a dominant ethnic group within the state (Yiftachel, 1998). In his words, Sri Lanka went from being a 'biethnic democracy' at the time of independence from British rule to a 'Sinhalese ethnocracy' (Yiftachel, 2006: 23). The driving force for a harsh military response to Eelam militancy from 1983 up to 2009 is this belief that Sri Lanka is a Sinhalese Buddhist state. In October 2008, the then chief of the SLA, General Sarath Fonseka, brazenly avowed that 'this country belongs to the Sinhalese and they (Tamils) must not try to demand undue things' (Patranobis, 2008).

No comparable vitriol can be heard from any agent of state in the Philippines. While Malacañang has always been dominated by groups subscribing to the majority Roman Catholic faith, Philippine nationalism is not primarily drawn from Christian fundamentalism or supremacy. Deep anti-Muslim prejudices in the Christian North and Centre of the country do exist, but they are not elevated to the level of a state ideology. Quite contrary to Sri Lanka which is a declared Buddhist theocracy, the Philippines is constitutionally a secular state.

The Sri Lankan state's army and police are exclusively manned by Sinhalese and Muslims, with no Tamils at all, while the Philippine state has thousands of Muslim soldiers and officers who work alongside Christians in the military and the police. Sri Lanka may not be a genocidal state, but it certainly is an ethnocracy which is cruder in its violent intent towards minorities and more xenophobic towards foreigners than the Philippine state.

We recounted that GSL has three instruments with which to regiment and constrain the proactiveness of humanitarian IOs — *bureaucratic, communicative* and *direct strong-arm action* (see Chapter 4). GRP, on the other hand, uses subtler and softer institutional mechanisms like NDCC, RDCC, DSWD and LGUs to keep a check on the autonomy and proactiveness of IOs. Human rights activists were bitter that the Arroyo administration's 'spate of state killings are the worst since the dictatorship of Ferdinand Marcos' (Adriano, 2008), but none of the hit squads with apparent state intelligence connivance ever targeted humanitarian IOs or their personnel. The long list of 'security incidents' against humanitarians in Sri Lanka which are instigated by agents of state offers a sharp contrast.

The Sri Lankan state's culture of using physical threats and direct strong-arm action on IOs is a key reason why indicator c) in Summary Table 6.1 rates its pressures on IOs as 'Maximum', while giving the Philippine state only a 'High'. The Sri Lankan state's ability to punish and coerce IOs is a lot more advanced because it has only one war (against the LTTE) to handle. The Philippine state cannot apply the same level of concentrated material pressure on IOs as it is fighting two wars (vs. NPA and vs. MILF) in the country. The division of attention wrought by fighting two simultaneous wars blunts the sharper edges of the Philippine state's coercive blade to discipline IOs.

Thomas Risse-Kappen's state-society balance typology is useful to distinguish Sri Lanka from the Philippines. It has six ideal typical political forms, viz. state-controlled structures, state-dominated structures, stalemated structures, corporatist structures, society-dominated structures and fragile structures (Risse-Kappen, 1995: 3-33) A state-controlled structure is one in which civil society is very weak and totally repressed by the state. Sri Lanka is a state-controlled structure because the Buddhist clerical establishment, the private sector, local associations and unions are all heavily penetrated by the Sri Lankan state and lack any semblance of independence.

A state-dominated structure, on the other hand, is defined by Risse-Kappen as one in which there are intermediate organizations (political parties, chambers of commerce, unions etc.) to counter-balance state power to an extent. The Philippines fits better into this category as it has an organised Left with its own political parties, media outlets and mass following, all legacies of the 'People Power' movement that brought down the dictatorship of Ferdinand Marcos in 1986.

The Philippines also has a powerful set of financial elites based in Makati who have enormous control over the state's policies in Mindanao because of their investments in logging and mining. This capitalist class is opposed to the organised Left but is also against excessive state power that could jam its accumulation of wealth. In 2008, the Makati Business Club (MBC) lobbied hard with Malacañang to scupper the GRP's MOA-AD with MILF as the agreement would have handed over control of Mindanao's natural resources to the MILF on a 75:25 ratio, sapping the profits of the financiers (CBNa, 2008). No comparable private entity in Sri Lanka could dare to overturn the state's policy on the Eelam wars.

The Makati finance capitalists partner with foreign mining giants that covet Mindanao's treasure trove of copper, gold, nickel and zinc reserves whose estimated value is more than $1 trillion (SS, 2009). Besides BHP Billiton Inc., the world's largest mining company, Australia has as many as 13 other firms operating in the Philippines. In 2007, the Australian ambassador in Manila openly admitted that he was pouring sixty percent of 'development aid' for the Philippines into cities and municipalities in Mindanao, where 'we see a very big potential on energy and mining' (MC, 2007). Canada is the other major foreign player with mining interests in Mindanao. The operations of one Canadian firm, TVI Pacific Inc., in Mindanao have come under scrutiny for alleged 'militarisation of the region and related human rights abuses' (GOC, 2005).

In Chapter 2, I mentioned the Marxist contention that IOs can act as 'advance units' for MNCs interested in expanding their markets for consumers and raw materials. Both AusAID and CIDA, two big Western donor entities, illustrate this by tying their humanitarian and development aid through IOs and local NGOs to those parts of Mindanao where their mining MNCs have concrete commercial interests. Thus, although Australia and Canada rally under the banner of the 'global war on terrorism' and coordinate their aid with the US in Mindanao, they have their own capitalist interest to protect in Mindanao by means of relief and development assistance.

The MILF is cognisant of the collusion of global and local capital and its deleterious impact on Mindanao's environment and the armed conflict. It accuses 'capitalists, political dynasties and warlords, and some religious groups who have vast claims in the wealth of Mindanao especially in mining' (MILF, 2008) for derailing the peace process with the GRP, implying that all these entities have power over the state and can sway its position on the Moro wars. No comparable combination of forces exists in Sri Lanka to veto GSL's will.

Risse-Kappen's typology does not distinguish political structures by the division of powers within branches of the state (i.e. among the legislature, executive, judiciary, military etc.) In Sri Lanka, the executive has an unshakable solidity to it because of high concentration of power in the presidency. The other arms of the state are inferior in might and rarely go against executive fiat, especially not in the realm of national security and the Eelam wars. All decisions of whether to pursue war and how to conduct it are mainly in the hands of the presidency, with some inputs from the army. Sri Lanka has never undergone a military *coup d'etat* or a situation where the SLA disobeyed a reigning elected president.

The Philippines, however, has a history of coups and putsches. Alan Robles has justifiably argued that 'the AFP is the final arbiter in Philippine politics' (Robles, 2008: 371). The Arroyo administration was on permanent tenterhooks to satisfy the whims and demands of the AFP top brass and avoid another coup. Since the Damocles Sword of a coup is ever-present in the Philippines, decisions about war and peace in Mindanao are frequently made by the presidency in keeping with the mood of the AFP. I once met a Brigadier General of the AFP in charge of western Mindanao operations who boasted that 'I am the authority of this region and all IOs have to go through me, irrespective of whether they are accredited by the GRP in Manila.'

The fragmentation of the state in the Philippines into bits of power that are distributed rather than concentrated in the presidency means that the pressures on humanitarian IOs do not stem from a single centralised locus. It is also owing to this factor that indicator c) in Summary Table 6.1 ranks the Philippines as 'High', compared to Sri Lanka's 'Maximum'.

A related difference between Sri Lanka and the Philippines is over the means of coercion in the hands of provincial sub-units of government. Sri Lanka is a unitary state with no genuine autonomy for provincial or local self-government units, especially not in the North and East where the Sinhalese state has suspicions about the loyalty of Tamils to a unified country. In December 2008, the Chief Minister of the newly formed Eastern Provincial Council and TMVP leader Pilleyan publicly lamented, eight months into office, that 'I don't have any powers' (TG, 2008). The TMVP has therefore not managed to build up a state-like machinery of coercion in the East with which to terrorise civilians and dictate to humanitarian IOs the way the LTTE used to do when it was militarily strong.

In Moro areas of the Philippines, the opposite is true. The LGUs of ARMM and surrounding provinces have enormous economic, military and feudal cultural power that is capable of carving out highly repressive forms of local rule against civilians. The political quid pro quos between the Ampatuans and the Arroyo administration were so entrenched that LGUs became arbiters of Mindanawons' fates in ways that are unthinkable for Sri Lanka. Sri Lanka lacks a feudal class of rich landlords who can amass wealth and power and determine the direction of the Eelam wars.

The preponderant ability of LGU-controlled CVOs and CAFGUs to start mini-wars against the MILF or MNLF in the Philippines is unmatched by the fledgling TMVP in Eastern Sri Lanka and by any future Provincial Council in the North. Summary Table 6.1 therefore ranks provincial government pressures to hush up abuses against civilians in Sri Lanka as 'Low to Medium' and in the Philippines as 'High'.

Chapters 4 and 5 painted two different types of guerrilla organizations between the Eelam wars and the Moro wars. The LTTE was a Hitlerist movement based on fanatical worship of a single man, Prabhakaran, who was deified as a contemporary demigod who could perform miracles and save the Tamils. Extreme personalisation of power within LTTE was partly a response to the competition it faced from other Eelam militant outfits which also claimed the mantle of the sole spokesperson of Sri Lankan Tamils (Swamy, 1994).

Prabhakaran's obsession to eliminate enemy Eelam militant factions and maintain LTTE's monopoly over the Sri Lankan Tamil cause pushed him into becoming a harsh authoritarian figure who frequently purged his own ranks and terrorised Tamil civilians and CSOs to toe the line. The LTTE's culture of 'total war' by total control over Tamil people meant that its de facto state machinery oversaw and sought to mould humanitarian IOs in ways that would serve the politics of its Eelam cause. Keeping a constant vigil on CSOs and IOs was a specialised task of LTTE's intelligence wing, especially until the CFA period of 2002-06. Only in the last two years or so, with the LTTE losing militarily, did the iron hand of the organization lift on local activists and IOs.

The MILF is a far more decentralised guerrilla organization compared to the LTTE. It lacks a single focal leader and decides on all policy matters through consultation with battalion and brigade commanders from the Barangays. Especially since the death of its founder Hashim Salamat in 2002, MILF's direction has been steered by a college of senior leaders. The Central Committee, chaired by Al-Haj Murad, often has democratic disagreements and votes in favour or against an issue. Murad is not a megalomaniac and lacks Prabhakaran's absolutist traits.

Since the MILF arose in 1984 as a protest movement against the peace deals signed by MNLF supremo Nur Misuari with the GRP, it is careful to avoid the 'flair for self-promotion' and self-indulgence that Misuari took to after he became Governor of ARMM in 1996 (Gluckman, 1997). As a consequence, there is no one brain centre in MILF today who can assume dictatorial powers. MILF has so many internal centres of power that the AFP terms them 'renegades' and 'loose commanders' who often strike out on their own and take a lot of convincing by the Central Committee to retract their steps.

When the MOA-AD was stayed by the Philippine Supreme Court in August 2008, three MILF commanders indiscriminately attacked Christian civilians and killed several dozens of them out of frustration. Murad promised to take 'punitive action' if any of the three commanders was found guilty (Elusfa2, 2008), but the issue petered out without any further action because of the power and popular following of these field leaders. Aside from core political Islamist principles that are agreed upon by all commanders, MILF concedes leeway to the men on the spot to take most decisions. MILF insiders situate this feature of the organization within 'common Islamic tradition' (Almotaqa, 2007).

With several 'factions' spreading out into the remote rural Barangays of ARMM and surrounding provinces, the MILF has no single approach to humanitarian IOs in contrast to the LTTE's well-oiled strategy of bullying IOs to serve its strategic goals against the GSL. One cannot observe persistent MILF pressure on IOs as much as the LTTE exerted over the years. This is why Summary Table 6.1 ranks rebel pressures on IOs to be 'Medium to High' for Sri Lanka and only 'Low to Medium' for the Philippines. The one issue area on which LTTE and MILF approach parity position of 'Medium' is child conscription, as it relates to a military necessity for both organizations in their asymmetric warfare against conventionally superior state armies. In all other human rights issues, rebel pressures to lower emphasis on civilian protection were higher in Sri Lanka than in the Philippines.

In toto, was the 'mighty state-cum-rebel pressure complex' of Sri Lanka more of a 'Power' constraint on IOs than the 'three-layered material pressure cooker' of the Philippines? The judgement about which country is heavier on the rationalist weighing scale depends on which indicator of 'Power' is deemed to have how much of an independent impact on humanitarian behaviour. If donors and provincial governments (a, b and e in Summary Table 6.1) are considered to be calling the shots on IOs, then the Philippines could be considered to be a worse environment for humanitarian proactiveness than Sri Lanka. If host states and rebels (c and d) are keys to determining IO behaviour, then Sri Lanka is more inhospitable for humanitarians than the Philippines.

While humanitarians are caught between a rock and a hard place in material pressure terms between Sri Lanka and the Philippines, judging one country as more hostile to IOs than the other as a whole would be an oversimplification. Instead, we must stratify 'Power' into the relevant indicators and see how they apply to each comparative dyad of IOs.

Apart as Heaven and Earth

Why does UNICEF lead the ranking of IOs in Sri Lanka but remain second from the bottom in the ranking for the Philippines? In the language of a Chinese proverb, what sets one apart from the other like heaven and earth? Before embarking on hypothesis testing, we need to standardise the comparative ranking of UNICEF branches between the two countries. The proactiveness scales for measuring the dependent variable in Chapters 4 and 5 were not identical due to local contextual differences. The net weighted proactiveness score of UNICEF Sri Lanka comes from a set of measures that are not the same which went into calculating the score of UNICEF Philippines. To equalise the scores across country contexts, one has to eliminate those measures of the dependent variable which do not overlap between Sri Lanka and the Philippines.

Removal of the two unique measures, viz. participation in temple festival vigils from the Sri Lanka scale, and field staffer's human rights consciousness from the Philippines scale, will enable standardisation of the inter-branch UNICEF comparison. Following these excisions, the new net weighted proactiveness score of UNICEF Sri Lanka turns out to be 3.33 (out of a maximum of 6) and that of UNICEF Philippines amounts to 1.16 (out of a maximum of 6).[4]

A gap in proactiveness of 2.17 points is quite large and raises the puzzle of why two branches of the same humanitarian IO behave differently on civilian protection in two different war zones. R1 and R2 would answer that UNICEF Sri Lanka faces lesser material pressures and lesser need to compete for finances and political patronage compared to UNICEF Philippines. In keeping with the complexity of the variable 'Power', we can disaggregate it into its components and test these hypotheses.

Summary Table 6.1 reveals that donor pressures on IOs to lower emphasis on civilian rights are 'Low' in Sri Lanka and 'Maximum' in the Philippines. Moreover, donor inducements to IOs to increase emphasis on protection are 'Medium to High' in Sri Lanka and 'Low' in the Philippines. This disaggregated 'Power' indicator clearly shows that one reason why UNICEF Sri Lanka is so ahead of its Philippine branch in proactiveness is because the former is spared of the donor-dictated conservatism that is integral to the US' 'war on terrorism'.

Summary Table 6.1 also shows that provincial government pressures to hush up abuses of civilians are 'Low to Medium' in Sri Lanka but 'High' in the Philippines. Again, the variation in this disaggregated 'Power' indicator seems to correlate with UNICEF Sri Lanka's lead over UNICEF Philippines along the theoretically expected lines. The ferocity of LGUs that the latter has to face and remain gagged on child conscription cannot be matched by the TMVP's pressures on the former.

One indicator of 'Power', however, appears on surface to be contradicting R1 because state pressures to lower emphasis on civilian rights are 'Maximum' for Sri Lanka and only 'High' in the Philippines. How could UNICEF Sri Lanka have a top proactiveness score of 3.33 if it faces 'Maximum' state pressures to marginalise protection? The clue lies in the specialised mandate of UNICEF for children's rights. GSL made life miserable for IOs if they laid blame or worked against its military and political interests in the Eelam wars, but it also gave inducements to IOs to tarnish the image and reputation of the LTTE. Child conscription is an issue on which UNICEF Sri Lanka gets maximum goading, not maximum pressure, from the state. So central is it to the propaganda war for GSL that the landing page of the website of the Sri Lankan embassy in Washington D.C in March 2009 expressed 'hopes that new UNICEF media campaign will promote release of children' (GSL, 2009B).

Except the smaller-scale child conscription by TMVP, UNICEF did not face any pressures to hide or ignore this crucial aspect of civilian protection in the Eelam wars. Chapter 5 has shown the obverse to be true in the Philippines, with the GRP not being a consistent manipulator of UNICEF Philippines to sully the MILF's child conscription.

Only one indicator of 'Power' genuinely goes against the expected correlation with greater proactiveness of UNICEF in Sri Lanka vis-à-vis the Philippines. Rebel pressures to lower emphasis on civilian rights are 'Medium to High' in Sri Lanka but only 'Low to Medium' in the Philippines. Ipso facto, UNICEF Sri Lanka should be less proactive than UNICEF Philippines on this count. But even here, we already noted that rebel pressures on UNICEF could conditionally be equally 'Medium' in both countries. The first condition is the issue of child conscription, on which both LTTE and MILF were adamant that they will not brook interference, although both paid lip service to the ideal of leaving children alone. The second condition is the waxing and waning military strength and political control of LTTE in the last five years. LTTE's pressure on UNICEF to push child conscription under the carpet was 'High' only when the former was at its zenith between 2002 and 2005.

The MILF, on the other hand, has been consistently strong as a guerrilla force that rarely suffers big reversals at the hands of the AFP (ABS, 2009). The decline of LTTE and the steadiness of MILF meant that, at least since 2006, rebel pressures on UNICEF Sri Lanka and UNICEF Philippines were equally 'Medium'. With 'Power' indicators a), b), c) and e) all pointing to the theoretically expected correlation between rational pressures and proactiveness of the two UNICEF branches, and indicator d) remaining inconclusively equal between the two countries, we can conclude with confidence that rationalist explanation R1 has high validity in explaining the 2.17-point-gap between the branches.

In Chapter 2, we asked whether each country branch of an IO or INGO has a separate identity of its own. While there is enough explanatory variation in 'Power' across the two countries in the UNICEF dyad comparison, it is also necessary to see if some proportion of the 2.17-point-gap in proactiveness owes to differences in inter-branch culture.

The temporal change in UNICEF Sri Lanka's values over a span of a few years during the CFA period (see Chapter 4) spurred its rise to the top of the proactiveness ranking. UNICEF Philippines is still waiting for sparks to ignite its bureaucratically (and 'Power' politically) suppressed proactiveness. One UNICEF Philippines official, who I met after an interval of three years, could not have been clearer when he shared the following thoughts:

> Since I last spoke to you in 2005, there has not been much movement on the Moro people's culture, which does not look at 'child soldiers' from a critical point of view. As long as advocacy on this topic is considered an intrusion into Moro culture, we have to be careful.[5]

Around these same three years, UNICEF Sri Lanka was transformed into a proactive IO where district-level heads could take decentralised proactive protection initiatives without worrying about getting permissions for each and every action. UNICEF Philippines, on the other hand, remained in a remote-control mode where Mindanao-based personnel had to defer to the 'high command' in Manila before doing anything remotely 'political' in the field.

So, while not disputing the clear-cut explanatory value of 'Power', we will have to agree that a shift in 'Ideas' was essential for UNICEF Sri Lanka to emerge as a clear leader in proactiveness compared to the ossified UNICEF Philippines . Chapter 7 will reengage with the syncretic hypotheses RC1 and RC2 in conjunction with alternative Marxist and feminist explanations to extract more theoretical leverage on this point.

Identical Also-Rans

Why is UNDP Sri Lanka almost a mirror image of UNDP Philippines when it comes to proactiveness towards civilian protection? What drives the branches of this IO to be so similar in their conservatism despite facing seemingly different rational 'Power' pressure complexes?

The standardised cross-country net proactiveness score of UNDP Sri Lanka (derived from the same rules of odd-measure elimination as in the previous section) is 1.66 (out of a maximum of 6) and that of UNDP Philippines is also 1.66 (out of a maximum of 6).[6] Post-standardisation, there is not even the tiny .34 lead that UNDP Philippines had over UNDP Sri Lanka. The absolutely identical standing and scores of the two branches raise the possibility that 'Power' differences between the two countries have no impact on their proactiveness and that the clue to their equality in conservatism lies in 'Ideas'. Disaggregated tests of R1 and R2 are in order here.

To recall from Summary Table 6.1, donor pressures on IOs to lower emphasis on civilian rights are 'Low' in Sri Lanka but 'Maximum' in the Philippines. In Chapter 4, we noted that UNDP Sri Lanka lacks a donor deterrent to its proactiveness and even enjoys mild encouragement from donors to include human rights-related content into its 'livelihood projects' in the North and East. But in the Philippines, as a prop in the 'war on terrorism', UNDP is forced to adopt a 'developmentalist' profile that is blind to violent abuses against civilians in the Moro war theatres. The unambiguous cross-country variation in donor pressures and inducements would lead us to expect UNDP Philippines to be less proactive than UNDP Sri Lanka on this count.

Moreover, we saw that UNDP Philippines 'competes hard with other UN agencies to be the main beneficiary and shepherd of the MDAP and to stay as close as possible to the Philippine state.' (see Chapter 5) UNDP Sri Lanka, on the other hand, does not hold any official position or privileged status on the Donor Co-Chairs mechanism and is not hard pressed to vie with fellow UN agencies for donor funds. Political economy hypothesis R2 is thus also supportive of the theoretical expectation that UNDP Philippines is less proactive than UNDP Sri Lanka.

Cross-country variation on the indicator of provincial government pressures on IOs to hush up civilian abuses further supports the possibility of UNDP Philippines being less proactive than UNDP Sri Lanka. To recall from Chapter 4, the TMVP has not been handed sufficient autonomous power by the Sinhalese state. Whatever pressures UNDP Sri Lanka faces from the TMVP is thus in rudimentary stages (i.e. 'Low'). UNDP Philippines, on the hand, lives in mortal fear of the LGUs in ARMM and surrounding provinces. Most of the 'ACT for Peace' employees and local partners of UNDP are handpicked by LGUs to strengthen the patronage networks of the feudal *Datus*. Given the absence of such a sophisticated layer of local self-government in Sri Lanka, one is again led to expect that UNDP Philippines should be less proactive than its Sri Lankan counterpart.

What balances the previous three indicators is cross-country variation in state pressures on IOs to lower emphasis on civilian protection. There is no doubting the great pressure that GRP places on UNDP Philippines to stick to the 'peace and development' formula. However, in the cross-country context, the Sri Lankan state's pressures on IOs are 'Maximum' compared to the 'High' of the Philippine state. If UNDP Philippines is fully integrated into the GRP fold, then UNDP Sri Lanka is doubly so and with greater fear of 'PNG's and physical attacks on its personnel by agents of state. The terrorising atmosphere of Eelam War IV had, in particular, shaken UNDP Sri Lanka to total surrender to the state's wishes. Thus, this disaggregated indicator of 'Power' leads to the reverse expectation that UNDP Philippines should be more proactive than UNDP Sri Lanka.

The other indicator that helps balance the first three discussed in this section is cross-country variation in rebel pressures on proactiveness of IOs. UNDP Sri Lanka faced 'Medium to High' extent of pressures from the LTTE to 'coordinate' with the TRO and turn a blind eye to the guerrillas' excesses on civilians. Following the tsunami calamity of December 2004, I recall meeting harried UNDP officials who were being regularly 'summoned' to discuss their project priorities with the LTTE's district-level political heads in the East. But the pressure from the LTTE on UNDP Sri Lanka eased during Eelam War IV and settled at 'Medium'. Since this book has taken the long view of IO proactiveness over a course of five years, it is appropriate to label the extent of LTTE pressures on UNDP Sri Lanka as 'Medium to High'.

UNDP Philippines faces only 'Low to Medium' pressures from the MILF. To recall from Chapter 5, UNDP Philippines has managed to win the grassroots confidence of the MILF because of the MNLF connections of its PDAs. It is a beneficiary of more or less stable trust between the two Bangsamoro militant factions and escapes censure or restrictions from the MILF. UNDP Sri Lanka, on the other hand, lacked the *deus ex machina* of PDAs and hence ended up facing far more intense pressures from the LTTE. By this indicator's count, UNDP Sri Lanka should be less proactive than UNDP Philippines.

The comparison of UNDP's branches on rationalist grounds has thrown up a draw of sorts, with disaggregated 'Power' indicators a), b) and e) suggesting that UNDP Philippines should be less proactive than UNDP Sri Lanka, and indicators c) and d) conveying the converse. One could conclude that the reason why UNDP Sri Lanka and UNDP Philippines share the same proactiveness score of 1.66 is because the causal effect of the first set of three indicators is being cancelled out by the second set, which has the opposite effect. In other words, the reworded rationalist hypotheses R1 that we used in Chapter 5 — 'both IOs face the *same* extent of material pressures and inducements' — is being validated by the evidence. What is not being validated is the modified hypothesis R2 that both IOs face 'the *same* extent of competition and rivalry for funding and political patronage' (see Chapter 5).

To what extent are modified hypotheses C1 and C2 also causing UNDP Sri Lanka and UNDP Philippines to stay on parity at 1.66 points each? Both branches are carbon copies in their 'Ideas' about the appropriateness of being cosy with the state, and their identity as a 'needs-based' IO which should not bother about civilian protection. We saw in Chapters 4 and 5 that both branches have Byzantine SOPs which dehumanise civilians and glorify rigid routines. Both UNDP Sri Lanka and UNDP Philippines carry reputations of corruption, which is a classic trait of opaque, change-resistant bureaucracies. The money making opportunities for faceless UNDP bureaucrats through the aid business in both countries are simply too important to be ignored while assessing why they religiously stick to material relief and development projects.

Unlike UNICEF Sri Lanka, UNDP in neither of the two countries has taken opportunities afforded over time to reinvent itself by mainstreaming protection. UNDP Sri Lanka was exposed during the CFA period to the same radical company of Nonviolent Peaceforce and local activists who wanted to ally with IOs and improve chances of getting justice from armed actors. But it had enough reserves of conservatism in its culture and enough fear of repercussions from GSL and LTTE to not budge an inch from its comfort zone of material aid and 'livelihood' projects.

UNDP Philippines had an opportunity to take up a more proactive stance when the post-MOA-AD war broke out in late 2008 and both parties rode roughshod over the ZOPs that its PDAs had instituted. At least on behalf of its own creations, not to mention the hundreds of thousands of IDPs fleeing the fighting, UNDP Philippines could have engaged in dialogue with both parties and tried practical conscious presence techniques for the sanctity of ZOPs to be respected. That it chose not to do so was a small glimpse of how irredeemable UNDP is as an organization.

With little to distinguish the 'Ideas' of one branch from those of the other, the modified culturalist hypotheses C1 and C2 seem to be adding strength to the reworded rationalist hypothesis R1. We thus find grounds to once again deduce that the syncretic hypotheses RC1 and RC2 are valuable in explaining humanitarian behaviour. Chapter 7 will devote greater attention to the paradigmatic intersections and show that causes can be combinatorial because of joint structural 'conditions' that constitute them.

The Pace Setter and the Dawdler

Like the two UNICEFs, OXFAM-GB's two branches in Sri Lanka and the Philippines are divided by a big gulf in their relative proactiveness towards civilian protection. Seen in the single-country context, OXFAM-GB Sri Lanka came third in a ranking of five IOs. On the other hand, OXFAM-GB Philippines was a clear leader in its peer ranking, outdoing its nearest competitors by a record margin of 2.33 points.

If one calculates the standardised cross-country net proactiveness scores of the branches with the same method as the previous two sections, OXFAM-GB Sri Lanka stands at 2.33 (out of a maximum of 6) and OXFAM-GB Philippines has 4.0 (out of a maximum of 6).[7]

What explains the 1.67 points difference in proactiveness of the same organization in two different conflicts? Rationalist hypotheses R1 and R2 imply that OXFAM-GB Philippines faces lesser material pressures from donors, host states and rebels and faces lesser competition for funds and political patronage than its Sri Lankan counterpart.

On first glance, OXFAM-GB Philippines faces 'Maximum' donor pressures to lower emphasis on civilian protection while its Sri Lankan counterpart has to contend only with 'Low'. Theoretically, this should lead to OXFAM-GB Sri Lanka forging ahead of OXFAM-GB Philippines in proactiveness, although the opposite is true.

To recall from Chapter 4, with the exception of the multilateral European Union channel, all the single state donors in Sri Lanka have no vested interest in downplaying civilian protection or forcing recipient IOs to forswear human rights. The key state donor for OXFAM-GB is Britain, which has had many run-ins with GSL over civilian protection during Eelam War IV. The British government banned the LTTE as a terrorist organization, but it has also no strategic bonhomie with GSL that would impel it to mellow down the proactiveness of IOs like OXFAM-GB that depend on its funding.

The same British government's foreign policy in the Philippines, however, is drastically different because of the US-led 'war on terrorism'. Since 2003, the British embassy in Manila has been offering grants to humanitarian IOs and local NGOs under the rubric of a 'Strategic Programme Fund' to 'counter terrorism' and to promote 'economic reform' (UKG, 2009). One never hears any criticism of abuses of civilians in Mindanao from British diplomats, as this is very much in keeping with the overall strategy devised by the US to perpetuate the 'news blackout' about the excesses of the Moro wars. DFID's grants to OXFAM-GB Philippines are thus expectedly focussed on relief and development projects.

Yet, there is one crucial aspect about OXFAM-GB Philippines with regard to donors which offsets the effect of 'Maximum' donor pressures — its steadfast refusal to accept USAID's funding. As noted in Chapter 5, OXFAM-GB Philippines can fund itself with ease through financial transfers from its global headquarters in Oxford.

ECHO in the Philippines has acted at odds with the US-led donor coalition because of the European Commission's interest in acting as a third party 'guarantor' of the GRP-MILF peace process, thereby spreading the 'soft power' of Brussels in Southeast Asia. In my conversations with EC diplomats in the Philippines, I sensed a keen interest in parting ways with the US and carve out an independent European position on the Moro wars. In October 2008, the EC defied the US-led conservative block of donors and issued a strongly worded statement (EU, 2008A) and dished out large grants in support of civilian protection and human rights. OXFAM-GB is one of the prime beneficiaries of Brussels' latest multi-million Euro humanitarian aid package for the Moro war theatres (EU, 2008B), a pecuniary shot in the arm for the organization's proactiveness.

OXFAM-GB Philippines is thus not subject to 'Maximum' donor pressures like the other IO cases in the country. It has carefully chosen donors and avoided falling into the 'war on terrorism' claptrap. So, on indicators a) and b) of Summary Table 6.1, OXFAM-GB Philippines faces 'Low' pressures and 'Medium to High' inducements to be proactive. Thanks to diversified funding sources and lack of dependence on DFID, OXFAM-GB Philippines is able to maintain a radical autonomy from the hegemonic 'war on terrorism'. In terms of finances, both OXFAM-GB branches are secure and do not have to compete for scarce funds, but the Philippine branch has strategically manoeuvred itself with donors to keep its freedom.

Indicator c) of Summary Table 6.1 means that OXFAM-GB Sri Lanka faces 'Maximum' state pressures to stay out of politically incendiary issues of abuses of civilians by armed actors. OXFAM-GB Philippines, on the other hand, faces only 'High' state pressures to downplay protection. Chapters 4 and 5 illustrated episodes of harassment and intimidation of OXFAM-GB Sri Lanka's personnel by state agents, who have license to run a veritable reign of terror against CSOs and IOs. Every OXFAM-GB Sri Lanka official I have interacted with in the last six years trembles at the prospect of being 'booted out' of the country by GSL.

The state-structured political ambience is not as vicious for OXFAM-GB Philippines because of the countervailing strength of progressive political parties, trade unions and activists who often associate themselves with the organization as their international ally. In Chapter 5, we have shown how OXFAM-GB Philippines uses the media and the anti-establishment sector of Philippine society to hold its own against the GRP's pressures to regulate and regiment IOs into a 'developmentalist' straitjacket. By this indicator too, OXFAM-GB Philippines has a distinct advantage over its Sri Lankan counterpart to be more proactive.

On the indicator of rebels' pushing and pulling to quieten the proactiveness of IOs, OXFAM-GB Sri Lanka has to deal with 'Medium to High' pressures, while OXFAM-GB Philippines is faced only with 'Low to Medium' level of pressures. In its better days of military glory and political command over the North and East, we have seen that the LTTE used to dictate to OXFAM-GB Sri Lanka personnel what exactly 'our Tamil people' needed and what was superfluous. Since OXFAM-GB's field offices in the Eelam war theatres were principally staffed by educated Tamil professionals, the fear factor was all the greater because LTTE would not allow independent-minded humanitarian personnel to breathe freely in the communities.

With the MILF, OXFAM-GB Philippines has a relatively smoother relationship devoid of fear. As the larger proportion of IHL violations and excesses committed in the Moro war theatres are by the AFP and its paramilitaries, MILF does not mind radical IOs redressing abuses when 'the victims of crimes, injustices, and human rights violations are Muslims' (SS, 2008). When OXFAM-GB Philippines took a courageous stand on the polemics of whether or not the post-MOA-AD war of 2008 had sparked a 'humanitarian crisis', MILF-allied intellectuals cited it as a talking point to insist that GRP should be convinced to acknowledge the crisis (Jannaral, 2008).

I personally recollect visiting remote Barangays of central Mindanao and hearing positive comments about OXFAM-GB Philippines' 'humanitarian protection' trainings from MILF commanders on the ground. Since OXFAM-GB Philippines does not venture into advocacy or action against child conscription by the MILF, it basically faces only 'Low' rebel pressures in contrast to the 'Medium to High' that is the fate of OXFAM-GB Sri Lanka. Thus, this indicator of 'Power' also supports the theoretical expectation of OXFAM-GB Philippines being relatively more proactive than its Sri Lankan branch.

The lone disaggregated indicator of 'Power' which goes against the general trend is e), i.e. provincial government pressures to hush up abuses of civilians by paramilitaries. On this count, OXFAM-GB Sri Lanka has only 'Low to Medium' pressures while OXFAM-GB Philippines faces 'High' pressures. Earlier in this chapter, we noted that the TMVP's attempts to recreate the pressure complex of the LTTE in the East have not been fully successful because of the tight leash on which it is kept by the Sinhalese state. GAs from the central government bureaucracy and SLA officer corps have greater say in the priorities of IOs in the East than the TMVP. OXFAM-GB Sri Lanka, which keeps a safe distance from child conscription, is thus subject to only 'Low' pressures from provincial government units.

In Mindanao, the fear of the *Datus* is very evident among OXFAM-GB Philippines personnel on the ground. Great care is taken by the organization to oil a cooperative relationship with the LGUs in ARMM and surrounding provinces. The statement of an OXFAM-GB Philippines official that upsetting the LGUs would mean that 'we would be killed' (see Chapter 5) is an unambiguous acceptance of this constraint on the organization's proactiveness. On this count, therefore, OXFAM-GB Sri Lanka should be more proactive than its Philippine branch.

In summation, indicators a), b), c) and d) are overwhelmingly tilted in favour of OXFAM-GB Philippines to be far more proactive than OXFAM-GB Sri Lanka. Only indicator e) has some mitigating countervailing power, possibly reducing the gap in cross-country proactiveness to 1.67 points instead of, say, 2.0 points or more. Rationalist hypothesis R1 is thus once again finding validation as a good explanation for why OXFAM-GB Philippines is the pace setter in civilian protection while its Sri Lankan counterpart merely dawdles.

Is there a possibility that culturalist hypotheses C1 and C2 might throw a spanner in the direction in which R1 is carrying OXFAM-GB Philippines miles ahead of OXFAM-GB Sri Lanka? If it is found that the 'Ideas' of OXFAM-GB Philippines are more bureaucratic, state-subservient and change-resistant than those of OXFAM-GB Sri Lanka, then it would lead to falsification of C1 and C2 and establish R1 as an undisputed explainer.

Chapters 4 and 5 revealed contrasting organizational cultures between the two branches of OXFAM-GB. The Sri Lankan branch is mired in the 'cosiness of received wisdom' (see Chapter 4) and shared beliefs that acting to protect civilians is too risky a proposition to be even mentally entertained. Leadership changes at the Colombo and Oxford levels have caused fluctuations in OXFAM-GB Sri Lanka's attitude to protection, reinforcing a fatalistic culture of blaming external material constraints for the organization's failure to be proactive on civilian rights. The self-identification within the organization as a relief agency and the perception that civilian protection should be left to specialised 'protection organizations' are so deeply entrenched in OXFAM-GB Sri Lanka that even a possible easing of the material pressures might not trigger a change in proactiveness.

OXFAM-GB Sri Lanka also has serious staffing lacunae that prevent it from mainstreaming protection. The organization's 'staff security' adviser is also its 'protection person'. Protection of civilians is therefore understood inside the organization as, at best, an extension of 'field security' for staff members. Humanitarian IOs often have highly unreasonable and rigid 'field security' protocols for their own personnel which restrict their movements in time and space and distance them from the sufferings of ordinary civilians. That

OXFAM-GB Sri Lanka's internal division of labour conflates 'field security' of its own personnel with protection of civilians means that its planning is far removed from the suffering of the latter, especially since September 2008 when the organization was ordered out of the Wanni by GSL and had no 'field security' problem to speak of in the active war theatre.

In contrast, OXFAM-GB Philippines has a culture that is not slavish to state sovereignty and material power structures that inhibit proactiveness. Endowed with an enduring faith in its agency, OXFAM-GB Philippines counteracts 'Power' by gravitating to alternative power centres. Since 2003, OXFAM-GB Philippines has gone further to the Left in the ideological spectrum of humanitarian IOs than any other case studied in this book. Its staff recruitment and sub-contracting criteria in Mindanao now include awareness of IHL, human rights laws and commitment to siding with those who are being dehumanised by war. Its leaders are more committed to peace with justice than those of OXFAM-GB Sri Lanka.

In Chapter 5, we showed that OXFAM-GB Philippines' shift towards embracing protection of civilians as an imperative during 2003-04 came as a result of its association with progressive activists from the grassroots who were struggling to maintain ceasefires, halt violence and prevent abuses. OXFAM-GB Philippines' personnel heard voices from the battlefields that protection was a desideratum that preceded development, relief or reconstruction. They had the humility to listen to civilians and to relay back their concerns to the Manila office, which in turn was ready to engineer the 'shift in thinking' for the whole branch.

OXFAM-GB Sri Lanka had no such metamorphosis not due to more preponderant material pressures but rather because of bureaucratic resistance to altering the course of humanitarian 'business as usual'. If UNICEF Sri Lanka could have its own reincarnation during the CFA period when material pressures of the state and rebels were quite onerous, then why could not OXFAM-GB Sri Lanka? The answers are given by temporal culturalist hypothesis C4. OXFAM-GB Sri Lanka's organizational culture was too static and dehumanised to undergo transformation on the lines of its Philippine branch.

We have to conclude that the 1.67-point lead of OXFAM-GB Philippines over OXFAM-GB Sri Lanka is caused by a mixture of R1, C1, C2 and C4. Not one of these hypotheses can alone claim credit for explaining the wide variation in proactiveness of this IO across countries. Once again, the evidence has pointed to the relevance of syncretic hypotheses RC1 and RC2, whose ramifications will be vetted in Chapter 7.

The Quibbler and the Charlatan

ICRC Sri Lanka and ICRC Philippines present similarities and contrasts in inter-branch humanitarian behaviour. The former's within-country proactiveness ranking is second only to UNICEF Sri Lanka, with a net weighted score of 3.0 (out of a maximum of 7). The latter's in-country ranking is also second, but with a lower net weighted score of 2.33 (out of a maximum of 7). The standardised relative proactiveness scores of the two branches, calculated with the same rule as in the previous three sections of this chapter, do not change these values. ICRC Sri Lanka has the same 3.0 (out of a maximum of 6) while ICRC Philippines has the same 2.33 (out of a maximum of 6).[8]

What explains the .67-point lead of ICRC Sri Lanka over ICRC Philippines? Rationalist hypotheses R1 and R2 would answer that ICRC Philippines must be facing greater material pressures and competing harder for scarce funds and political patronage than ICRC Sri Lanka. By the count of indicator a) from Summary Table 6.1, ICRC Sri Lanka faces only 'Low' level of donor pressures to downplay civilian protection in the Eelam wars while ICRC Philippines has to reckon with 'Maximum' donor demands to de-emphasise the protection crises of the Moro wars.

Lacking economic or geopolitical interest in covering up GSL's blood-soaked counter-insurgency, the US and European states have not dithered in responding favourably to ICRC Sri Lanka's funding appeals for its protection budget. Talking to ICRC Sri Lanka personnel leaves no doubt that the organization enjoys donor inducements to prevent or reduce IHL violations in the Eelam war theatres.

ICRC Philippines has a completely different relationship with the US and European donors flowing from their geostrategic objectives in Southeast Asia. The global 'war on terrorism' tested the ICRC's traditionally trustworthy relations with Washington and added a new wind of caution to this already cautious IO. The George W Bush administration's rampant violations of IHL and human rights like water boarding, extraordinary renditions and outsourced gulags of secret CIA-run prisons confronted ICRC country missions with the dilemma of whether to go against its principal patron and expose these excesses using their organizational name and reputation.

The ICRC's President Jakob Kellenberger threatened to raise more vocal 'Public Denunciations' if US military policies did not improve. But the organization stuck to a minimalist stand for years even as the US and its allies, including GRP, committed systematic abuses against 'terrorists'. Afraid that the Bush administration might pull the plug from financing ICRC, the organization's top leaders 'were careful not (to) slip into an anti-Americanism' and were 'exceedingly attentive to inappropriate Jewish-American threats' (Forsythe, 2005: 138, 220).

The result of the early pressure placed on the organization globally by US neo-conservatives was a taming of the ICRC, which now 'defers to [the U.S.] policy of coercive interrogation while opposing it' (Forsythe, 2005: 101). The deference carried over to the 'second fronts' of the 'war on terrorism', including the Philippines, where ICRC has never issued a public denunciation even though serious abuses were being committed against civilians in Mindanao by the AFP and the Americans under *Balikatan* exercises in western and central Mindanao.

In Chapter 5, we saw that ICRC Philippines is proud of its 'global relationship with the US government' and has not had any problem raising funds for its budgets in Mindanao because of the tacit understanding that it would not wash dirty linen in public about the effects on civilians of the AFP's counter-insurgency. ICRC Sri Lanka has never had to enter such a bargain with donors and is relatively freer on this count to try and alleviate persecution of civilians.

Chapter 5 revealed that ICRC Philippines has been competing hard in the humanitarian market for the last two years to finance the 'scaling up' of its operations in the Moro war theatres. The organization's rational 'need' to grow in size and financial security drove its field personnel to crass self-advertising to catch the attention of donors. ICRC Sri Lanka, on the hand, already has a large expatriate presence in all districts of the North and East and does not need to trumpet its bravado and rapid response capability to raise funds. True to the prediction of R2, therefore, ICRC Sri Lanka is relatively more proactive than ICRC Philippines.

Indicator e) from Summary Table 6.1 also supports a) and b) in favour of ICRC Sri Lanka being ahead of ICRC Philippines in proactiveness. The latter has to face 'High' provincial government pressures to hush up abuses committed by paramilitaries while the former only has to deal with 'Low to Medium' pressures. ICRC Philippines has faced flak from the ARMM LGUs for not 'coordinating' its relief and rehabilitation projects with them during the post-MOA-AD war in central Mindanao. In October 2008, I met one fuming aid 'coordination' official from the RDCC-ARMM who said that he was enraged at ICRC's expatriate personnel in the field who do not inform him of their movements and activities in the war zones in advance. While it is standard practice for humanitarian IOs to inform AFP and MILF commanders beforehand about their plans to enter sensitive areas for relief distribution, the LGUs expect that they too should be kept in the loop.

Following ICRC Philippines' fiasco in Datu Piang (see Chapter 5), I heard from DSWD officials of ARMM that they would 'take action' against the organization for ploughing its own furrow and scoring brownie points through fallacious claims. After some ICRC Philippines personnel were abducted for ransom in Sulu by the Abu Sayyaf in January 2009, the IO announced a temporary pullout from the Moro war theatres. DSWD officials were nonchalantly 'unaffected' by ICRC's loss and added that 'they (ICRC) are so-called freelancers (and) go to wherever they want to go' (Carcamo2, 2009). It was a rebuff to the organization and a show of strength that those IOs which do not defer to LGU wishes will be abandoned.

ICRC Sri Lanka, on the other hand, is spared of intrusive surveillance and unwarranted demands from local self-government units and should therefore be more proactive than ICRC Philippines.

On the count of indicator c) from Summary Table 6.1, ICRC Sri Lanka should face 'Maximum' state pressures while ICRC Philippines is only confronted with 'High'. But the reality is more complex because of ICRC's specialised mandate and utility for states and violent non-state actors. When GSL decided to evict all other humanitarian IOs from the Wanni as fighting escalated in Eelam War IV, it allowed ICRC Sri Lanka to remain because of 'the agreement of both parties' (LN, 2009), i.e. GSL and LTTE. The humanitarian functions of overseeing the exchange of combatants' bodies and manning of crossing points between government-controlled and rebel-controlled lines etc. which ICRC Sri Lanka performs were beneficial to both warring parties.

Another factor that mitigates the 'Maximum' state pressures on ICRC Sri Lanka is its direct implementation of relief and protection projects in the North and East, without having to rely much on the Sri Lanka Red Cross (SLRC). The SLRC has not been extensively used by ICRC as its local implementing partner in the North and East and its charitable activities are largely confined to the Sinhalese South which is not directly affected by the Eelam wars. ICRC Philippines, on the other hand, relies on the PNRC a lot in central and western Mindanao and ends up being pulled into the GRP's orbit because of the politicisation of the local Red Cross.

Taking the peculiarities of ICRC into account, it is still fair to say that ICRC Sri Lanka faces more state pressures than ICRC Philippines, but only by a slight margin. Indicator c) inclines ICRC Sri Lanka to be less proactive than ICRC Philippines, but we must bear in mind that the 'fear factor' of the state is not that varied between the two countries. A senior ICRC Philippines official who had previously served in the protection section of ICRC Sri Lanka offered the following analysis:

> Compared to the GSL, GRP is somewhat less aggressive in pressurising and limiting the human rights components of IGOs and INGOs, but it bears reminder that the level of the armed conflict in Sri Lanka is several notches above that in Muslim Mindanao right now. Essentially, I would

characterise both GSL and GRP as extremely reluctant to grant access to conflict areas to IGOs and INGOs.[9]

Another rationalist indicator of 'Power' which theoretically leads to the expectation that ICRC Sri Lanka be less proactive than ICRC Philippines is rebel pressures to lower emphasis on civilian rights. By the schema of Summary Table 6.1, ICRC Sri Lanka faces 'Medium to High' pressures from the LTTE while ICRC Philippines has to deal only with 'Low to Medium' pressures from the MILF.

This again needs qualification due to the utility that rebel groups see in having the ICRC around when armed conflict is high. ICRC Sri Lanka has acknowledged that during the peak of Eelam War IV, it received 'security guarantees' from the LTTE to remain in the Wanni and provide relief to the swarming IDPs (ICRC, 2008C). Hoping that ICRC would highlight the extreme violence being faced by Tamil civilians under the onslaught of the GSL in Eelam War IV, the LTTE did not antagonise or pressurise the organization after 2006. Therefore, rebel pressures on ICRC Sri Lanka over our five-year-span were 'Medium'.

The MILF's attitude to ICRC Philippines has been cagey in recent years because of the organization's usage of the PNRC for aid delivery in ARMM and surrounding provinces. The PNRC Chairman criticised MILF's 'rogue' commanders for killing Christians in Lanao del Norte after the MOA-AD's failure in 2008 and reiterated that 'we are all Filipinos first before we are Christians or Muslims.'[10] This terminology is unacceptable for the MILF's Bangsamoro nationalists, who claim they are 'Moros first.' Since PNRC never dares to critique the AFP or LGUs for their abuses of civilians, MILF considers the ICRC with some degree of suspicion that it is a tool of the GRP.

This suspicion was visible in the case of the Datu Piang 'rescue' episode narrated in Chapter 5. Yet, MILF's desire to internationalise the sufferings of the Moros means that its pressure on ICRC is only mild. Thus, on disaggregated indicator d) of Summary Table 6.1, we can safely posit equally 'Medium' pressures that do not tilt either branch of ICRC to be more or less proactive than the other.

The overall scorecard of rationalist pressures on ICRC Sri Lanka and ICRC Philippines have indicators a), b) and e) unambiguously in favour of the former being more proactive, indicator c) slightly in favour of the latter being more proactive, and indicator d) being a draw. Since the lead of ICRC Sri Lanka over ICRC Philippines is a mere .67 points, there need not be a decisive convergence of all or most 'Power' indicators to favour greater proactiveness of the former over the latter. Rationalist indicators of 'Power' that represent parts of hypotheses R1 and R2 do seem to be explaining why ICRC Sri Lanka marginally leads ICRC Philippines in proactiveness.

It is necessary for us to ensure that culturalist hypotheses C1 and C2 do not contradict the variation between the two ICRC branches that R1 and R2 are predicting. In the domain of 'Ideas', ICRC Sri Lanka is expected to have a bureaucratic culture that is less resistant to change, and beliefs that are less subservient to state sovereignty than those of ICRC Philippines.

From Chapter 4, we saw that ICRC Sri Lanka is a 'bottom up kind of organization' which allows its district-based offices to chalk out locally-relevant strategies to improve the civilian protection climate. While ICRC Sri Lanka's typical organizational culture is to be standoffish towards local rights defenders and activists, this has been sometimes overcome by conscientious individual representatives who are in charge in district-level offices of the North and East.

ICRC Philippines, on the other hand, has yet to throw up imaginative personalities who worked around the organization's legalistic rules and cooperated with protection networks on the ground in ARMM and surrounding provinces. There is little doubting that ICRC Philippines has a poor image in the eyes of local activists in the Moro war theatres, while ICRC Sri Lanka has not angered rights defenders in the Eelam war theatres to the same extent.

Having said so, the stark reality of ICRC Sri Lanka over the last five years has been one of a quibbler which prefers to cite the relevant legal clause when faced with a serious incident of violence against civilians. It comes a cropper in terms of practical actions to protect civilians. ICRC Sri Lanka is almost indistinguishable from ICRC Philippines in its caution of not naming and shaming perpetrators of atrocities for fear of losing its 'neutrality'. That ICRC Sri Lanka never issued a single 'Public Denunciation' in spite of the killings of thousands of civilians in Eelam War IV sits as a black mark on its record.

All things considered, ICRC Sri Lanka has a slight advantage over ICRC Philippines in terms of 'Ideas'. Both branches manifest the global ICRC culture of reticence, indifference to victims of violence who fall into legal gaps, and failure to cooperate with radical local human rights activists. What sets ICRC Philippines apart is its willingness to exploit the sufferings of civilians in the Moro wars and resort to charlatanry in order for the organization to expand its operations. ICRC Sri Lanka may be a quibbler with legal niceties, but it has at least not degraded itself like its Philippine counterpart.

Since culturalist hypotheses C1 and C2 give ICRC Sri Lanka the edge in proactiveness, they are reconfirming the predictions of R1 and R2. It can be said that 'Power' and 'Ideas' are jointly causing ICRC Sri Lanka's .67-point lead over ICRC Philippines. The finding once again brings to fore the value of syncretic hypotheses RC1 and RC2, which will be evaluated in Chapter 7.

The Victim and the Instrument

The in-country proactiveness rankings of SCSL and SCF USA in the Philippines (henceforward SCF) vary, although they are both branches of the same global INGO. SCSL is ranked fourth among our five IO cases in Sri Lanka, with a net proactiveness score of 2.0 (out of a maximum of 7). SCF fares better at second rank with a net proactiveness score of 2.33 (out of a maximum of 7). But when the scores of the two branches are calibrated for cross-country comparison, we find that SCSL stands unchanged at 2.0 (out of a maximum of 6), while SCF falls to 2.0 (out of a maximum of 6).[11]

What explains this uniformity despite the fact that there are obvious differences in 'Power' pressures between the two countries? To answer this, we need to examine how each disaggregated indicator of 'Power' plays out for the two branches of Save the Children. Modified R1 and R2 would lead us to expect that the material pressures and the needs to compete for funds and patronage are the same between SCSL and SCF.

Indicator a) from Summary Table 6.1 conveys that donor pressures on SCSL to lower emphasis on civilian protection are 'Low' while they are 'Maximum' for SCF. In Chapter 4, we noted that SCSL 'is not subject to donor pressures to neglect civilian protection', be it USAID or individual European states. The highlighting of child conscription by the LTTE as an international *cause celebre* means that funding and encouraging child rights-based humanitarian IOs to end the practice is extremely popular among donor states. SCSL not only faces 'Low' pressures from donors to devalue civilian protection but also enjoys the converse positive inducements from them to pursue protection of children in armed conflict.

SCF, on the other hand, is squarely an instrument of the US-led 'war on terrorism' in the Philippines and has been incorporated into the vocabulary and infrastructure of military humanitarianism in the Moro war theatres. By virtue of its total dependence on USAID, SCF is compelled to cooperate with 'peace and development' and 'Growth with Equity' (GEM) formulae that turn a blind eye to civilian protection. SCF is the leader of ASCEND Mindanao, a children's educational funding programme of USAID which keeps a safe distance from 'conscription' and 'violence against children' even while being implemented in the most militarised provinces of Sulu, Maguindanao and North Cotabato (ASCEND, 2008). The same USAID in Sri Lanka is happy to sponsor SCSL specifically for 'protection of children' in the East. So, on 'Power' indicators a) and b), SCSL should be more proactive than SCF.

Indicator c) of Summary Table 6.1 conveys that SCSL faces 'Maximum' state pressures to go quiet on civilian protection while SCF only has to bear with 'High' state pressures. Like a possessed soul, GSL has tormented SCSL in the media and through forcible actions that no other IO in the country has had to weather. It is due to the sustained victimisation by the state that SCSL has had to moderate its tone and actions in the North and East as Eelam War IV dragged on. Not once has SCSL openly said that the SLA is actually involved in child conscription of its own to assist the TMVP (Foster, 2006) or done anything concrete on the ground to stem this practice.

SCF, on the other hand, faces lesser pressure from GRP because of its willingness to work as a prop for the US military and the AFP's 'war and terrorism.' The organization has not particularly been targeted or kept under watch by the AFP or civilian intelligence agencies of the state. Since SCF in the Philippines is SCF USA and a reliable implementing partner of USAID, the organization only faces the generic 'High' state pressures that apply across the board to all humanitarian IOs. Thus, on the count of indicator c), SCF should be more proactive than SCSL.

'Power' indicator d) of Summary Table 6.1 follows the logic of c) because IOs in Sri Lanka are facing 'Medium to High' rebel pressures while those in the Philippines have to deal with only 'Low to Medium' level rebel demands. However, this generic variation does not apply to Save the Children's branches because they are, by definition, both 'child rights organizations' mandated to counter child conscription by armed actors.

SCSL shirked from mobilising mothers' self-help groups which wanted to organise and demand that their children be returned by the TMVP for fear of being further branded as a 'pro-LTTE' IO. When I worked in Batticaloa and Trincomalee districts as a civilian peacekeeper, SCSL was noticeably absent from child protection initiatives which would anger the LTTE. Although a partner of UNICEF Sri Lanka, SCSL always preferred to take a backseat on child conscription by the LTTE due to security fears of its largely Tamil staffers in the North and East. Until 2006 or so, SCSL did face 'High' rebel pressures, but the intensity fell to 'Medium' as LTTE became too preoccupied with defending its shrinking territory against the SLA.

SCF in the Philippines has also had to cope with 'Medium' level of pressures from the MILF because of the Islamist movement's apprehension that child rights IOs would 'tamper' with the culture of *jihad* among the Moros by 'putting wrong ideas' into their heads. As in the case of SCSL, SCF tries to keep a low profile in advocacy for civilian protection and defers to UNICEF Philippines to make the public statements against child conscription by the MILF (MT1, 2008). The levels of rebel pressures both branches face are essentially equal.

'Power' indicator e) favours humanitarians in Sri Lanka to be more proactive than their branches in the Philippines. But again, since Save the Children is a specialised 'child rights' IO, the pressures it faces from sub-units of the state are not necessarily the same as the generic levels recorded in Summary Table 6.1.

In Sri Lanka, TMVP is determined to raise a fighting force comprising children so that it can establish itself as a long-term military alternative to the LTTE, with sufficient cadres in the East. In 2004, I was personally involved with local activists in getting several children released from the clutches of the TMVP, whose leaders in Batticaloa were under SLA protection and guidance. Blessed with the state's imprimatur, TMVP used its newfound status as the ruling party in the Eastern Provincial Council to deter any IO from trying to enter villages and assisting families whose children were in its custody. So, SCSL has actually faced 'Medium' (not 'Low') provincial government pressures that are backed by the central government in the East.

SCF in the Philippines is subject to far greater pressures from the ARMM LGUs than SCSL in Eastern Sri Lanka. The absolute limits placed on SCF to avoid tackling issues that tread upon the interests of the *Datus* are much bigger than the fear factor of the TMVP for SCSL. Institutionally too, the control of RDCC and DSWD by the ARMM LGUs gives more leverage to the *Datus* over SCF. It is therefore apt to conclude that SCF faces 'High' provincial government pressures compared to SCSL's 'Medium' pressures. So, on this count, SCSL should be more proactive than SCF.

Overall, the rationalist variables determining the relative proactiveness of the two branches of Save the Children have not unequivocally upheld the predictions of R1 that the two face the same amount of material pressures. Indicators a), b) and e) suggest that SCSL should be more proactive than SCF, while indicator c) conveys the opposite. Indicator d) suggests equality in the level of rebel pressures and can be taken out of the equation. Is the combined force of a), b) and e) being neutralised by the power of c) so that the two branches share the same proactiveness score of 2.0 each? In other words, are pressures and inducements on the two branches of donors and provincial governments cancelled out by the pressures of the host state (central government)?

Answering this requires assigning quantitative proportional weights to donor pressures, local self-governing units' pressures and state pressures, an impossible mission for a qualitative study. What we can do at this juncture is to move ahead and test culturalist hypotheses C1 and C2 and see if they come up with a clearer verdict on why SCSL and SCF are tied at 2.0 points. According to the modified C1 and C2, the two branches are equal in their cross-country proactiveness because they share the same bureaucratic culture, identity and beliefs about the supremacy of state sovereignty.

From Chapter 4, we learnt that SCSL views itself as neither completely a 'rights organization' nor an all-out 'service delivery' organization. Its relief and development specialists do not evince much enthusiasm for proactive behaviour. The unified mission structure of SCSL hampers clarity in approach to civilian protection by lumping SCF USA and SCF UK — two conservative branches — with SCF Norway and SCF Sweden, which are said to have greater 'expertise' and predilections for civilian protection. While none can doubt the victimisation of SCSL by the Sri Lankan state, the organization has enough internal dissensions and bureaucratic hurdles to stay at fourth place in the in-country proactiveness ranking.

SCF in the Philippines is very similar in its organizational culture to SCSL. Just as SCSL claims to be 'a bit of both', i.e. a rights-cum-relief organization, SCF is content to 'wear multiple hats' (see Chapter 5) with no priority for civilian protection. As with SCSL, SCF is attempting a merger with SCF Sweden to become a 'unified mission' so that the latter's 'protection expertise' will lift the branch's proactiveness. The belief that particular branches of the Save the Children family have more knowledge and better strategies to implement protection projects is shared both by SCSL and SCF Philippines.

Both branches also rely on 'indirect' approaches to problems of violence against children by armed actors and justify their inaction with technocratic alibis like 'mandate limitations' and 'data unavailability'. Bureaucrats in both branches 'projectify' protection and look at it less as a cross-cutting consciousness that must percolate throughout the organization and more as a set of programmes that have to be financially supported by donors.

Even on the attitude towards 'local culture', SCSL and SCF are dead ringers. The former concurs with UNICEF Sri Lanka that it would have been inappropriate and risky for IOs to go against 'Tamil culture' prior to the 2002 CFA, when children were willingly donated to the LTTE for the self-determination struggle. The latter justifies its failure to tackle the MILF's conscription of children by expressing deference to Islamist Moro values about childhood and adulthood. Fear of inciting 'cultural resistance' from local communities and essentialisation of conservative traits as a whole community's 'culture' motivate both branches.

To sum up, a test of the modified culturalist hypothesis C2 reveals rough similarity in the 'Ideas' driving both branches of Save the Children. One can conclude here that the parity of 2.0 points between SCSL and SCF is caused by their sameness of bureaucratic culture and identity. But if modified C2 is true here, then so should modified R1. Suppose we were to argue that 'Power' indicators a), b) and e) are not neutralising c), i.e. that one of the Save the Children branches has to be more proactive than the other, then rationalist hypothesis R1 would stand falsified and C2 could be crowned as the superior explanation. The only option we are left with is to leave the unsolved question of the explanatory potential of 'Power' in the case of SCSL and SCF to future researchers who could replicate the observations and determine if the disaggregated indicators could be cancelling each other out.

The undersong from the paired cross-country comparisons of IOs in this chapter is that the 'real world' is complex enough to evade the simplistic fits of hypotheses. Weighing, validating or falsifying hypotheses with subjectively collected data is a probabilistic endeavour and cannot be foolproof. The next chapter will wade into the complexity of IO behaviour and consider theoretical intersections and interstices that can give researchers a broader generalisable handle over humanitarians as political actors.

7

THE 'TRUTHS' ABOUT
HUMANITARIAN BEHAVIOUR

Insufficiency of Stand-Alone Explanations

The philosopher David Hume was sceptical of the notion of causation as an objective reality or 'matter of fact.' He considered causal connections to be no more than 'belief', 'feeling', 'imagination', 'presumption' or 'impressions' that exist in the 'memory' and 'senses' of the researcher who observes repeated empirical associations between two variables. As an empiricist, Hume reminded positivists that they have no more than a 'distant notion' of the 'Power' by which cause can necessarily produce an effect (Hume, 1999: 67-82). His negation of 'necessary connexions' meant that all inductively derived theories purporting to be explanations of natural or human behaviour are, at best, probabilistic approximations of the truth.

Ideologically rigid political scientists who plant their feet firmly within one of the four paradigmatic camps laid out in the Introduction go against Hume's word of caution. They assert knowledge of the necessary cause of all political behaviour and name it with one simple word- either 'interests', 'ideas', 'institutions' or 'structures'. This book purposefully avoided simplistic *a priori* essentialisms that one of the four paradigms is the master key to unravelling the mysteries of all political behaviour or just the empirical puzzle of why some humanitarian IOs are more proactive than others.

Essentialist political scientists usually pick favourable research topics and cases that would be easy fits for their pet theory.[1]

Some scholars combatively take on 'hard cases' to prove that their paradigm can not only explain its traditional 'bread and butter' topics but also those monopolised by the opposing camp (Grieco, 1990; Finnemore, 2003). The problem with spirited defenders of their respective paradigms is that they interpret data with high subjectivity and prejudice to make it conform to their camp's theoretical expectations.

Selection and interpretation bias are two common pitfalls of ideologically motivated scholarship which seeks conformity of all empirically observed political behaviour to a desired theory. This book avoided both flaws. It chose humanitarian IOs as cases so that they do not impair fair competition among all four paradigms of political science. Then, it interpreted evidence from first-hand personalised experience of the war zones of Sri Lanka and the Philippines without being convinced that any single paradigm has the password to the truth.

The empirical chapters of the book reconfirmed my initial hunch that stand-alone explanations for humanitarian behaviour cannot yield anything close to even the 'distant notion' of causation that Hume would grant to positivists. Charles Ragin has argued that complexities arise even within a simple probabilistic generalisation when the researcher does a thorough investigation or detailed study at the case level (Ragin, 1989). John Stuart Mill's 'chemical causation' (Mill, 2002) or Ragin's 'multiple causation' comes into view when one studies the particularity and diversity of cases in a small-N research design.

'Multiple causation' is the intersection of a set of causes which combine to generate an outcome. The task of the qualitative comparative researcher is to accept the complexity but find some order in these combinations. Even after eschewing mechanistic simplicity of cause and effect, the comparativist must find a pattern in the combinations that can be predictive so that one can nail down 'a method to the madness' of complex social behaviour (Ragin, 1989).

The empirical chapters of this book frequently found that rationalist hypotheses R1, R2, R3 or R4 were incapable of clearly accounting for the entire difference in proactiveness scores, especially that between two distantly placed IOs in the rankings. For instance, in Sri Lanka, we saw that the gap of 2.64 points between UNDP and UNICEF was not being fully explained by differences in rationalist 'Power' pressures on the two organizations. So, we moved on to test differences in culturalist 'Ideas' between the two organizations and found that C1 and C2 were indeed causing UNICEF to be leap years ahead of UNDP in proactiveness.

The issue that we left hanging in Chapter 4 was whether C1 and C2 on their own can explain the 2.64-point gap between the two organizations, without needing R1. We could not give 'Ideas' a clean and decisive victory over 'Power' at that stage because of the methodological constriction of within-country comparison.

But Chapter 6's cross-country comparisons conclusively validated the relevance of R1 for explaining the relative proactiveness of UNICEF Sri Lanka over UNICEF Philippines and the parity between UNDP Sri Lanka and UNDP Philippines. In both these inter-branch comparisons, we found that culturalist variables C1 and C2 were 'adding strength' to the rationalist variables (see Chapter 6) and jointly causing the observed differences in proactiveness.

Chapter 3 listed two types of combinatorial hypotheses as answers to the empirical puzzles spurring this book. RC1 projected a scenario where both rationalist and culturalist variables were working on one IO in the same direction, while the same paradigmatic variables worked in the exact opposite direction on the other IO. This combination of 'Power' and 'Ideas' is the most potent in terms of plausibly causing a large gap in proactiveness between the two IOs because rationalist variables and culturalist variables are working together in the same directions.

Some dyadic pairs in Chapter 6 conformed to this combination. For example, UNICEF Sri Lanka faced the following combination: lesser material pressures plus beliefs and norms are less bureaucratic and stress human rights. UNICEF Philippines, on the other hand, faced the complete converse combination: greater material pressures plus beliefs and norms are bureaucratic and stress state sovereignty. Similarly, the record-breaking gap of 2.33 points in the dyad of OXFAM-GB Philippines vs. OXFAM-GB Sri Lanka was explained by a clean one-directional combination of 'Power' and 'Ideas' that advantaged the proactiveness of the latter over the former. The former faced the following combination: lesser material pressures plus beliefs and norms are less bureaucratic and stress human rights. The latter faced the exact opposite combination: greater material pressures plus beliefs and norms are bureaucratic and stress state sovereignty. RC1 is therefore being validated in dyadic comparisons of IOs that have wide gaps in proactiveness scores.

What about dyads where the proactiveness gaps are narrowly in favour of one branch over the other? Can we expect RC1 to be the correct multiple causal combination in these comparisons as well? If we look at ICRC Sri Lanka vs. ICRC Philippines, there is a small .67-point proactiveness lead to the former, which faces the following combination: lesser material pressures plus beliefs and norms are less bureaucratic and stress human rights. The latter faces the obverse combination again: greater material pressures plus beliefs and norms are bureaucratic and stress sovereignty. What is varied about RC1 in this dyad compared to dyads that have bigger gaps in points is the *value* that each part of the combination takes. Calls of 'Lesser' and 'Greater', 'More and 'Less', in this dyad refer to small differences between the two ICRC branches.

Thus, apart from validating RC1, the examples from Chapter 6 are illustrating the importance of the specific values that 'Power' and 'Ideas' take in any combinatorial explanation. The larger the value of a combination in RC1, the bigger is the expected gap in proactiveness between two IOs. This being a qualitative study, it is infeasible to determine which independent variable has higher variance in its causal effect and which independent variable has lower variance.

It is this methodological drawback which produced the 'confused message' of R1 in the dyadic pair of SCFSL vs. SCF (see Chapter 6). Nonetheless, we can be confident that RC1 is a superior explanation that accounts for more of the dependent variable than any of the temporally static variables — R1, R2, C1 or C2 — taken singly.

Of the numerous paired comparisons in this book, there is no instance where the four static rationalist and culturalist variables, standing alone, could satisfactorily account for all the variation in the dependent variable. However, when we move away from comparative statics to the temporal rationalist and culturalist variables, i.e. R3, R4, C3 or C4, we do find some instances where one or two of them belonging to the same paradigmatic camp have complete explanatory power for an IO's change in proactiveness over time.

We found in Chapter 4 that 'a combination of R3 and C4 seem to have caused the temporal change in UNICEF's proactiveness' in Sri Lanka. But in the case of SCSL's withdrawal into a shell as a result of the state's threats, we found that 'R3 had a causal impact on the organization's proactiveness even though C3 or C4 remained constant during this time.' Likewise, in the case of OXFAM-GB Philippines 'progressive reinvention', we found that 'since there was no corresponding decrease in material pressures and inducements on OXFAM-GB in 2003-04 (rationalist temporal hypothesis R3), the only plausible cause for the turnaround is offered by C4' (see Chapter 5).

Again, while studying the regressive turn in UNICEF Philippines over time due to changes in leadership beliefs, we noted that 'even as rationalist material pressures on UNICEF remained more or less constant over the last few years, the culture of the organization had become more "developmentalist" due to leadership "hang ups".' These deductions validate temporal culturalist hypotheses C3 and C4 as capable of causing change in the organization's proactiveness 'by themselves.'

The lesson from these temporal paired comparisons for theory is that not every instance of causation of humanitarian behaviour is necessarily combinatorial, 'chemical' or multiple. When an IO changes its proactiveness over time, it could be because of a change in a combination of independent variables or simply because of a change of a single independent variable. Unless more iterations of such temporal paired comparisons are performed, it will be difficult to pinpoint under what circumstances an IO can change due to variation in a single independent variable as opposed to change due to variation in a combination of independent variables. Future research should probe this aspect deeper with more qualitative temporal comparisons of IOs in Sri Lanka and Philippines as well as other internal war theatres.

Does multiple causal hypothesis RC2 find any validation from the cases chosen in this book? Suppose we pair up for comparison SCSL and ICRC Philippines. The former seems on first impression to be facing greater material pressures than the latter, while having a relatively less bureaucratic organizational culture than the latter. From Chapter 6, we noted the following results of SCSL's disaggregated 'Power' indicators: 'Low' donor pressures, 'Medium to High' donor inducements, 'Maximum' state pressures, 'Medium' rebel pressures and 'Medium' provincial government pressures. ICRC Philippines, on the other hand, had the following results from its disaggregated 'Power' indicators: 'Maximum' donor pressures, 'Low' donor inducements, 'High' state pressures, 'Medium' rebel pressures and 'High' provincial government pressures. The overall material pressures it faces are clearly greater than those faced by SCSL. On the culturalist side, SCSL could be deemed to be more bureaucratic than ICRC Philippines because of the former's more ambivalent identity and moribund internal mission structure.

If RC2 is true, then ICRC Philippines should be more proactive than SCSL. The standardised cross-country proactiveness scores are 2.33 (out of a maximum of 6) for ICRC Philippines and 2.0 (out of a maximum of 6)[2] for SCSL. By a slender margin of .33 points, RC2 is being validated. The important message of RC2 is that even if an IO faces greater material 'Power' pressures than its peer, it can be more proactive by virtue of having more progressive 'Ideas'. The key here is to know *how much more* progressive 'Ideas' are required to offset the proactiveness deficit caused by having to face greater 'Power' pressures. ICRC Philippines is not progressive in culture by a big margin to SCSL and yet manages to sneak ahead by .33 points. In Chapter 8, we will revisit this finding because of its practical implications for humanitarian policy.

The main theoretical proposition emerging from this book is that stand-alone explanations that rest only on rationality or only on culture are often insufficient to account for the full range of humanitarian behaviour towards civilian protection. For the sparring protagonists of the 'Third Debate' of IR theory to proclaim from their respective pedestals that rational 'interests' are the sole determinants of all political phenomena or that cultural 'Ideas' are the only meaningful causes is nothing but empty posturing intended to force the complex social world into a 'box' defined by a school of thought, as I had submitted by citing Thomas Kuhn's philosophy in Chapter 2.

By finding that *international humanitarian organizations set priorities and act according to them in response to both 'Power' and 'Ideas' rather than exclusively one or the other*, I am not claiming to render the 'Third Debate' futile but only clarifying that it cannot afford to rely on singular causal conceptions of rationality *or* culture. Instead of a univariate explanation that is deterministic or dogmatic, this book found more credibility in a bivariate explanation that is still parsimonious.

The sign of a good research design, according to Gary King, Robert Keohane and Sidney Verba, is if it can extract parsimonious explanations that explain a lot with a little (King, 1994). A bivariate explanation for humanitarian behaviour that rests on 'Power' and 'Ideas' is nowhere near to throwing the kitchen sink at the dependent variable. I avoided including all possible explanatory variables for humanitarian behaviour thanks to the Third Debate's spotlight on only two major causes — rationality and culture.

Had it not been for the contest set up by the Third Debate, this book would have lacked the for-and-against quality of relating theories to empirics and weighing their comparative worth. Had there been no titanic clash between rationalists and culturalists and if the Debate was stuck in the intra-rationalist 'neo-neo' polemics, the very conceptualisation of my research question and topic would have been different. The line up of rationality against culture gives researchers the extra option of evaluating holistic ontologies instead of remaining lodged within the individualistic rationalism of the 'neo-neo' ilk.

What IR scholarship needs is not defenestration of the Third Debate but its reorganization into contestation about the *conditions* under which even ontologically polarised paradigms like rationalism *and* culturalism could come together and jointly determine political behaviour. The search for these conditions need not be motivated by an intentional desire to build bridges between the two camps of the Debate.

To begin one's research by donning the garb of a healer or a match maker and to then torture data to conform to syncretic hypotheses will be an infringement of the methodological principle of eclecticism needed in theory-testing research. Theory-building research could justify staunch attachment to rationalism or culturalism, but theory-testing has to be designed not to fix the facts for a paradigm but to find the multiple 'truths' about political behaviour and come up with solutions to real world problems like the global crisis in civilian protection.

Beyond the Third Debate

James Fearon has drawn a helpful distinction between a *cause* and a *condition* in small-N qualitative research. He defines the former as a regular factor that produces a regular outcome, akin to Hume's 'cause' as a 'connexion' researchers make because of regular occurrence of two phenomena. A condition, on other hand, is to Fearon a non-regular event or factor that leads to a specific outcome (Fearon, 1991). I visualise a condition as a more generic system, order or structure that does not have to 'occur' in an observable sense but which is omniscient and which enables causes to occur either singly or in combination.

For causes to take the form that they do, they must be conditioned by a larger locale in which they can find meaning.

What might be the *conditions* that facilitate two apparently polarised ontologies like rationalism and culturalism to combine and determine the priorities of humanitarian IOs in war zones? This book often referred to 'structures' of different sorts that set the bounds within which humanitarians made their choices and set priorities. It broached, *inter alia,* the 'structure of political power — both domestic and international', the 'structure of rules, principles, norms and decision-making procedures', 'rational structures imposed by relationally dominant armed actors in a conflict zone', 'international governing structures', 'class prejudices and structures', 'alternative statist support structures', 'Power' structures', 'state-controlled structures' and 'state-dominated structures.'

The structures that litter this book are both material and non-material, although the impression may have arisen that mainly rationalist 'Power' complexes that weigh down on the agency of humanitarian IOs were being recognised as structures. Mention was made in the Introduction of a 'structure of rules' or a 'structure of ideas' that explain all political behaviour to some social scientists.

The empirical chapters also calculated the compound of culturalist variables derived from C1, C2, C3 and C4 and made determinations for each IO case whether it was more or less bound by bureaucratic SOPs, conservative values and rigidity. Taken individually, these culturalist variables were tested and projected as causes of IO behaviour. But taken as a whole, they represent the structure of 'Ideas' just as rationalist variables taken as a whole were called a complex or 'structure of political power.'

While elaborating on structuralism as a paradigmatic camp in the Introduction, I referred to 'complex versions of Marxism' that accord equal explanatory weight to ideational and material factors in the formation and evolution of structures. If one were to place humanitarians within a grand structure or system, the most obvious home would be the capitalist world-system, which champions both the material interests of a global capitalist class (Robinson, 2004) and the concomitant ideology of liberalism.

The entire foreign aid artifice upon which humanitarian IOs thrive is a distinct invention of the capitalist world-system. If we scan the horizon of aid donors who played a central part in pressurising or inducing humanitarian IOs for or against proactiveness, all of them share the common feature of being capitalist states (or conglomerates of capitalist states like the EU) that serve as nodes or 'moments' for the accumulation and global flow of capital (Rupert and Smith, 2002: 7). None of the international humanitarian IOs used as cases in this book have ever been funded by non-capitalist states or foundations. If it were not for the rise of the capitalist world-system, there would never be this $15 billion per annum 'aid industry' and its spin-off, the humanitarian business.

In Chapter 6, I mentioned that India has not managed to develop a strong foreign aid bureaucracy or system to channel aid to Sri Lanka via IOs like advanced capitalist donor states. Geography and cultural affinities between India and Sri Lanka have led the donor principals in Sri Lanka to confer and consult with India, but the reason why India itself has not succeeded in turning into a major player of the humanitarian aid game has to do with its weaker capitalist structures. India is nowhere close to the US, EU or Japan in terms of having a vastly powerful capitalist class that possesses global footprints and interests. The material and ideational thrust of India's capitalist class is inward and oriented towards the domestic market within the country. For India's ruling elites to imagine playing a humanitarian role in Sri Lanka via IOs, it will perhaps take another generation of capitalist growth.

The same trajectory fits the case of Malaysia vis-à-vis the Moro wars in the Philippines. Due to a preponderance of state power and one party rule, Malaysia has not carved out a genuinely independent capitalist class with a stake in export markets and raw material extraction in neighbouring countries of Southeast Asia. Malaysia's rise as an Asian Tiger economy was managed through 'statist economic development, a top-down model of capitalist transformation that kept the domestic bourgeoisie politically dependent' (Hilley, 2001: 51). Lacking a self-sustaining capitalist class that seeks regional expansion, Malaysia has — like India vis-à-vis the Eelam wars — not developed into a major humanitarian donor state to compete with the US, the EU, Australia and Canada.

Why are capitalist states most prone to giving humanitarian aid? In Chapter 3, I elaborated on a circular process in which 'aid that is transferred by USAID or ECHO to war zones in the Global South via humanitarian IOs eventually returns to the Global North in the form of earnings for Western corporations.' The penchant of most IOs for material relief and assistance is thus tied into the search of the capitalist world-system for opening up new markets. Through humanitarian aid and 'post-war reconstruction' packages, the capitalist world-system lengthens its shadows and deepens its appeal.

These correlations can best be exemplified by the case of Japan, one of the leading donor states in both the Eelam wars of Sri Lanka and the Moro wars of the Philippines. Japan's profile as Asia's most prominent giver for humanitarian and development IOs arose in a context in the late 1980s, when it sought to open up new markets. Bryan Johnson has summed up the motivations of Japanese capitalism behind its aid empire:

Japan has been using its aid mainly as a kind of subsidy to Third World purchasers of Japanese exports. These subsidies then are labelled aid to the poor (Johnson, 1990: 1).

I did acknowledge other motivations for Japanese humanitarian aid to Sri Lanka and the Philippines that are cultural and geopolitical respectively. But the thrust of Japan's status as a bankroller of humanitarian IOs comes from the needs of its commercial capitalist class.

The second layer of the capitalist-world system's imprint on the humanitarian enterprise comprises the greed and corruption in IOs which we unveiled in the empirical chapters of this book. Donor capitalist greed finds a recursion in the financial improprieties and scandals that dog the humanitarian business. A humanitarian regime that is sustained by a for-profit world-economy can be not-for-profit only on paper.

Why would rationalist and culturalist variables be enabled to combine and determine the priorities of humanitarian IOs by the 'condition' of a capitalist world-system? To reiterate, the structure of the world-system is a reflection of both material and ideational forces. The very roots of humanitarian organizations lie in a partnership of 'Power' and 'Ideas', which are actually inseparable just as a mode of production is the mirror of the social relations or institutions of production.

Therefore, only under a capitalist world-system which furthers material interests with a charitable liberal ideology can two seemingly opposed paradigms with contrasting ontologies like rationalism and culturalism combine to cause humanitarian behaviour.

Structural Marxism can be visualised as one of the alternative explanations for humanitarian behaviour besides rationalism and culturalism. But a 'condition', as defined here, is a far larger category than an alternative explanation. It is not directly testable with social scientific hypotheses, but that deficiency does not deny its existence or preponderance at a level above that of causes. The proposition being made is that the capitalist-world system structures the A to Z of the humanitarian enterprise and hovers above causes like rationality and culture, which are both components of the larger world-system.

The other 'condition' that is a facilitator of rationalist and culturalist causes of the behaviour of humanitarian IOs is the global structure of patriarchy, which depends on gendered and unequal relationships that affect every part of the planet. Predating the capitalist world-system, the structure of patriarchy has a special impact in war zones where humanitarians throng. Armed conflict breaks down the certainties of the pre-existing gender relations in a society and throws up more adverse forms of violence that is targeted at particular sexes.

It is fashionable among all humanitarian IOs to advertise that they are into 'gender' programming since this category is on the wish list of donors. But interventions based on stereotypes have never empowered women and men to protect themselves against harassment and abuse.[3]

In Chapter 4, we briefly touched upon the curious phenomenon of a 'gender specialist' in OXFAM-GB Sri Lanka, who had succeeded in captaining the organizational ship away from civilian protection into 'gender programming'. OXFAM-GB Sri Lanka has offices in all three Eastern districts of the country, where a horrific form of gender-based violence has emerged since the coronation of the TMVP as the state-sanctioned Tamil political party-cum-militia. TMVP cadres harnessed their legitimacy as state-recognised 'elected' representatives of the Tamil people by embarking on unchecked sexual predation against young Tamil women in the East. A number of such incidents were reported to humanitarian IOs that were organising the IDP camps (LST, 2008B: 9), but few could think of innovative solutions to this reign of sexual terror.

Although OXFAM-GB had a 'gender specialist' expatriate boss in Colombo, it did not translate this possible advantage into concrete action to address the scourge of sexual assaults organised by the TMVP and the security forces. The organization's literature is full of glowing reports about how it is promoting 'gender equality' and 'rights of women' in the East, but the talk is as usual unmatched by deeds. All the OXFAM-GB Sri Lanka personnel I met over several years perceived of 'gender' programming in purely socio-economic terms, i.e. giving out more loans to IDP women or organising them into cooperatives to give them a means of livelihood. When the biggest threat to women in the East was sexual assault, OXFAM-GB chose not to go anywhere close to this explosive issue. When three rapes were reported in Haiti's relief camps after the shattering earthquake of early 2010, a senior UN official who had earlier been the WFP's Regional Director for Asia, gave away the same patriarchal heedlessness with a remark that the 'figure almost elates me' (Lee, 2010).

Part of the casual attitude of humanitarian IOs to gender-based violence owes to their affirmation of cultural stereotypes about war-affected communities. Just as child conscription became a cultural minefield for UNICEF and Save the Children in Sri Lanka and the Philippines, sexual violence in wars registers in the minds of humanitarians from their essentialisation of 'local culture'. So, if it is taboo in Sri Lankan Tamil society for a victim of rape to be identified or treated, then IOs go along with it so as not to generate any controversy that might harm the organization's reputation. Even IOs which have female expatriate personnel distance themselves from gender-based violence that is perpetrated by armed actors because of the same combinatorial causes of 'Power' and 'Ideas'.

In 2006, some publicly unnamed IOs in Eastern Sri Lanka were found to be forcing local Tamil women working on their payrolls to 'appear in pornographic videos in exchange for cash handouts' (Kamalendran, 2006). Unless humanitarians were hardwired with patriarchal values, they would not commit such heinous actions by taking advantage of the breakdown of protections during war. Sexual misconduct targeting local women by expatriate IOs happens in Sri Lanka and the Philippines on a large scale but gets under-reported due to suppression of such stories in the media by the public relations machinery of the aid industry.

Patriarchy is an overriding theme that 'conditions' IO behaviour by imposing itself on their rationality and culture. One sees shades of patriarchy in the material as well as ideational complexes which determine humanitarian behaviour in both countries studied in this book. Since women are not generally active in fighting on the battle fronts, except within the LTTE, IOs develop a patronising frame to define, classify and 'protect' female civilians. In the process, they solidify the conservative gender hierarchies that prevail in both Sri Lankan and Philippines societies.

Humanitarians justify inaction or insensitivity to sexual violence and stereotyping on rational or cultural grounds, but do not realise that they reify the global structure of patriarchy. As in most other war zones, I also observed IOs in Sri Lanka and the Philippines to almost entirely entrust men (usually, politically well connected local males) to lead the relief distribution and to 'take charge' of protection of IDP camp inmates. Here again, we find that there is a 'condition' that structures the causes of humanitarian behaviour.

The Third Debate of IR theory, which was the axle of this book, relegates Marxism and feminism to the dustbin of 'non-scientific' approaches (Ling and Agathangelou, 2004) and prefers to concentrate on causal theories and paradigms. Since Marxism and feminism do not easily meet the scientific methods of hypothesis testing and falsification, they have been viewed with wariness by the parties to the Third Debate.

What this book has done is to take readers into the heart of the Debate but also beyond it by proposing 'conditions' that structure causes. If it were not for the particular material and ideational configurations of the capitalist world-economy and of patriarchy, the humanitarian enterprise, its rationality and culture would all be unrecognisable. Marxism and feminism do not contradict the rationality and culture of humanitarians but rather uncover the systems that constitute them.

Another way of envisaging the inter-relationships of conditions and causes of humanitarian behaviour is to look at the capitalist world-system and patriarchy as antecedent variables to the explanatory variables of rationality and culture.

Neither 'interests' nor 'Ideas' can be what they are and combine to be the proximate causes of humanitarian behaviour without being preceded by the two structural conditions. Figure 7 depicts the theoretical connections that do the bulk of explaining in this book in pictorial form.

The Third Debate's one-upmanship duels between rationalists and sociological culturalists have fostered rival claims that interests are antecedent to norms or that norms precede interests in causation (Moravcsik, 1997, Finnemore, 1996). The poverty of this jousting is that it misses the centrality of structures like patriarchy and the capitalist world-system, which are first-order explanations. This book is a caveat against theorists of IR losing their way by confining their vision to the Third Debate's second-order causes and marginalising feminism and Marxism, whose primeval explanatory concepts have undeniable traction.

To propose that rationality and culture of humanitarians emanate from capitalist and patriarchal structures is to also draw attention to unequal relationships that inhere in such structures. For rational self-interest of an individual or an organization to take the modalities that it does depends on the kinds of relationships that exist between political actors. IOs are subordinate to capitalist donors, militarist states and rebel groups in power terms, but are superior to civilians who are made to be dependent on the aid barons. The location of IOs in a relationship hierarchy holds the key to its rationality as well as its culture. When an IO defines its identity, values, beliefs and norms, it is in keeping with its position within the hierarchy of political relationships at the local war zone level and at the global military-humanitarian complex level.

This book has demonstrated that neither self-interest nor values is independent of structural relations via which political actors interact with each other. Humanitarianism is a gestalt phenomenon- a whole comprising unjust power relationships manifested as macro-structural conditions that is greater than the sum of its second-order parts of self-interest and norms. If one adds up rational self-interest and cultural values, the sum will fall short of humanitarianism unless we were to multiply the former two with their structural forbears.

The Introduction to this book undertook to carry understanding of humanitarian behaviour to a 'deeper level of abstraction' beyond the immediate causes of rationality and culture. I have thereupon taken humanitarianism to its structural wellsprings instead of leaving it loosely grounded at the half-baked stage of the 'Third Debate' of IR theory.

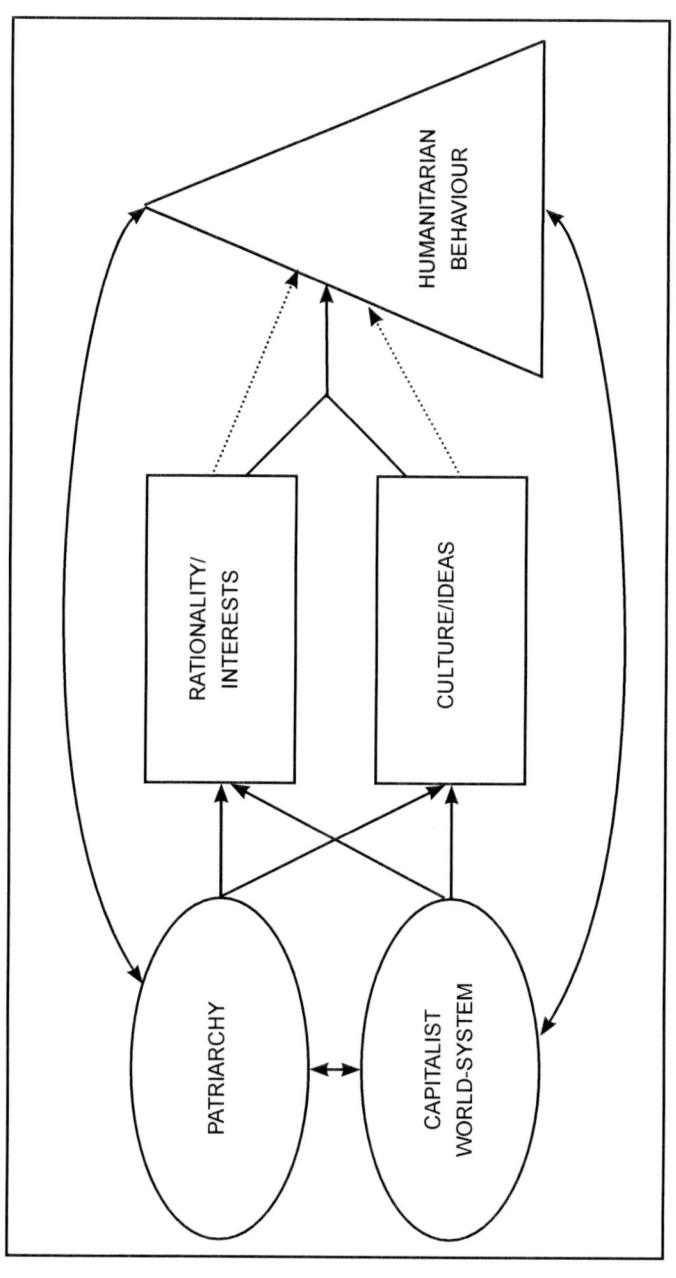

Figure 7. Ultimate and immediate determinants of humanitarian behaviour[4]

Transferable Causes and Conditions

This book picked only ten humanitarian IOs as cases on the basis of methodological rules of exclusion. These ten IOs comprise a small sample in the universe of humanitarian IOs (and their branches) that runs into the hundreds if one counted every war zone in the world. To what extent can one claim that the combination of 'Power' and 'Ideas', which were found to be causes in these ten cases, will determine the behaviour of the entire universe of cases?

If we re-examined the case selection criteria from Chapter 3, it becomes evident that these ten IOs have traits representative of the general humanitarian stock in trade. They are large, well-funded, globally branched and staffed by the same professional class of 'aid workers' that globe-trots from one humanitarian 'mission' to the other. These ten IOs had nothing unique about them to make them behave in ways that are atypical in the humanitarian industry.

So, it is safe to assert that *all* humanitarian IOs, governmental and non-governmental, respond to a mixture of 'Power' and 'Ideas'. The exact combination of disaggregated indicators of 'Power' and 'Ideas' will obviously vary from one organization and war zone to the other, but the theoretical framework of rationality-cum-culture as a cause of the behaviour of *all* humanitarians should apply without exceptions. Having said so, the salutary caveat of King, Keohane and Verba that conclusions in social science are uncertain because all research designs are inherently imperfect is worth bearing in mind (King, 1994). In quantitative social science, uncertainty can be measured through tests like 'regression diagnostics' and numerically stated. In a qualitative comparative research design like mine, one needs to revisit the process by which causal inferences were obtained.

In Chapters 4, 5 and 6, I employed a standard technique of listing the indicators of 'Power' and 'Ideas' and evaluating how each explanatory variable fared in the case of a particular IO or branch. The judgements of whether an indicator was 'Low', 'Medium', 'High' or 'Maximum' were made on the basis of personal observation, conversations with stakeholders, news reports, grey literature etc. That all these sources were subjective cannot be denied. Subjectivity in a war zone is even more unreliable because of the political purposes that lurk behind talk, news and action relating to the conflict. To minimise respondent bias in both coding of the dependent variable and in judging the values of explanatory variables for each IO case, I relied on a cross-checking method (see Chapter 3).

In spite of these precautions, it is possible that there are errors in the assessments of the values of both dependent and independent variables. To reiterate, many of the tables constructed in the analytical parts of this book are perceptual. IO pairs whose proactiveness gaps are tiny could end up being ranked upside down if the perceptions of my coders were replaced by those of others. Observers, including myself, who granted slightly greater or lesser pressures or bureaucratic culture to one organization could be countered by others who might have witnessed episodes of different behaviour by the same organization's personnel.

What can be assured is that the measurements and associations established in this book are roughly accurate, i.e. methodologically reliable. The likelihood of systematic bias having crept into the findings is zero. The likelihood of reverse causation or endogeneity (degree of proactiveness of an IO causing its rationality or culture) is theoretically zero. The chances of the values of an IO's 'Power' indicators covarying with the values of its 'Ideas' (collinearity) are also dim because we found multiple combinations of the two explanatory variables that defy any straightforward correlation between rationality and culture.

There is one major scope limitation of this study concerning the geographical backdrops in which humanitarian IOs ply their wares. In Chapter 6, we classified Sri Lanka and the Philippines as 'state-controlled' and 'state-dominated' polities respectively. Further, in Chapter 4, we contrasted an internal war like Sri Lanka's which has a belligerent and powerful state as a party to the conflict with internal wars in other parts of the world where state authority has broken down.

Findings about humanitarian behaviour in contexts of a strong centralised state may not carry over to war theatres where state structures have been pulverised. The picture of humanitarians as 'lords of poverty' or 'lords of conflict' (Hancock, 1997) assumes that war zones are *terra nullius* which are taken over by merchants of aid. But both Sri Lanka and the Philippines have hyper-nationalist and militarily strong states that never allow IOs to rule like feudal satraps.

The most visible difference between geographical backdrops like Sri Lanka and the Philippines on one hand and, say Somalia or Afghanistan, is in the meaning of 'Power' pressures on IOs. In the latter cases, the composition of the 'Power' complex that pressurises and induces IOs will not include the state or its provincial units. Even with the culturalist variables, if we recall the language of C1 and C3, the point of reference had to do with state and sovereignty. The same humanitarian IO branch in the Philippines and in Afghanistan will likely have quite different cultural attitudes towards sovereignty because of the considerable weakness of the state in the latter country.

There is also a possibility that internal wars with weak states or semi-independent rebel groups might throw up a totally alternative explanatory variable, maybe institutions, which we subsumed under the 'condition' of structures in this study. With these caveats and uncertainties in mind, I can only assert that the main thesis of humanitarian IOs responding to both 'Power' and

'Ideas' will hold good for *all* humanitarian IOs in internal wars that have loci of strong *de facto* or *de jure* power centres. As no theoretical research has ever been done to explain humanitarian behaviour even within the smaller universe of internal wars in strong states, this book breaks new ground.

As to the key proposition of this chapter that the capitalist world-system and patriarchy 'condition' the causes of humanitarian behaviour, the near universality of these two systems permits us to generalise the proposition to *all* humanitarian IOs operating in *all* internal wars. Although inter-state wars fell outside the subject matter of this book, I find no reason to limit the claim about structural 'conditions' of humanitarian behaviour only to internal wars. So, the external validity claim can be restated to say that the capitalist world-system and patriarchy are conditions of humanitarian behaviour in *all* contemporary wars.

8

HUMANITARIANISM, MILITARISM AND THE STRUGGLES FOR PEACE

The Military-Humanitarian Complex

When SCF Philippines gladly teamed up with the US navy and the AFP to implement the psychological component of the 'war on terrorism' in western Mindanao (see Chapter 5), the organization's personnel did not agonise over the propriety of the action. Far from being chary of losing its vaunted 'neutrality', SCF Philippines sensed a strategic opportunity to cement its relationship for long-term funding from USAID by acting as a complement to American militarism.

When I enquired about the ethics and the practical consequences of a supposedly 'neutral' humanitarian IO partnering so openly with *Balikatan* war games, SCF personnel argued that 'they (US military) do their work and we have to do our's.'[1]

Military humanitarianism is a feint to exacerbate a violent environment by injecting more armaments and combatants that prolong war. SCF Philippines was a willing participant in this nefarious plan for the ARMM and surrounding provinces, but kept its head down and focussed on its own work as if it was logically separable from that of the US marines and the AFP. It was neat division of labour between an imperial military presence and its benign charitable instrument.

The ICRC too, constantly touted as the 'gold standard of humanitarian action' (Weiss, 2007: xii) and neutrality, has no qualms about being primarily funded by the US government in the Philippines, although Washington is a party to the Moro wars. Just as private military firms (or mercenaries) have been outsourced some of the tasks of the 'war on terrorism' (Scahill, 2007), humanitarian IOs find themselves being useful in a 'win-win' way for Western military interventions.

Why do humanitarian IOs jettison their so-called core value of 'neutrality' by clamouring for great power military interventions, accepting funds from partisans and agreeing to be used as their pawns for achieving victory in total wars? Is the reason limited to the fear factor of donor pressures on humanitarians to prostitute themselves or does it have a deeper ideological rationale?

Conor Foley has argued that, beginning in the 1990s, some humanitarian IOs grew politicised and began lobbying great powers to militarily intervene in countries where there are 'humanitarian crises'. In doing so, Foley says, aid workers 'became part of the front line' of a 'global war' by liberal interventionists who were in power in the USA, UK and France (Foley, 2008). What he fails to analyse are the ideological roots of liberal interventionism and the conditional prerequisite of a capitalist world-system that have forever influenced the culture of humanitarian IOs.

Sarah Lischer has summed up the liberalism that is the binding glue of the humanitarian regime as follows:

> Most Western NGOs have an implicit (and perhaps unconscious) bias towards liberal ideals of individual rights and economic freedom. David Forsythe explains that, far from remaining neutral, many NGOs champion 'a type of social liberalism focussed on the worth and well being of the human person...which translates into policy preferences'. These otherwise laudable values may be identified with Western occupiers, and thus taint the perceived neutrality of humanitarian organizations (Lischer, 2007: 109).

Contrary to Foley's claim that the 'majority of aid workers' were only very reluctantly becoming instruments of liberal interventionism in the post-Cold War era, Lischer is pointing to the liberal backbone that is congenital to the humanitarian enterprise. Foley's defensive account of humanitarians perpetrates the myth that IOs are 'motivated by genuine altruistic concern' (Foley, 2008: 219)[2] and attempts to delink the aid business from capitalist imperialism. But this sympathetic portrayal of humanitarians is betrayed by Foley's own admission that, in Afghanistan (the so-called 'good war' of Western liberals), IOs and NATO troops shared the same objectives of 'strengthening law and order, weakening the warlords, combating corruption and supporting human rights' (Foley, 2008: 219).

Like true-blooded liberals, these IOs casually shrugged away the material and human destruction, mass displacement and loss of life brought about by the US-led war on Afghanistan and went along with assisting occupation forces.

If two actors — humanitarian organizations and imperialist militaries — profess common goals of so-called alleviation of *les miserables* but work together to accentuate civilian suffering through war, one should acknowledge that these IOs and great powers are willing partners in crime. Mild critics of humanitarianism like Foley fail to address the ideological affinity between aid agencies and their capitalist donor states.

All the humanitarian IOs studied in this book, with exceptions like OXFAM-GB Philippines, have by virtue of their origin and evolution always been torchbearers of the liberal geoculture that long preceded the end of the Cold War. What happened after 1991 was actually a meeting of minds between the innate liberalism of humanitarian IOs and a new breed of 'liberal interventionist' ruling classes in the West who felt triumphant about their victory over communism (Fukuyama, 1993).

Historian Michael Howard has argued that a 'liberal conscience' has been critical to framing US and European ideas about war since the nineteenth century. Although this 'conscience' generally sat in the anti-war corner of Western debates about improving the world, it clamoured for war to 'free' subjugated minorities in the Ottoman, Habsburg and Russian empires (Howard, 1978). Freedom of the individual and free markets had so captivated liberals that they continued supporting Western military destabilisation of the Global South right through the ages of empire and decolonisation.

With the rise of neoliberalism as a market fundamentalist version of classical liberalism, the justification for invading or occupying unstable or conflict-prone parts of the world to prepare them for integration into the global economy grew stronger after 1991. David Rieff writes that humanitarian intervention is 'of a piece with the profound assault on sovereignty contained in the neo-liberal project of economic globalisation' (Rieff, 2000). Thus, liberal humanitarian IOs found in Western liberal interventionism after 1991 not only openings to enhance their budgets and projects in war zones but also a basic convergence of ideology under the overall condition of the capitalist world-system.

Military affairs scholar Jan Willem Honig pieces together this ideological convergence to analyse why contemporary wars and military interventions are loaded with liberal and humanitarian overtones:

> With the end of the Cold War, when the West seemingly saw off its last major ideological competitor, liberal ideas and values have been offered an unprecedented opportunity to assert themselves and finally make our military establishments a true and global 'force for good' (Honig, 2008).

Invading or bombing countries in the name of human rights matched the liberalism of humanitarian IOs, who willingly became auxiliaries of armies performing 'good' liberal services on behalf of the 'free world' of donor states.

Gary Bass, a cheerleader for liberal imperialism, has even geopoliticised military interventions by recommending that great powers of the 'free world' divide the planet into 'spheres of humanitarian interest' and intervene in their respective domains to uphold democracy and human rights. Classifying the world into 'free' and 'unfree' countries, Bass reminds today's 'leading democracies' about their duty to intervene and 'save' individuals in the 'unfree' part who are being oppressed by their cruel governments (Bass, 2008).

The US-led 'war on terrorism', which I found to be the most prominent 'Power' factor in determining humanitarian IO priorities in the Philippines, is not a deviation from the liberal conscience but its apotheosis. John Mearsheimer, the guru of neorealism, has labelled the neo-conservative architects of the 'war on terrorism' Wilsonian liberals with teeth (Mearsheimer, 2005). Richard Seymour maintains that liberalism and neo-conservatism united under the banner of promoting democracy and human rights because 'the vocabulary of totalitarianism has never been far away when liberals and neoconservatives talk about foreign policy' (Seymour, 2008: 250). To both neo-cons and pro-'war on terror' liberals, 'Muslim totalitarianism is the presently regnant form of this totalitarian menace' — a successor to the twentieth century threats of Bolshevism and fascism (Seymour, 2008: 253).

Since 'liberal-humanitarian' interventionists always looked up to Western militaries to 'liberate' people in the Global South from genocidal violence or repressive governments, they took an instant liking for the 'war on terrorism' and justified it by equating Hitler, Stalin, Saddam Hussein and all other 'Islamo-Fascists' from the Taliban to the Abu Sayyaf.[3]

Even when confronted with the excessive destruction of lives in Afghanistan, Iraq and other 'second fronts' in the 'war on terrorism', 'liberal-humanitarian' intellectuals argued that 'freedoms' would only come at a price. Principal among them was Michael Ignatieff, who redefined liberalism as 'lesser evilism'. According to this widely-cited liberal-humanitarian, the violence, torture, violation of international laws, and fuelling of existing local wars by the US-led 'war on terrorism' are necessary evils and means to defeat an even greater evil — al-Qaeda. (Ignatieff, 2005).

Humanitarian personnel may not be as open in canvassing for imperial wars of aggression as Ignatieff, but their entire being is suffused with the same liberal philosophy of 'lesser evilism'. The empirical chapters of this book gave examples of the ethical dilemmas confronting humanitarians about whether or not to 'compromise' with those who wield extraordinary power in return for 'access' to civilian populations in war zones.

The balance sheet calculation goes somewhat as follows: 'if we accept money from a party to the conflict or set up a relief camp as per its dictates or allow aid to be siphoned off for combatants on its side, the actions may prolong the war or give the patron an unfair advantage in the fighting, but the compact is worth it because we can keep our programmes running so that millions of IDPs or refugees will not starve or go shelter less.'

That the Faustian bargain of humanitarian IOs with foreign or domestic armies could have cataclysmic consequences for the protection of civilians in a war zone is evident from this book. But few, if any, humanitarian IO personnel worry about the disastrous impact of becoming agents of state (capitalist donor or host) because their genuflection opens 'access' to civilian communities who might otherwise perish due to forcible displacement.

The biggest myth sustaining liberal humanitarianism is the notion that aid agencies 'save lives' in emergencies and that any price is worth paying for it to continue this way. Ironically, for most humanitarian IOs, the business of saving lives does not include protection of civilians from violence and abuse.

Feeding, clothing, sheltering and development — priorities that suit psychological warfare specialists — are the priorities for most humanitarian IOs when they assemble a response to emergencies. Protection rarely features in the act of 'saving lives' because the military allies of the IOs are supposed to be handling that side of the work. Thanks to this liberal faith in Western militaries, neither ICRC Philippines nor SCF Philippines will ever openly acknowledge that US neo-imperialism in Mindanao has made the Moro wars bloodier and more intractable.

In Chapter 1, I divided military humanitarianism (great power-driven interventions in the Global South) from the attempt to mainstream human rights into humanitarian IOs as two different external modalities through which the protection crisis in internal wars is sought to be addressed. The empirical chapters of this book, particularly those profiling the 'war on terrorism' in the Philippines, have closed the theoretical gap between the two modes by mooting a *military-humanitarian complex* that is joined at the hip by rational material interests and the capitalist geoculture of liberalism.

This complex is conspicuous in a geographical backdrop like the Philippines because the US military directly performs humanitarian services and also depends on humanitarian IOs to be at its beck and call for winning 'hearts and minds' of civilians.

But the same liberal interventionist culture and rational calculations matter in contexts like Sri Lanka, where the collusion of humanitarian IOs is not with a global great power donor like the US but with an aggressive ethnocratic state that can expel them from the country by whim. In this case too, the choice is between losing 'access' to civilian beneficiaries and accepting the lesser evil of being commandeered by the host state to serve its military-strategic goals.

Even if the GSL was hell bent on total war as the solution to Tamil separatism, humanitarian IOs had no qualms about abetting this agenda.

At the time of writing, IO cases of this book were queuing up to fund and supply SLA's detention camps, in which Tamil civilians fleeing the dense fighting of the Wanni were interred indefinitely with no freedoms (Montlake, 2009). On being challenged as to how the UN could justify being used by the GSL so blatantly against the interests of civilians, the organization's relief coordinator argued that 'the UN wouldn't want to punish those in the camps' (Lee, 2009). In the culture of humanitarian IOs, losing access to beneficiaries is equated with punishment, thereby elevating the value of their material relief to life-saving proportion.

What these humanitarians did not acknowledge was that lives were actually being destroyed due to physical violence against detainees in these very camps by the SLA and its intelligence agents. While the UN-assisted camps went by GSL's innocuous-sounding tag, 'welfare centres', state agencies overseeing them were 'secretly subjecting LTTE suspects to arbitrary detention or possible enforced disappearances' (Hogg, 2009).

In Chapter 4, I quoted an OXFAM-GB Sri Lanka official likening the 'welfare centres' to Nazi concentration camps. But neither his organization nor any other humanitarian IO has yet found the guts or the creativity to counter this policy of the belligerent Sinhalese state. If liberalism is anti-totalitarian, why are liberal humanitarian IOs silently abetting state-sponsored totalitarianism in the North and East of Sri Lanka? The only plausible answer is that the IOs are integrated cells of the *military-humanitarian complex*. This complex is universal to contemporary internal and inter-state wars, but stands out in bold relief in countries like the Philippines, where the 'war on terrorism' makes extensive use of liberal humanitarian propaganda.

In Chapter 3, I mentioned one strand of liberal theory that humanitarian aid is a 'sop to the western conscience.' What this book has done is to demonstrate that it is an ideological ally of Western liberal imperialism that has global consequences for war-torn societies, and not merely a sop to pacify public opinion in Western donor societies.

French pacifist Jean Bricmont has argued that a new form of 'humanitarian imperialism' has come into being since NATO's bombing of Serbia in 1999, wherein great powers selectively and hypocritically use the pretext of human rights and 'saving lives' to undertake aggression and consolidate empires (Bricmont, 2006). Non-state actors have been roped into this imperialist project of aggravating wars and militarising parts of the Global South. Both the bureaucratic culture and the cost-benefit rationality of these non-state IOs are products of the worldwide quest for neo-colonial domination by capitalist donor states which wear the liberal masks of 'civic action' and 'peace and development' but unleash havoc through wars and neoliberal exploitation.

Far from having any 'moral authority' (Barnett and Finnemore, 2004), humanitarian IOs are basically aides in empire-extension — a finding that would not be obvious if one remained glued to the confines of the 'Third Debate' of IR theory. In this book, I argued that most humanitarians were 'hunters' who enable more efficient forms of abuse and atrocities against civilians in Sri Lanka and 'props' for the 'war on terrorism' in the Philippines. These localised instances of oppression and impunity are part of a larger structural condition of the contemporary world where violence is permitted and abetted for geopolitical and geo-economic ends.

Only by nesting the aid industry and humanitarian IOs in their structural seedbeds of capitalist empire and patriarchy can one approach a fuller understanding of their nature and purpose. Lacking a structural theoretical handle on humanitarians is a handicap plaguing most practitioner literature about 'mainstreaming' protection. Workshops, consultancies and trainings abound in giant humanitarian IOs to try to move the wheels and get their field personnel to become more proactive on protection, but none of these initiatives have looked inward at the humanitarian trade to see how it is integrated with global structures of violence and domination. This book goes a long way in uncovering this fundamental connection.

Is Mainstreaming a Pipe Dream?

It is now more than fifteen years since the UN and international human rights organizations launched the 'mainstreaming' campaign to push humanitarian IOs in a proactive direction. Several quasi-legal milestones have been achieved along the way, including the Guiding Principles on Internal Displacement, R2P' and the formation of the International Criminal Court[4] Scholastic and practitioner debates now centre on how touch-me-not national sovereignty is being bent, at least in a select few cases, in a new era of global justice, and what its implications are for war and peace (Kukathas, 2006; Kochler, 2003; Chaulia1, 2008). The topic of humanitarian interventions has also been studied keenly as a subset of these larger questions, especially on the implications of 'coalitions of the willing' flouting international laws to disallow sovereignty from being misused to commit atrocities on civilians (Hehir, 2008; Davis, 2004).

Despite the proliferation of literature about humanitarianism, the focus of most writings on the subject remains state-centric. The morality, legality and power politicking behind growing calls for humanitarian interventions are all studied from the perspective of foreign policies of states. Non-state humanitarian actors — IGOs and INGOs — are not given enough attention by social scientists although they have been practising their version of 'intervention' in internal and inter-state wars long before 'R2P' was even coined.

I attribute the neglect of the non-state aspect of humanitarianism to widely shared beliefs among academics that humanitarian IOs are apolitical or that they lack material power to change the behaviour of armed actors who perpetrate abuses on civilians.

The onus of the burgeoning 'humanitarian intervention' scholarship is on states and their foreign military policies because only great power states are seen as having the clout to solve or exacerbate the protection crisis in war zones. This book has revealed how valuable field-based IOs are to the military-humanitarian complex. Unlike great power military machines, humanitarian IOs by themselves can never bring about 'regime change' or decisively enable one warring party's victory over its rivals. But what the IOs offer is a force multiplier to global, national and even sub-national militaries to achieve their more grand IOs geopolitical or geo-economic aims. This book is a reminder to political science scholars that ignoring non-state IOs is an obfuscation of the subalterns or foot soldiers of the aid regime that service the military-humanitarian complex.

By 'bringing organizations back in', we can acknowledge that non-state humanitarian actors have agency and are capable of having an impact on the global protection crisis. The positioning of humanitarian IGOs and INGOs as dependent variables in this research design does not condemn them to be permanently pressured, induced and inscribed upon by the structural conditions or the proximate causes.

Especially in the realm of culturalist 'Ideas', we noted that humanitarians create some of the structures that cause their behaviour. Bureaucratic ideas, practices and procedures are dead weights on most humanitarian IOs that could be shed with ingenuity, creativity and pluck. OXFAM-GB Philippines or •UNICEF Sri Lanka led the proactiveness rankings in their respective countries precisely because they arrived at a self-appreciation of their agency even in a highly structured war zone.

The OXFAM-GB Philippines case is the most instructive of how agency can skirt the structural impediments to proactiveness. We noted in Chapter 6 that the EU has struck a discordant note in the US-dominated 'war on terrorism' donor coalition in the Philippines and how OXFAM-GB benefited from this intra-capitalist rivalry by finding diplomatic and financial space for its proactiveness. However solid and undivided the capitalist world-system appears, there are always splits and schisms motivated by competition among capitalist states and classes.

A progressive IO which can strategically grasp these underlying realities can exploit the ruptures in the world-system and carve out room in which to become more responsive to civilian protection. IOs must be alive to intra-capitalist competition and alternate forms of masculinity and feminity in order to activate their own agency.

Capitalising on divisions among donor states is not a very likely outcome unless cultures of IOs transform. For the engine of agency to move, nothing short of a cultural renaissance will be required in IOs. The rare success stories of IOs that managed to reinvent themselves in this book to become more proactive carry crucial lessons.

Firstly, local activists, CSOs, human rights defenders and movements for non-violent justice exist in every war zone. They are the best knowers and solvers of the menace of fear and violence hanging over war-terrorised societies. *Qua* locals, they have the highest stakes in keeping ceasefires, ending wars, restoring justice and rebuilding societies for durable peace. For an IO to 'mainstream' protection, it has to open channels to this wealth of local knowledge. Otherwise, it risks remaining stuck in the bubble of 'developmentalism' and aid, which are blind to the protection crisis.

To listen and learn from local organisers and ordinary civilians coping against adversity is a virtue, one that does not come easily to humanitarian IOs brimming with boorish expatriate 'experts'. Some humanitarians I met in Sri Lanka even asked me if there is a 'magic technique' to find genuine local activists, since they were unable to locate any. With suspicions about the 'neutrality' of many local activists drummed into their minds, humanitarians shy away from them or even tattle on them to friendly officers or commanders of state and non-state militaries.[5]

Many episodes in this book elaborated the bureaucratic insouciance of expatriate humanitarians towards civilians who are in urgent need of international protection. Part of this sclerosis in IOs comes from being aloof from radical local activists, who could advise responses that do not re-traumatise the victims of abuse. Divorced from local movements, IOs usually fund insensitive 'psycho-social' or 'developmental' approaches adopted by conservative local NGOs. Overcoming superciliousness and respecting radical local activists is a step that can do marvels for the proactiveness of a humanitarian IO.

The implication of the two progressive turns from our ten IO cases — UNICEF Sri Lanka and OXFAM-GB Philippines — is that local peace and human rights defenders are agents of change who can transform not only IOs but also the brutal milieu of war through coordinated grassroots actions. The extraordinary pluck and perseverance of local activists have saved the lives of thousands of civilians in both Sri Lanka and the Philippines over the last few decades. IOs need to accept this fact and strengthen the hands of concerned citizens who strive for non-violent solutions. The more aloof humanitarians remain from citizen activists, the greater the likelihood that IOs will not be able to clean up their imperialist footprints.

The second lesson for progressive reincarnation within IOs is to reconceptualise peace as a corollary of justice. My diagram in Chapter 1 shows how central the question of human and people's rights is to the solution of internal wars. Very few humanitarians think about these linkages because they buy into the capitalist ideas that peace will come from economic development and 'poverty reduction'.

Both the North and East of Sri Lanka and the south-western parts of the Philippines happen to have lower socio-economic indices than relatively prosperous parts of their countries inhabited by ethnic majorities. The reason for regional imbalances in economic prosperity between majority and minorities in both countries is war and systematic identity-based discrimination by state structures. The 'peace and development' formula conveniently bypasses politically-motivated and imposed impoverishment of minority regions and argues the opposite, i.e. that war is being caused by poverty.

Especially in ethnocracies like Sri Lanka, impoverishment is the result of war and not vice-versa. Humanitarian IOs that also double up as development organizations during lulls in fighting will need to undergo a fundamental internal catharsis to be able to make the correct diagnosis of why a society has been sundered and forced to sink into misery. Failing such a reappraisal, 'mainstreaming' of protection will remain a sideshow and humanitarians will continue with their 'business as usual' of delivering material aid and pat themselves that it is their contribution to 'supporting peace' (Spillmann, 2001).

A third lesson for mainstreaming to work out in humanitarian IOs is that bureaucratic 'projectification' of action is a recipe for sclerosis. As the international humanitarian regime evolves with its own rules, regulations and standards, it has become narrowly over-specialised. The logic of inter-organizational competition to vie for scarce donor funds spurs technically standardised 'project' proposals and area experts to manage each component of emergency response ('clusters' in UN argot). When a project hits the ground with technical categories like 'inputs', 'outputs', 'outcomes', 'objectives', 'indicators' and 'impact', actions of the IO become circumscribed by these guidelines.

In 2002, when a tireless local activist approached UNICEF and Save the Children in Eastern Sri Lanka with innovative ideas, she had no receptivity because both these IOs had ongoing 'projects' that did not match her fresh thinking. What is worse, they suggested that she write a 'project proposal' and submit it for funding. She was aghast at this 'projectification' of all solutions and told me that 'the moment these humanitarians begin using their 'project' language, I know that they will ruin my idea and raise money out of it.'[6]

The leitmotif of this book is that creativity is the *piece de resistance* of mainstreaming protection. Perhaps expecting die-hard bureaucratic IOs to adopt it is wishful thinking. When I worked in the Protection Department of a giant humanitarian INGO, the International Rescue Committee in 2003, I was instructed by superiors that 'process' and 'procedure' should be followed while performing any activity and that the 'rules' are even more important that the outputs because they ensure that the whole organization is talking and acting in one step. The irony of a Department with a proceduralist bureaucracy setting forth to make the organization more proactive on political rights of civilians is supreme. Instead of freeing an organization for creativity, proceduralist mainstreaming adds to the calcification.

Humanitarian IOs that learn the three lessons outlined in this chapter will be able to also enjoy some fringe benefits of a less stressful work culture. It is a misnomer that humanitarian aid workers face emotional, mental and physical stress only because of the rational 'Power' pressures in a war zone (Fawcett, 2003). IOs' spiritual health, sorely missing from their lackadaisical attitudes to the value of civilian life, can be restored if excess bureaucratisation of the workplace is eased. It is only through release from bureaucratic pathologies that humanitarian IOs can discover their own agency.

Humanitarians are so caught up in enacting their routines and living in the lap of luxury that they normalise the abnormality of war. Life in a war zone becomes king-size life for expatriate humanitarians, who occupy the best mansions and drive around in the fanciest of vehicles. Though nowhere as privileged as an international bourgeoisie, humanitarians develop a culture of grandeur amidst the ruins of war. Like an upwardly mobile middle class in an impoverished society, they become inured to the abuses borne by ordinary civilians.

Humanitarian IOs have umpteen times hidden behind the excuse of rational power pressures for not being more proactive. Even the so-called 'muscularist' IOs like MSF defend their failures to act for civilian protection by holding that 'an organization simply cannot provide humanitarian aid and at the same time fight against impunity' (Fournier, 2009). This book has gone against the grain of such conventional platitudes and shown how IOs which undergo reinventions of culture can assist local protection networks to counter abuse of civilians.

A Black Swan to End Humanitarianism?

Given the entrenched power of the structural edifices of the capitalist world-system and patriarchy, however flexible they are at the margins, is humanitarianism ever going to be passé? There are two routes through which the humanitarian IO mode of external involvement in internal wars could become a relic.

Firstly, if humanitarian IOs outlive their usefulness to donor states, which represent the inner elite circle of the global capitalist class, they could be discarded for other types of actors. Already, the training of armies to handle humanitarian functions has reached an advanced stage in Western military formations like NATO, which set the pace of 'humanitarian soldiering' during the Kosovo war of 1999 (Huysmans, 2002).

The reason why donor states might choose to have their armies do both the 'shock and awe' bombardments and the mopping-up through humanitarian aid is the comparative advantage in rational efficiency of militaries over slow-moving bureaucratic IOs. Around the world, state armies are pressed into service by their governments for disaster rescue and relief after natural calamities due to these qualities. In war zones, armies can kill efficiently with one hand and feed with alacrity with the other if they fully develop dual capacities. When NATO found UN agencies and INGOs under-prepared to succour the victims of its war on Serbia, it simply decided to sideline the IOs and deployed its own troops to build and manage refugee camps.

Some humanitarian IOs with radical roots (e.g. OXFAM-GB Philippines) could be thorns in the flesh for imperial designers if they are allowed to be key players in aid delivery and civilian protection. In war theatres like Mindanao, if more IOs imitate OXFAM-GB and undergo cultural metamorphosis, it would become harder for the 'war on terrorism' to succeed. To avoid the hassle of having to separate the 'good' apples from the 'bad' ones, Western strategic planners could prefer to get rid of humanitarian IOs altogether and rely on direct funding of local NGOs that are selected for their loyalty to 'peace and development' frameworks.

What could prevent wholesale shut down of humanitarian IOs is the old need for a cloak of legitimacy over geo-strategic interventions by great powers. IOs fit the bill because of their multilateral character, which helps to disguise unilateral wars, invasions or destabilisation of countries in the Global South.

For example, after the end of the 22-day Israeli war on the Gaza Strip of 2008-09, which was backed militarily and diplomatically by the US government, Washington promptly announced 'neutral' humanitarian assistance worth $20.3 million to the battered area via UNRWA, UNOCHA and ICRC (DOS, 2009). So mobilised is the anti-Israeli and anti-American sentiment in the Gaza Strip that the US or Israeli armies could not have distributed the relief on their own. The curved arrows in my diagram in Chapter 7 conveyed how humanitarian behaviour reinforces patriarchy and the capitalist world-system in war zones. As long as IOs fulfil this 'mandated' responsibility, they will not be totally abjured by donor states.

In Afghanistan and Iraq, which were brought under US military occupation in 2001 and 2003 respectively, invading Western armies engaged in direct relief delivery because many parts of these countries were unsafe for civilian IOs (Bristol, 2006). So, what is emerging is a pattern of use or disuse of IOs, depending on the security situation in a particular war and the legitimacy needs of powerful actors. IOs are necessary in certain war contexts but can be bypassed in others. The realisation that armies could completely replace civilian non-state humanitarian IOs is at the heart of the anxieties of aid agencies that are opposing encroachment on to their turfs (Gordon, 2004). Humanitarianism, as a liberal interventionist ideology, will obviously not wither away even if the IGO and INGO form of delivering aid might rust and lose its appeal in the future.

The second route through which humanitarian IOs could fade in future wars is self-mobilisation for self-protection of war-hit communities under local activist leadership. When one spends time in a war zone like the North and East of Sri Lanka or south-western Philippines, stories of betrayal and callousness of humanitarians towards civilians facing mortal danger come in the hundreds. Humanitarian IOs can pose as 'saviours' of the last resort for civilians, but people who are left in the lurch multiple times by these organizations know better.

Since IOs are the only manifestations of the so-called 'international community' with which ordinary civilians come face-to-face in war zones, the bitterness that accumulates against them in the minds of people is tremendous. I was often confronted with critical questioning as to how long I intended to stay in Sri Lanka or the Philippines as an international civilian peacekeeper when the norm of humanitarian IOs is to simply execute an aid 'project' and then pack their bags for greener pastures, leaving civilians to their fates as battle lines inch closer.

The single biggest complaint about humanitarians that I heard in both the Eelam war and Moro war theatres from activists and displaced civilians was that they abandon people when they most need them to be present for protection. Many civilians express gratitude to humanitarian IOs that provide them material relief during flight, but they are equally critical of aid agencies for failing to stand by them and act as a deterrent to abuses by armed actors.

Every war produces revolutionary potential among civilians to organise and protect themselves from state armies and rebel groups. When bare survival is threatened, there is no limit to human ingenuity. I recall visiting villages of central Mindanao where locals narrated how they set up informal signalling systems to intimate the community well before armed groups find their prey in that area. The UN family has developed a detailed methodology for 'Humanitarian Early Warning Analysis' in war zones, but it lacks the creativity of a self-devised community-level protection network that is not reliant on project proposals and donor grants. The 'early warning' systems that humanitarian IOs employ are from global headquarters, district or provincial capital towns and cities of the war-affected country — a different kettle of fish from the ones that spontaneously emerge in communities staring at extermination in war.

The overthrow of 'developmentalist' humanitarian IOs by a well-knit community intervention scheme for self-protection is not far-fetched. I recall hearing from a senior activist leader in Mindanao in 2006 that the United States Institute of Peace had been 'isolated' by local civil society after it tried to bypass existing protection networks at the grassroots level by setting up its own 'peace facilitation' groups. In Chapter 5, I reported the will of local activists in Maguindanao province of Mindanao to 'isolate' the ICRC if it did not join hands to bring hostilities to a complete halt. These examples show that it is possible for protection of civilians to be freed from the gyves of IO projects and programmes.

The idea of monitoring and resisting humanitarianism is popular among peace and human rights activists in Sri Lanka and the Philippines. Due to methodological and theoretical limitations, I did not problematise the concept of 'Power' in this book. But it deserves mention that organised local activists in war zones believe that they have a special 'Power' to end wars and abuses by means of their tactful and exemplary actions. Activists inspired by Mahatma Gandhi's maxim —, 'be the change you want to see in the world' (Kumar and Whitefield, 2007), have moral power that the IOs lack. The modalities of resistance to military humanitarianism and humanitarian imperialism will vary from one violent context to the other, but it persists in the minds of progressive local civil societies of every war zone.

Jeffrey Isaac contends that empiricist methodology limits political scientists to 'power over', i.e. domination of a stronger actor over a weaker one, and leads to bypassing 'power to', i.e. the 'powers possessed by subordinate groups, whose behaviour is not simply heteronomously caused by the actions of the dominant' (Isaac, 1987: 195).

As my ontology and normative position are rooted in validating the dignity of civilians in war, it was necessary to step out of the empiricist-cum-positivist skin in the later parts of the book to reflect upon structural 'conditions' that are not amenable to cause-and-effect simplicity. The possibilities of resistance to humanitarianism can only be apparent if the structural 'conditions' of the capitalist world-system and patriarchy are laid bare and if activists' 'power to' transform their communities is recognised.

Can popular movements or uprisings erupt against humanitarian IOs for their failure to do what people seek the most in a war zone, i.e. protection? Philosopher Nassim Taleb has a theory that historic changes can come from unexpected, hard-to-predict and rare events such as the appearance of a black swan in 1697 in Australia, which was considered impossible until that moment (Taleb, 2007). When the chips are really down and death is in the air- a typical day or night for communities in a war zone- there is no limit to human ingenuity or spontaneity.

The mistake that many smug humanitarians commit is to assume that the war-battered are supplicants for the crumbs of bread being thrown at them from the aid basket and will therefore not bite the hand that feeds them. Humanitarians like to believe that their emergency rations or tarpaulin for temporary shelters are so 'life saving' that people will never rise up against their givers.

As long as civilians believe that IOs are doing them noble favours by coming to their rescue during calamities, the myth that lives are being 'saved' through supposedly benign external interventions will save humanitarians from popular wrath. But when the hegemony of humanitarianism is broken and its violent structural roots are exposed, the global protection crisis will find grassroots-based solutions.

EPILOGUE

Decolonising International Organizations

Why have people and states been coming together to form international organizations, federations and associations for centuries? It is owing to needs that arise in history which cannot be met with resources or actions available within one's own society or country. Collective organizations are products of collective needs and aspirations that are felt simultaneously at a moment in time by political elites and/or peoples across national boundaries.

A befuddling number of collective organizations catering to a panorama of specialised thematic functions and purposes dots the international landscape today and testifies to the vast variety of collective needs and aspirations that have accumulated over the course of inter-social and inter-state interactions.

While each collective organization reflects the shared values of its members, personnel or supporters, universal IGOs such as the United Nations rely on least common denominator aspirations that are so basic that every single state, and the societies they govern, can identify with them. I interpret these core aspirations to be life, liberty and the dignity of the human person. When the UN was created in 1945, its framers drew on a globally shared desire of rulers and ruled to prevent war and to ensure peace and security so that human beings can live and die peacefully. Out of absolute war-weariness at the end of World War II came a global consensus that we needed a permanent organization that can address the big question of international relations — how to limit the use of force so that the 'peoples of the United Nations' can be spared extreme violence and 'untold sorrow' (UN, 1945).

Like all IOs, the UN has since inception been subject to the manipulation of its more powerful members and constituencies. The fact that the IMF and the World Bank became the dominant specialised agencies of the UN system while the ILO got sidetracked as an aspirational entity with negligible influence on macro-economic policies of states shows how much this universal organization became captive to special interests.

Throughout the Cold War, the UN's founding missions of preventing war and protecting fundamental human rights were paralysed by great powers that used their veto 279 times in the Security Council between 1945 and May 1990 (Orford, 2003: 3). For its first 45 years in existence, the UN stood by helplessly as proxy wars consumed many parts of the Global South in the East vs. West confrontation.

The shift in great power alliance patterns after 1991 and the wave of liberal triumphalism pushed the UN and its sub-IGOs into an 'era of humanitarian intervention' (Orford, 2003: 3). The unipolar moment, which lasted for about a decade after the collapse of the USSR, and the neoliberal ascendance in global markets catapulted humanitarianism as a new colonising principle that was outsourced to UN agencies, INGOs and hybrids like the ICRC. Dashing hopes that a post-Cold War UN would be able to prevent wars and genocides, violent conflicts continued to rage in the last two decades in the absence of democratisation of the world order of states and of the capitalist world-system. Aid agencies and development organizations strode the Global South like mini-colossuses that derived their authority not from moral power but the donor power of capitalist states and international financial institutions.

The collective aspirations and morals enshrined in the UN Charter and the Universal Declaration of Human Rights fell by the wayside in the uninterrupted takeover of IOs by the strong after 1945. The narrower the set of interests that universal organizations are yoked to, the less likely they are to serve the *summum bonum*. The whole history of professional humanitarian IOs since World War II is one of instrumentalisation sugar-coated with philanthropic and charitable rhetoric. IOs have not only been harnessed for partisan ends by donors, host states and violent non-state actors, but also engendered through their own reserves of grants and 'projects' a wholesale 'NGOisation' of the Global South. The macro impact of development and humanitarian aid has been to de-radicalise societies that are struggling for peace, human rights and justice.

The liberal IR theorist's celebration of IOs as mediums to promote international cooperation and peace hides the reality of collective organizations being used to defeat the desire of peoples around the world to have peace with justice.

Revolutionary transformations that could have empowered civilians to protect themselves and forge lasting solutions to violent conflict were stanched by the overpowering pull of well-paying 'NGO jobs' that opened the doors for an 'international career' in the aid business. When post-colonial states became repressive, militaristic and ethnocratic, often with the approbation of great powers and multinational corporations, the collective need and aspiration of peoples was to resist the encroachment on their freedoms and dignities.

Existing humanitarian and development IOs, drenched in liberal values, could not perceive this need and continued to sing along with their sponsors the old tunes of 'capacity building' of (capitalist friendly) states in the Global South. New IOs like Nonviolent Peaceforce that reflect the current moral and material aspirations of societies, especially those which have been devastated by war, are yet to mature into system-changing forces. Small-scale consortiums of civil society organizations and activists from around the world which are free from the humanitarian impulse and dedicated tox, civilian protection, justice and peace are being created thanks to the global communications revolution. Since they contain the seeds of decolonising international collective organization, attempts will be made by the powers that be to co-opt them into their arsenal of humanitarian and development IOs.

The challenge for activists in the coming decades will be to shield their organizations and movements from the all-encompassing dragnet of donor states, belligerent state and non-state elites, and the freewheeling capital accumulationist class. The only guarantee that they will survive the barrage of structural 'conditions' which has colonised IOs for hundreds of years is if they discover their agency — i.e. nurture progressive organizational culture, minimise bureaucratisation and firewall themselves from the military — humanitarian complex.

APPENDIX

Calibrated Tables for Cross-Country Comparisons
Table 7.1. Sri Lanka, coding group I.

Action	UNDP	UNICEF	ICRC	OXFAM-GB	SCSL
Participates in or provides inputs to protection sector meetings of IGOs and INGOs falling under Humanitarian Coordination, convened by UNOCHA.	1	.5	.5	1	1
Intercedes for justice on behalf of relatives of abducted or harassed civilians with relevant armed actors or authorities.	0	1	1	0	0
Participates in or provides inputs to protection/ human security meetings of IGOs and INGOs at district level in Batticaloa, Trincomalee and/ or Jaffna.	1	.5	.5	1	1
Makes field visits to areas known to be critical to show conscious international presence and deter violence/civilian abuse.	0	0	0	1	0
Shares sensitive information on protection/ human rights and cooperates with relevant human rights defenders at the local, national and international levels.	0	0	0	0	0
Has signed civil society petitions and/or issued any press releases of its own that oppose atrocities or call on armed parties to respect civilians and pursue non-violent paths.	0	0	0	0	0
Total score for each organization	2	2	2	3	2

Table 7.2. Sri Lanka, coding group II.

Action	UNDP	UNICEF	ICRC	OXFAM-GB	SCSL
Participates in or provides inputs to protection sector meetings of IGOs and INGOs falling under Humanitarian Coordination, convened by UNOCHA.	0	.5	.5	1	1
Intercedes for justice on behalf of relatives of abducted or harassed civilians with relevant armed actors or authorities.	0	1	1	0	0
Participates in or provides inputs to protection/ human security meetings of IGOs and INGOs at district level in Batticaloa, Trincomalee and/ or Jaffna.	0	.5	.5	0	1
Makes field visits to areas known to be critical to show conscious international presence and deter violence/civilian abuse.	1	1	1	0	0
Shares sensitive information on protection/ human rights and cooperates with relevant human rights defenders at the local, national and international levels.	1	1	1	1	0
Has signed civil society petitions and/or issued any press releases of its own that oppose atrocities or call on armed parties to respect civilians and pursue non-violent paths.	0	0	0	0	0
Total score for each organization	2	4	4	2	2

Table 7.3. Sri Lanka, coding group III.

Action	UNDP	UNICEF	ICRC	OXFAM-GB	SCSL
Participates in or provides inputs to protection sector meetings of IGOs and INGOs falling under Humanitarian Coordination, convened by UNOCHA.	0	.5	.5	1	1
Intercedes for justice on behalf of relatives of abducted or harassed civilians with relevant armed actors or authorities.	0	1	1	1	0
Participates in or provides inputs to protection/ human security meetings of IGOs and INGOs at district level in Batticaloa, Trincomalee and/ or Jaffna.	0	.5	.5	0	1
Makes field visits to areas known to be critical to show conscious international presence and deter violence/civilian abuse.	0	1	0	0	0
Shares sensitive information on protection/ human rights and cooperates with relevant human rights defenders at the local, national and international levels.	1	1	0	0	0
Has signed civil society petitions and/or issued any press releases of its own that oppose atrocities or call on armed parties to respect civilians and pursue non-violent paths.	0	0	1	0	0
Total score for each organization	1	4	3	2	2

Table 7.4. Philippines, coding group I.

Action	UNDP	UNICEF	ICRC	OXFAM-GB	SCSL
Participates in and provides inputs to protection/human rights advocacy on Moro wars at the Manila level.	1	0	0	1	1
Intercedes for justice on behalf of relatives of abducted or harassed civilians with relevant armed actors or authorities.	0	0	1	0	0
Participates in or provides inputs to protection/human rights meetings at the Mindanao level.	0	.5	0	1	0
Makes field visits to areas known to be critical to show conscious international presence and deter violence/civilian abuse.	0	0	1	1	0
Shares sensitive information on protection/human rights and cooperates with relevant human rights defenders at the local, national and international levels.	1	1	0	1	1
Has signed civil society petitions and/or issued any press releases of its own that oppose atrocities or call on armed parties to respect civilians and pursue non-violent paths.	0	0	0	0	0
Total score for each organization	2	1.5	2	4	2

Table 7.5. Philippines, coding group II.

Action	UNDP	UNICEF	ICRC	OXFAM-GB	SCSL
Participates in and provides inputs to protection/human rights advocacy on Moro wars at the Manila level.	1	0	0	1	1
Intercedes for justice on behalf of relatives of abducted or harassed civilians with relevant armed actors or authorities.	0	0	1	0	0
Participates in or provides inputs to protection/human rights meetings at the Mindanao level.	0	.5	0	1	0
Makes field visits to areas known to be critical to show conscious international presence and deter violence/civilian abuse.	0	0	0	0	0
Shares sensitive information on protection/human rights and cooperates with relevant human rights defenders at the local, national and international levels.	0	0	0	1	1
Has signed civil society petitions and/or issued any press releases of its own that oppose atrocities or call on armed parties to respect civilians and pursue non-violent paths.	0	0	1	1	0
Total score for each organization	1	.5	2	4	2

Table 7.6. Philippines, coding group III.

Action	UNDP	UNICEF	ICRC	OXFAM-GB	SCSL
Participates in and provides inputs to protection/human rights advocacy on Moro wars at the Manila level.	0	0	0	1	1
Intercedes for justice on behalf of relatives of abducted or harassed civilians with relevant armed actors or authorities.	0	0	1	0	0
Participates in or provides inputs to protection/human rights meetings at the Mindanao level.	0	.5	0	1	0
Makes field visits to areas known to be critical to show conscious international presence and deter violence/civilian abuse.	1	0	1	0	0
Shares sensitive information on protection/human rights and cooperates with relevant human rights defenders at the local, national and international levels.	1	1	0	1	1
Has signed civil society petitions and/or issued any press releases of its own that oppose atrocities or call on armed parties to respect civilians and pursue non-violent paths.	0	0	1	1	0
Total score for each organization	2	1.5	3	4	2

Table 7.7. Standardised net weighted proactiveness scores of IO branches across Sri Lanka and the Philippines.

Organization	Sri Lanka	Philippines
UNICEF	3.33	1.16
UNDP	1.66	1.66
OXFAM-GB	2.33	4.0
ICRC	3.0	2.33
Save the Children	2.0	2.0

NOTES

Preface

[1] Technically, this map does not accurately represent the territorial and political boundaries of Sri Lanka. It has been designed purely for the convenience of readers of this book.

[2] Technically, this map does not accurately represent the territorial and political boundaries of the Philippines. It has been designed purely for the convenience of readers of this book.

Introduction

[1] This book follows the standard notation by distinguishing 'international relations' from 'International Relations'. The former refers to real world practices, whereas the latter means the academic sub-field of political science that vets these practices.

[2] A survey of top IR journals in the US in the late 1990s and found that Marxism and feminism featured only in 2.6 to 4.2 percent of articles, while rationalist theories figured in 77 to 63 percent of articles and reflectivist/constructivist theories appeared in 7.8 to 25 percent of articles (Weaver, 1998; Smith, 2002).

Chapter 1

[1] For a case study on the politics behind the onset of a 'protection deficit' in humanitarian organizations (Loescher, 2001).

Chapter 2

[1] The London-based think tank, One World Trust, issues annual Global Accountability Reports of select IOs. The 2008 report ranks humanitarian IGOs and INGOs like UNHCR, UNICEF, IOM, ICRC, CARE International and Catholic Relief Services for their accountability to internal and external stakeholders (OWT, 2008).

[2] These two antithetical positions observed among humanitarian IOs were first formalised by David Rieff (Rieff, 2003).

[3] James Fearon and Alexander Wendt argue that the ontological division between rationalists as individualists and constructivists as holists is overly philosophical and

unhelpful. To them, it is better to assume a posture of agnosticism about 'what society is really made of' (Fearon & Wendt, 2003, p.53).

4 Sarah Lischer cites US military interventions in Kosovo, Afghanistan and Iraq to argue that 'humanitarian organizations fulfil military or political goals for sponsoring governments' (Lischer, 2007, p.100).

5 Numerous Western INGOs and Foundations participated in Cold War campaigns (Osgoode, 2002).

Chapter 3

1 For the ICRC's contention that it is a unique organization (Rona, 2004).

2 The exception is Medecins Sans Frontieres, one of the few giant humanitarian INGOs whose bulk of the funding comes from private sources rather than governments.

3 For an example of humanitarian IOs complementing International Financial Institutions to dis-empower war-hit civilians (Chaulia, 2006).

4 The UNDP Administrator at the time of writing this book, Kemal Dervis, worked for 24 years at the World Bank.

Chapter 4

1 See (Dias, 2007) The final assault of the Sri Lankan military which annihilated the LTTE in May 2009 involved grave breaches of civilian life and liberty. The horrors of this *coup de grace* need to be added to the overall death tally.

2 For the gruesome spectacle of discovery of fresh mass graves from time to time (Subramanian, 2005).

3 Identities of coders throughout this book have been kept confidential owing to high security risks to their lives.

4 For an overview of the selectivity and double standards on human rights in American foreign policy (Mertus, 2004).

5 Conversation with author on 24 July 2008, in Colombo.

6 Conversation with author on 19 August 2008, in Trincomalee.

7 Conversation with author on 14 August 2008, in Colombo.

8 Conversation with author on 24 July 2008, in Colombo.

9 Ibid.

10 For the authoritarian centralisation in LTTE's de facto state apparatus (Stokke, 2006).

11 Tamil Makkal Viduthalai Pulihal (TMVP) is Karuna Amman's breakaway faction of the LTTE, which works for the SLA and is now in charge of a new layer of local administration on behalf of GSL in the East.

12 Conversation with author on 24 July 2008, in Colombo.

13 Conversation of a UN human rights official with author on 23 July 2008, in Colombo.

14 Conversation with author on 29 July 2008, in Colombo.

15 The Government Agent (GA) is the chief administrative officer of the Sri Lankan state at the district level.

16 Conversation with author on 30 July 2008, in Colombo.

[17] Conversation of senior UN official with author on 7 August 2008, in Colombo.

[18] Conversation with author on 7 August 2008, in Colombo.

[19] Conversation with author on 5 August 2008, in Batticaloa.

[20] The European Union banned LTTE in 2006 after several previous appeals for it to stop 'use of violence and terrorism' and 'recruitment of children as soldiers' (AT, 2005).

[21] Conversation with author on 7 August 2008, in Colombo.

[22] Conversation of UNICEF official with author on 7 August 2008, in Colombo.

[23] Conversation with author on 23 July 2008, in Colombo.

[24] Conversation with author on 24 July 2008, in Colombo.

[25] In a key document, the organization pledged that 'special attention will also be paid to ensuring that civil and political rights are fully respected in UNDP's sustainable human development programming and implementation' (UNDP, 1998).

[26] Conversation with author on 27 July 2008, in Batticaloa.

[27] Conversation with author on 29 July 2008, in Colombo.

[28] Ibid.

[29] Conversation with author on 30 July 2008, in Colombo.

[30] Conversation with author on 7 August 2008, in Colombo.

[31] Conversation with author on 17 July 2008, in Batticaloa.

[32] Ibid.

[33] Conversation with author on 7 August 2008 in Colombo.

[34] Conversation with author on 21 July 2008, in Trincomalee.

[35] Conversation with author on 9 August 2008, in Colombo.

[36] Conversation with author on 29 July 2008, in Colombo.

[37] Conversation with author on 5 August 2008, in Batticaloa.

[38] Conversation with author on 14 August 2008, in Colombo.

[39] Conversation of ICRC representative with author on 4 January 2005, in Batticaloa.

[40] Conversation of ICRC personnel with author on 1 August 2008, in Colombo.

[41] Conversation with author on 14 August 2008, in Colombo.

[42] Conversation of ICRC official with author on 1 August 2008, in Colombo.

[43] Conversation of local employee of SCSL with author on 17 August 2008, in Batticaloa.

[44] During my two years' stint in Sri Lanka, I heard countless outbursts of Sinhalese chauvinists against Norwegians, 'bloody Europeans', Christian NGOs and 'American bastards' for allegedly sympathising with and supplying weapons to the LTTE.

[45] Conversation with author on 19 August 2008, in Colombo.

[46] Conversation with author on 29 July 2008, in Colombo.

[47] Ibid.

[48] Conversation with author on 29 July 2008, in Colombo.

[49] Ibid.

[50] Conversation with author on 1 August 2008, in Colombo.

[51] Ibid.

[52] Ibid.

[53] Conversation with author on 19 August 2008, in Colombo.

[54] Ibid.

[55] Conversation with author on 14 August 2008, in Colombo.

[56] In the Philippines, which we will go to in Chapter 5, only SCF USA operates in the field, while SCF UK has a research presence.

[57] I was told by a former colleague at Nonviolent Peaceforce that ECHO officials in Brussels conveyed to her in 2008 that protection is 'not a life saving issue' in war zones and hence, not a priority.

[58] Conversation with author on 19 August 2008, in Colombo.

[59] Conversation with author on 26 July 2008, in Trincomalee.

[60] Conversation with author on 8 August 2008, in Colombo.

[61] Ibid.

[62] Conversation with author on 19 August 2008, in Colombo.

[63] Conversation with author on 19 August 2008, in Colombo.

[64] An International Eminent Persons Group led by senior judge was appointed in 2007 to observe investigations of high profile human rights violations in Sri Lanka, including the Muthur massacre of ACF personnel. It was disbanded due to lack of cooperation from GSL (Karunakharan, 2008).

[65] Conversation with author on 19 August 2008, in Colombo.

[66] Conversation with author on 8 August 2008, in Colombo.

[67] Conversation with author on 5 August 2008, in Colombo.

[68] Conversation with author on 8 August 2008, in Colombo.

[69] Conversation with author on 19 August 2008, in Colombo.

[70] Conversation with author on 27 July 2008, in Batticaloa.

[71] Conversation with author on 19 August 2008, in Colombo.

[72] For instances of humanitarians taking over government tasks and virtually ruling war-torn parts of Africa (Juma & Suhrke, 2003).

[73] In October 2007, the UN High Commissioner for Human Rights Louise Arbour upbraided GSL that 'people from across a broad political spectrum have expressed to me a lack of confidence and trust in the ability of existing relevant (government) institutions to adequately safeguard against the most serious human rights abuses' (UN, 2007).

[74] Conversation with author on 19 August 2008, in Colombo.

Chapter 5

[1] For detailed descriptions of the serious violations committed by both sides in the most recent war of late 2008 (PAHR, 2009).

[2] The MILF counts the military conflict of 2003 as another all-out war, but President Arroyo repudiated the label and instead termed it 'active defence' (Alanto, 2009; AAIW, 2003).

[3] For an example of this phenomenon (Panti, 2008).

[4] For an elaboration of how former Philippine president Gloria Arroyo attached herself as 'little sister' to 'big brother' George W Bush (Choudry, 2004).

[5] The concomitant annual increase in US military aid to GRP since 2001 is a whopping 551% (Padilla, 2006, p.132).

6 For the view that the Abu Sayyaf is a 'CIA creation' (Juan, 2007).

7 In late 2009, the Ampatuans' militias were implicated in a massive attack on rival Moro politicians and journalists that killed 57 persons in broad daylight. President Arroyo was then compelled by national outrage to finally crack down on the Ampatuan empire and terminate their pre-eminence through direct military action of the AFP.

8 Conversation with author on 29 September 2008, in Cotabato.

9 Conversation with author on 29 September 2008, in Cotabato

10 ECHO returned to Mindanao with grants for relief and civilian protection in October 2008 (ECHO, 2008).

11 Conversation with author on 24 September 2008, in Cotabato.

12 Conversation with author on 3 October 2008, in Cotabato.

13 Conversation with author on 3 October 2008, in Cotabato.

14 Conversation with author on 18 August 2006, in Quezon.

15 Conversation with author on 29 September 2008, in Cotabato.

16 Conversation with former GRP-UNDP Programme staff members on 7 August 2006, in Cotabato.

17 Conversation with volunteers of a human rights CSO on 29 June 2006, in Cotabato.

18 Conversations with Executive Director of a 'peace and development' NGO on 2 August 2006, in Jolo.

19 Conversation with author on September 27 September 2008, in Cotabato.

20 Ibid.

21 Conversation of author with an OXFAM employee on 29 September 2008, in Cotabato.

22 Conversation with author on 10 July 2006, in Pikit.

23 Conversation with author on 2 October 2008, in Manila.

24 Ibid.

25 Conversation of ICRC official with author on 22 June 2006, in Makati.

26 Ibid.

27 Conversation with author on 2 October 2008, in Manila.

28 Humanitarian jargon for 'Situation Report'.

29 Conversation with author on 10 October 2008, in Manila.

30 Conversation with author on 10 October 2008, in Manila.

31 Ibid.

32 Bantay Milikan, a women's watchdog organization, has been marginalised and kept on the AFP's watch list in western Mindanao because of its vociferous mass mobilisation against *Balikatan* (Chaulia, 2007).

33 Conversation with author on 10 October 2008, in Manila.

34 Conversation with author on 2 October 2008, in Manila.

35 Ibid.

36 Conversation with author on 2 October 2008, in Manila.

37 Conversation with author on 22 June 2006, in Makati.

38 Conversation with author on 2 October 2008, in Manila.

39 Conversation with author on 22 June 2006, in Makati.

[40] Conversations with a Mindanao-wide movement of local activists in June 2006 in Cotabato.

[41] Conversation with author on 2 October 2008, in Manila.

[42] Conversation with author on 10 October 2008, in Manila.

[43] Ibid.

[44] Ibid.

[45] Ibid.

[46] Ibid.

[47] Ibid.

[48] Ibid.

[49] Conversation with author on 30 September 2008, in Cotabato.

[50] Ibid.

[51] Ibid.

[52] Conversation with author on 30 September 2008, in Cotabato.

[53] Conversation with author on 30 September 2008, in Cotabato.

[54] On 15 September 2008, the EU 'expressed concern about the escalation of violence in Mindanao, and the growing number of civilian casualties and displaced persons. It particularly condemned the indiscriminate killing of civilians and called for those responsible to face the due process of law' (PIA, 2008).

[55] Conversation with author on 30 September 2008, in Cotabato.

[56] Conversation with author on 9 October 2008, in Manila.

[57] Conversation with author on 10 October 2008, in Manila.

[58] Conversations of UNICEF official with author in July 2006 in Cotabato.

[59] Conversation with author on 30 September 2008, in Cotabato.

[60] One multi-country analysis by sociologists rates both the Philippines and Sri Lanka as semi-peripheral states in the capitalist world-system (Kick, 2000, p.242).

Chapter 6

[1] Japan is the exclusive exception since it insists that recipient IOs concentrate only on development and relief distribution.

[2] Canada is a partial exception since it occasionally allows recipient IOs to work on protection and human rights while staying rooted under the canopy of 'peace and development'.

[3] The one partial exception was child conscription by the LTTE, which GSL wanted IOs to highlight, although it discouraged exposure of the same problem if the perpetrator was the TMVP.

[4] See Appendix for calculations.

[5] Conversation with author on 30 September 2008, in Cotabato.

[6] See Appendix.

[7] See Appendix.

[8] See Appendix.

[9] Conversation with author on 2 October 2008, in Manila.

[10] Cf. (PNRC, 2008) The PNRC Chairman is also an avid supporter of *Balikatan* and

a long-time crusader for retaining US military bases in the Philippines.
[11] See Appendix.

Chapter 7

[1] During the neo-neo debate of IR, neorealists intentionally chose hard core 'security' topics because they often vindicated their hypotheses, while neoliberal institutionalists intentionally chose 'international political economy' topics which supported their theories more (Baldwin, 1993, p.7).

[2] See Appendix.

[3] For an example from Africa (Chaulia, 2006).

[4] Dotted arrows leading singly (without combining) from Rationality or Culture to Humanitarian Behaviour are more likely to be relevant when the comparisons are temporal, but not always so. The curved arrows leading from Humanitarian Behaviour to Patriarchy and the Capitalist World-System signify a feedback loop, wherein IOs strengthen their own structural conditions by means of their actions in war zones which are in sync with the overall design of an iniquitous world order.

Chapter 8

[1] Conversation of a SCF employee with author on 28 September 2008, in Cotabato.

[2] A one-stop-shop liberal treatise defending the US invasion of Iraq on humanitarian grounds is contained in (Cushman, 2005) For the neo-con concept of Islamo-fascism (Podhoretz, 2007).

[3] All four armed conflicts that were under the ICC's investigations by mid-2009 were technically internal wars — Northern Uganda, Democratic Republic of Congo, Central African Republic and Western Sudan (Darfur).

[4] For an analysis of how humanitarian IOs boost the intelligence-gathering capacities of great powers and armed actors (Demars, 2001).

[5] For a critique of the neoliberal development agenda in the Global South (Craig & Porter, 2006).

[6] Conversations with author in 2003 and 2004 in Batticaloa.

BIBLIOGRAPHY

Institutional Sources

Abadi, D. (2007) *How OIC is Used to Perpetuate Philippine Colonialism in Mindanao and Malaysian Colonialism in Sabah,* Cotabato: Moro National Liberation Front.

ACT. (2008) *Action for Conflict Transformation (ACT) for Peace Programme,* Davao: Programme Management Office.

AI. (2008) *Shattered Peace in Mindanao: The Human Cost of Conflict in the Philippines,* London: Amnesty International.

Alanto, B. (2009) 'Remembering the 'Day of Treachery' and its Implications', *Luwaran,* 13 February.

Andrews, F. (2002) *The Philippine Insurrection (1899-1902): Development of the US Army's Counterinsurgency Policy,* Baton Rouge: Louisiana State University.

Annan, K. (2005) *Report of the Secretary-General on the Protection of Civilians in Armed Conflict,* New York: United Nations.

Asani, A. (1980) *Moros, Not Filipinos,* Manila: MNLF Secretariat.

ASCEND. (2008) *Assistance for the Comprehensive Education Development of Mindanao (ASCEND Mindanao),* Manila: US Agency for International Development.

Barnaby, W & Paul, H. (2005) *Managing the Risks of Corruption in Humanitarian Relief Operations,* London: Overseas Development Institute.

Butts, K. & Turner, C. (2004) *Trilateral Strategic Defence Capability Planning Symposium,* Carlisle Barracks: US Army War College.

Cagoco-Guiam. (2002) *Child Soldiers in Central and Western Mindanao: A Rapid Assessment,* Geneva: International Labour Organization.

Camacho, A. (2004) *Issues and Recommendations on Child Soldiers in the Philippines,* Quezon: University of Philippines.

Carames, A et al. (2007) *DDR Processes in the Philippines (Mindanao-MNLF),* Barcelona: School for a Culture of Peace.

Chimni B. (2000) 'Globalisation, Humanitarianism and the Erosion of Refugee Protection', Oxford: Refugee Studies Centre, Working Paper 3.

CIDA. (2006) *Canada's Development Partnership with Mindanao,* Manila: Canadian International Development Agency.

CSUCS. (2008) *Child Soldiers Global Report: Philippines*, London: Coalition to Stop the Use of Child Soldiers.

Danida. (1999) *Evaluation of Danish Humanitarian Assistance Volume 6: Great Lakes*, Copenhagen: Ministry of Foreign Affairs.

Darcy, J. (1997) *Human Rights and International Legal Standards. What Do Relief Workers Needs to Know?*, London: Overseas Development Institute.

Donini, A & Niland, N. (1996) *The Rise and Fall of Humanitarianism*, Helsinki: United Nations University.

DOS. (2007) *Extrajudicial Killings in the Philippines: Strategies to End the Violence*, Washington, D.C.: US Department of State, 14 March.

DOS. (2009) *President Authorises $20.3 Million Emergency Assistance for Gaza*, Washington, D.C.: United States Department of State, 30 January.

ECHO. (2008) *When the Mindanao Conflict Comes Back into the Spotlight*, Brussels: European Commission's Humanitarian Aid Office.

EU. (2008a) *Declaration of the Presidency on Behalf of the European Union Concerning the Situation in Mindanao*, Brussels: Council of the European Union, 15 September.

EU. (2008b) *European Commission Provides € 1.0 Million to Help Promote Dialogue and Confidence-Building in Mindanao*, Manila: Delegation of the European Commission to the Philippines.

FIC. (2007) *Humanitarian Agenda 2015. Sri Lanka Country Study*, Medford: Feinstein International Centre.

FIC. (2009) 'Norwegian Government: Unacceptable Suffering Among Civilians in Sri Lanka', Oslo: Government of Norway, 27 January, GN.

GOC. (2005) *The Activities of the Canadian Mining Company TVI Pacific Inc. in the Philippines*, Ottawa: House of Commons.

GRP. (2003) 'Ople Lauds Malaysian Role in Mindanao Peace Initiatives', Malacañang: Manila, 24 February.

GRP. (2008a) *RDCC-ARMM TMG Meets with UN Team*, Manila: Philippines Information Agency.

GRP. (2008b) *RP-US 'Balikatan 2008' Emphasises Humanitarian Assistance*, 4 February, Manila: Republic of the Philippines.

GRP. (2008c) *Army to Conduct SALAAM Training in Iligan*, 13 November, Manila: Philippine Information Agency.

GSL. (2000) *India Will Take the Lead to Support*, Colombo: Government of Sri Lanka.

GSL. (2009a) *Akashi Commends Government's Success in War Against Terrorism*, Geneva: Permanent Mission of the Republic of Sri Lanka.

GSL. (2009b) Sri Lankan Ambassador Calls for End to Use of Child Soldiers. [Online], Available: *http://www.slembassyusa.org/press_releases/winter_2008/sl_ambassador_calls_27feb09.html* [7 March 2009]

Honig, J. (2008) *Course Description for 'Contemporary War and the Liberal Conscience'*, Stockholm: Swedish National Defence College.

ICG. (2008) *Sri Lanka's Eastern Province: Land, Development, Conflict*, London: International Crisis Group.

ICRC. (2002) *Discover the ICRC*, Geneva: International Committee of the Red Cross.

ICRC. (2005a) 'Philippines: ICRC Urges Respect for Humanitarian Law', Geneva: International Committee of the Red Cross, 12 February.

ICRC. (2005b) *Humanity in the Midst of Conflict*, Makati: International Committee of the Red Cross.

ICRC. (2008c) 'ICRC Continues Humanitarian Work in LTTE-Controlled Area', Geneva: International Committee of the Red Cross.

ICRC. (2008d) *ICRC Deplores Misleading Public Use of its Confidential Findings on Disappearances*, Colombo: International Committee of the Red Cross.

ICRC. (2008e) *The ICRC in Sri Lanka*, Geneva: International Committee of the Red Cross.

IDRC. (2001) *The Responsibility to Protect. Report of the International Commission on Intervention and State Sovereignty*, Ottawa: International Development Research Centre.

Jacobsen, K. (1999) 'A Safety First Approach to Physical Protection in Refugee Camps', Cambridge: Inter-University Committee on International Migration, Working Paper 4.

Johnson, B. (1990) *Japanese Foreign Aid: Defining America's Interests*, Washington, D.C.: The Heritage Foundation.

Kenny, K. (2000) 'When Needs are Rights: An Overview of UN Efforts to Integrate Human Rights in Humanitarian Action', Providence: Thomas J. Watson Institute for International Studies, Occasional Paper 38.

Lohman, W. (2009) *Spratly Islands: The Challenge to US Leadership in the South China Sea*, Washington, D.C.: The Heritage Foundation.

LST. (2008a) *Civil Society Solidarity with International Humanitarian Organizations*, Colombo: Law and Society Trust.

LST. (2008b) *Afraid Even to Say the Word: Elections in Batticaloa District*, Colombo: Law and Society Trust.

MERN. (2003) *Principles of Conduct for Non-Government Humanitarian Agencies in Mindanao*, Davao: Mindanao Emergency Response Network.

MILF. (2008) 'MILF: Filipino Oligarchs Sabotage Peace Deal', *Luwaran*, 17 October.

Minear, L. (1999) 'Partnerships in Protection. An Overview of Emerging Issues and Work in Progress', Boston: Humanitarianism and War Project, Independent Background Paper.

NDCC. (2008) *Guidelines in the Coordination of the Delivery of Humanitarian Services to Disaster Victims and Internally Displaced Persons*, Quezon: National Disaster Coordinating Council.

OECD. (2006) *Whole of Government Approaches to Fragile States*, Paris: Organization for Economic Cooperation and Development.

OWT. (2008) *The 2008 Global Accountability Report*, London: One World Trust.

OXFAM. (2003) *OXFAM's Work in Philippines in Depth*, Oxford: OXFAM.

OXFAM. (2006) *OXFAM's Work in Sri Lanka in Depth*, Colombo: OXFAM.

OXFAM. (2008) 'Protect Civilians from Deprivation and Harm', *Quezon: OXFAM-GB*, 11 August.

Padilla, A. (2006) *Aid and Conflict: The Philippine Case*, Quezon: The Reality of Aid.

PAHR. (2009) *Mindanao Fact Finding Mission: Unraveling Stories of Human Rights Violations,* Manila: Philippine Alliance of Human Rights Advocates.

Pandith, S.(2002) 'Japan- Lanka's Friend in Need' *Colombo: Government of Sri Lanka,* 19 February.

PDF. (2008) 'Working Group on Millennium Development Goals and Social Progress', Manila: Philippines Development Forum, Annex 1

PIA. (2008) *European Union Heads of Mission Visit Mindanao,* Manila: Philippine Information Agency.

PNRC. (2008) *Gordon Condemns Lanao Killings as Acts of Inhumanity,* Manila: Philippine National Red Cross.

Rabasa, A. (2001) *Southeast Asia After 9/11: Regional Trends and US Interests,* Santa Monica: RAND Corporation.

Ramsey, R. (2007) *Savage Wars of Peace: Case Studies of Pacification in the Philippines, 1900-1902,* Fort Leavenworth: Combat Studies Institute.

Riehl, V. (2001) 'Who is Ruling South Sudan? The Role of NGOs in Rebuilding Socio-Political Order', Uppsala: Nordic Africa Institute, Report No.9.

Rona, G. (2004) *The ICRC's Status: In a Class of its Own,* Geneva: International Committee of the Red Cross.

Sabasinghe, D. (1985) *Now, a Sri Lankan Free Market Economic Miracle,* Washington, D.C.: The Heritage Foundation.

Santos, S. (2002)'The Recent MILF Agreements, Belligerency Status, International Law and the Philippine Constitution', *Kalilintad.*

Save. (2004) *Provincial Reconstruction Teams and Humanitarian-Military Relations in Afghanistan,* London: Save the Children.

Save. (2006) *Save the Children in Sri Lanka Concerned about Increased Violence and Killing of Children,* Colombo: Save the Children in Sri Lanka, 16 June.

Save. (2007) 'Save the Children in Sri Lanka Refutes Providing Funds to the LTTE', *Colombo: Save the Children in Sri Lanka,* 1 November.

Save. (2008a) *Where We Are: Sri Lanka,* London: Save the Children.

Save. (2008b) 'Save the Children Instructed to Withdraw from Tamil Tiger's Stronghold in Sri Lanka', *Colombo: Save the Children in Sri Lanka,* 1 October.

SCF. (2004) *Philippines Country Brief.* London: Save the Children.

Schenkenberg, E. (1997) *No Longer an Option But a Necessity: Cooperation Between Humanitarian and Human Rights Organizations,* London: Overseas Development Institute.

TRO. (2008) *Tsunami Projects in Northeast of Sri Lanka- A Review on 3rd Anniversary,* Killinochchi: Tamils Rehabilitation Organization.

UKG. (2009) *Strategic Programme Fund,* Manila: The British Embassy in the Philippines.

UN. (1945a) *Charter of the United Nations,* New York: United Nations.

UN. (1995b) *Statement on the Role and Functioning of the Resident Coordinator System,* Geneva: United Nations.

UN. (2001) 'UN Employees Investigated for Accepting Bribes', *UN Wire,* 20 February.

UN. (2004) *UNDAF in the Philippines,* Manila: United Nations Country Team.

UN. (2007) 'UN, Sri Lanka Should Cooperate on Human Rights, High Commissioner Says', *UN News Centre*, 15 October.

UN. (2008) 'Report of the Secretary-General on Children and Armed Conflict in the Philippines', New York: United Nations.

UNDP. (1998) *Integrating Human Rights with Sustainable Human Development*, New York: UN Development Programme.

UNDP. (2007a) *UNDP and Civil Society in Sri Lanka: Partnerships in Crisis Situations*, Colombo: UN Development Programme.

UNDP. (2008a) *UNDP in Sri Lanka*, Colombo: UN Development Programme.

UNDP. (2006a) *Development Support Services Centre*, Makati: UN Development Programme.

UNDP. (2006b) *Protecting and Promoting the Universal Values of Human Rights and Rule of Law*, New York: UN Development Programme.

UNDP. (2007b) *UNDP Country Programme, Sri Lanka (2008-2012)*, Colombo: UN Development Programme.

UNDP. (2008b) *Letter to Centre for Ethnic Studies*, Colombo: UN Development Programme.

UNDP. (2008c) *UNDP Philippines Country Office*, Makati: UN Development Programme.

UNICEF. (2007) *History of UNICEF in Sri Lanka*, Colombo: UN Children's Fund.

UNICEF. (2008) *Fact Sheet. Action Plan for Children Affected by War*, Colombo: UN Children's Fund.

UNOCHA. (2008) *Donor Response to 2007 Common Humanitarian Action Plan*, Colombo: UN Office for the Coordination of Humanitarian Affairs.

USAID. (2004) *US Foreign Aid: Meeting the Challenges of the Twenty-First Century*, Washington, DC: USAID.

USAID. (2006) *USAID/Philippines Operational Plan*, Silver Spring: US Agency for International Development.

USAID. (2008) *USAID and Save the Children Extend Programme to Improve Protection of Children in Eastern Sri Lanka*, Colombo: US Agency for International Development.

USAID. (2009) *Innovative USAID Programmes in ARMM*, Manila: US Agency for International Development.

USG. (2003) 'US, Philippines Strong Allies in War against Terrorism,' *Manila: Embassy of the United States of America*, 20 May.

USG. (2006) *Securing Peace in Mindanao through Diplomacy, Development and Defence*, Manila: Embassy of the United States of America, August.

UTHR. (2008) 'Unfinished Business of the Five Students and ACF Cases- A Time to Call the Bluff', *Jaffna: University Teachers for Human Rights*, 1 April.

Waduge, S. (2008)'What Have the LTTE's NGO/INGO Friends Been Doing in Sri Lanka?', *Colombo: Ministry of Defence*, 10 April.

Walkup, M. (1997) *Policy and Behaviour in Humanitarian Organizations: The Institutional Origins of Operational Dysfunction*, Gainesville: University of Florida, Unpublished Dissertation.

Wijesinha, R. (2009) *The Naïveté of the ICRC in Geneva*, Colombo: Ministry of Defence

Books

Aaron, R. (1954) *The Century of Total War,* London: Derek Verschoyle.

Amin, S. (1997) *Capitalism in the Age of Globalisation: The Management of Contemporary Society,* London: Zed Books.

Amoroso, D. (2003) 'Inheriting the 'Moro Problem': Muslim Authority and Colonial Rule in British Malay and the Philippines', in Go, J & Foster, A. (eds.) *The American Colonial State in the Philippines: Global Perspectives,* Durham: Duke University Press.

Anderson, M. (1999) *Do No Harm: How Aid can Support Peace- or War,* Boulder: Lynne Rienner.

Arendt, H. (1963) *Eichmann in Jerusalem: A Report on the Banality of Evil,* New York: Penguin.

Bacani, B. (2004) *Beyond Paper Autonomy. The Challenge in Southern Philippines,* Cotabato: Centre for Autonomy and Governance.

Baldwin, D. (ed.) (1993) *Neorealism and Neoliberalism: The Contemporary Debate,* New York: Columbia University Press.

Barkun, M. (1968) *Law Without Sanctions: Order in Primitive Societies and the World Community,* New Haven: Yale University Press.

Barnett, M. (2002) *Eyewitness to a Genocide: The United Nations and Rwanda,* Ithaca: Cornell University Press.

Barnett, M. & Finnemore, M. (2004) *Rules for the World. International Organizations in Global Politics,* Ithaca: Cornell University Press.

Bass, G. (2008) *Freedom's Battle: The Origins of Humanitarian Intervention,* New York: Alfred Knopf.

Becker, G. (1978) *The Economic Approach to Human Behaviour,* Chicago: University of Chicago Press.

Bentham, J. (1995) *The Panopticon Writings,* London: Verso.

Berman, S. (1998) *The Social Democratic Moment: Ideas and Politics in the Making of Interwar Europe,* Cambridge: Harvard University Press.

Birtle, A. (1998) *US Army Counterinsurgency & Contingency Operations Doctrine: 1860-1941,* Darby: Diane Publishing Company.

Blight, J. & Lang, J. (2005) *The Fog of War: Lessons from the Life of Robert S McNamara,* Lanham: Rowman and Littlefield.

Bob, C.(2005) *The Marketing of Rebellion: Insurgents, Media and International Activism,* Cambridge: Cambridge University Press.

Boli, J.& Thomas, G. (eds.) (1999) *Constructing World Culture: International Nongovernmental Organizations Since 1875,* Stanford: Stanford University Press.

Boggs, C. (1976) *Gramsci's Marxism,* London: Pluto Press.

Boot, M. (2003) *The Savage Wars of Peace: Small Wars and the Rise of American Power,* New York: Basic Books.

Brabant, K. (1997) *The Coordination of Humanitarian Action: The Case of Sri Lanka,* London: Overseas Development Institute.

Bricmont, J. (2006) *Humanitarian Imperialism: Using Human Rights to Sell War,* New York: Monthly Review Press.

Carpenter, C. (2006) *Innocent Women and Children: Gender, Norms and the Protection of Civilians*, Farnham: Ashgate Publishing.

Carr, E. (1939) *The Twenty Years' Crisis 1919-1939: An Introduction to the Study of International Relations*, London: MacMillan.

Chester, E. (1995) *Covert Network: Progressives, the International Rescue Committee, and the CIA*, Armonk: M.E.Sharpe.

Clarance, W. (2006) *Ethnic Warfare in Sri Lanka and the UN Crisis*, London: Pluto Press.

Claborne, C. (ed.) (1997) *The Papers of Martin Luther King, Jr.: Birth of a New Age*, Berkeley: University of California Press.

Cohen, S. (2001) *India: Emerging Power*, Washington, D.C.: Brookings Institution Press.

Coley, A. (2008) *Logics of Hierarchy: The Organization of Empires, States, and Military Occupations*, Ithaca: Cornell University Press.

Craig, D. & Porter, D. (2006) *Development Beyond Neoliberalism? Governance, Poverty Reduction and Political Economy*, London: Routledge.

Crozier, M. (1964) *The Bureaucratic Phenomenon*, London: Tavistock Publications.

Cushan, T. (ed.) (2005) *A Matter of Principle: Humanitarian Arguments for War in Iraq*, Berkeley: University of California Press.

Dai, X. (2007) *International Institutions and National Policies*, Cambridge: Cambridge University Press.

Daley, P. (2008) *Gender & Genocide in Burundi: The Search for Spaces of Peace in the Great Lakes Region*, Bloomington: Indiana University Press.

Davis, M. et al (eds.) *International Intervention in the Post-Cold War World: Moral Responsibility and Power Politics*, Armonk: M.E.Sharpe.

DiPrizio, R. (2002) *Armed Humanitarians: U.S. Interventions from Northern Iraq to Kosovo*, Baltimore: Johns Hopkins University Press.

Dogan, M. & Pelassy, D. (1990) *How to Compare Nations: Strategies in Comparative Politics*, Chatham: Chatham House.

Donini, A. (2008) 'Through a Glass, Darkly. Humanitarianism and Empire', in Gunewardena, N & Schuller, M. (eds.) *Capitalising on Catastrophe. Neoliberal Strategies on Disaster Reduction*, Lanham: Altamira Press.

Downes, A. (2008) *Targeting Civilians in War*, Ithaca: Cornell University Press.

Dowding, K. (1996) *Power (Concepts in Social Thought)*, Minneapolis: University of Minnesota Press.

Doyle, M. (1997) *Ways of War and Peace: Realism, Liberalism and Socialism*, New York: W. W. Norton.

Enloe, C. (1998) 'All the Men Are in the Militias, All the Women Are Victims: The Politics of Masculinity and Femininity in Nationalist Wars', in Lorentzen, L & Turpin, J. (eds.) *The Women and War Reader*, New York: New York University Press.

Easton, D. (1990) *The Analysis of Political Structure*, London: Routledge.

Fawcett, J. (2003) *Stress and Trauma Handbook: Strategies for Flourishing in Demanding Environments*, California: World Vision International.

Fearon, J. & Wendt, A. (2003) 'Rationalism v. Constructivism: A Sceptical View', in Carslnaes, W.et al (eds.) *Handbook of International Relations*, London: Thousand Oaks.

Finnemore, M. (1996) *National Interests in International Society*, Ithaca: Cornell University Press.

Finnemore, M. (2003) *The Purpose of Intervention: Changing Beliefs about the Use of Force*, Ithaca: Cornell University Press.

Foley, C. (2008) *The Thin Blue Line: How Humanitarianism Went to War*, New York: Verso Books.

Forsythe, D. (2005) *The Humanitarians: The International Committee of the Red Cross*, Cambridge: Cambridge University Press.

Foucault, M. (1995) *Discipline and Punish: The Birth of the Prison*, New York: Vintage.

Frohardt, M. et al. (1999) *Protecting Human Rights: The Challenge to Humanitarian Organizations*, Providence: Thomas J. Watson Jr. Institute for International Studies.

Fukuyama, F. (1993) *The End of History and the Last Man*, New York: Harper Perennial.

Garret, G. & Weingast, B. (1993) 'Ideas, Interests, and Institutions: Constructing the European Community's Internal Market', in Goldstein, J. & Keohane, R. (eds.) *Ideas and Foreign Policy: Beliefs, Institutions and Political Change*, Ithaca: Cornell University Press.

Geertz, C. (1973) *The Interpretation of Culture*, New York: Basic Books.

Gerge, A. (1979) 'Case Studies and Theory Development: The Method of Structured, Focused Comparison', in Lauren, P. (ed.) *Diplomacy: New Approaches in History, Theory and Policy*, New York: Free Press.

Green, D. & Shapiro, I. (1994) *Pathologies of Rational Choice Theory: A Critique of Applications in Political Science*, New Haven: Yale University Press.

Grieco, J. (1990) *Cooperation Among Nations: Europe, America and Non-Tariff Barriers to Trade*, Ithaca: Cornell University Press.

Goti, J. (1996) *Game Without End: State Terror and the Politics of Justice*, Oxford: Oxford University Press.

Gramsci, A. (1992) *Prison Notebooks*, New York: Columbia University Press.

Gramsci, A. (1971) *State and Civil Society*, New York: International Publishers.

Gunaratna, R. (1993) *Indian Intervention in Sri Lanka: The Role of India's Intelligence Agencies*, Colombo: South Asian Network on Conflict Research.

Gurr, T. (2000) *People Versus States: Minorities at Risk in the New Century*, Washington D.C.: United States Institute of Peace Press.

Hancock, G. (1997) *Lords of Poverty: The Power, Prestige and Corruption of the International Aid Business*, New York: The Atlantic Monthly Press.

Harvey, D. (1996) *Justice, Nature and the Geography of Difference*, Oxford: Blackwell.

Hay, C. (2006) 'Political Ontology', in Goodin, R. & Tilly, C. (eds.) *The Oxford Handbook of Contextual Political Analysis*, Oxford: Oxford University Press.

Hayter, T. (1971) *Aid as Imperialism*, Gretna: Pelican Publishing.

Hehir, A. (2008) *Humanitarian Interventions After Kosovo: Iraq, Darfur and the Record of Global Civil Society*, New York: Palgrave Macmillan.

Hilley, J. (2001) *Malaysia: Mahathirism, Hegemony and the New Opposition*, New York: Zed Books.

Howard, M. (1978) *War and the Liberal Conscience*, New Brunswick: Rutgers University Press.

Hume, D. (1999) *Enquiry Concerning Human Understanding*, Oxford: Oxford University Press.

Hyndman, J. (2000) *Managing Displacement: Refugees and the Politics of Humanitarianism*, Minneapolis: University of Minnesota Press.

Ignatieff, M. (1995) *Blood and Belonging: Journeys into the New Nationalism*, New York: Farrar, Straus and Giroux.

Ignatieff, M. (2005) *The Lesser Evil: Political Ethics in an Age of Terror*, Princeton: Princeton University Press.

Jacobson, H. (1984) *Networks of Interdependence: International Organizations and the Global Political System*, New York: Alfred Knopf.

Juan, S. (2007) *US Imperialism and Revolution in the Philippines*, New York: Palgrave Macmillan.

Juma, M. & Suhrke, A. (eds.) (2003) *Eroding Local Capacity. International Humanitarian Action in Africa*, Uppsala: Nordic Africa Institute

Kennedy, D. (2005) *The Dark Sides of Virtue: Reassessing International Humanitarianism*, Princeton: Princeton University Press.

Keohane, R. & Nye, J. (1977) *Power and Interdependence: World Politics in Transition*, Boston: Little, Brown & Company.

Keohane, R. (1984) *After Hegemony: Cooperation and Discord in the World Political Economy*, Princeton: Princeton University Press.

Keohane, R. (1989) *International Institutions and State Power: Essays in International Relations Theory*, Boulder: Westview.

Keohane, R. (1993) 'Institutional Theory and the Realist Challenge After the Cold War', in Baldwin, D. (ed.) *Neorealism and Neoliberalism: The Contemporary Debate*, New York: Columbia University Press.

Kier, E. (1999) *Imagining War: French and British Military Doctrine Between the Wars,* Princeton: Princeton University Press.

King, G. et al (1994) *Designing Social Inquiry: Scientific Inference in Qualitative Research*, Princeton: Princeton University Press.

Kinsella, H. (2005) 'Securing the Civilian: Sex and Gender in the Laws of War', in Barnett, M. & Duvall, R. (eds.) *Power in Global Governance*. Cambridge: Cambridge University Press.

Klein, N. (2007) *The Shock Doctrine: The Rise of Disaster Capitalism*, New York: Metropolitan Books.

Knorr, K. & Rosenau, J. (eds.) (1969) *Contending Approaches to International Politics*, Princeton: Princeton University Press.

Kochler, H. (2003) *Global Justice of Global Revenge? International Criminal Justice at the Crossroads*, Springer: New York.

Kouchner, B. & Bettati, M. (1987) *The Duty of Interference: Can We Leave Them to Die?,* Paris: Denoël.

Kuhn, T. (1962) *The Structure of Scientific Revolutions*, Chicago: University of Chicago Press.

Kumar, S. & Whitefield, F. (2007) *Visionaries: The 20th Century's 100 Most Inspirational Leaders*, White River Junction: Chelsea Green Publishing.

Laitin, D. (1986) *Hegemony and Culture: Politics and Religious Change among the Yoruba*, Chicago: University of Chicago Press.

Lakatos, I. (1970) 'Falsification and the Methodology of Scientific Research Programmes', in Worrall, J. & Currie, G. (eds.) *The Methodology of Scientific Research Programmes*, Cambridge: Cambridge University Press.

Lindlof, T. (2008) 'Idiographic vs. Nomothetic Science', in Donsbach, W. (ed.) *The International Encyclopaedia of Communication*, Oxford: Blackwell.

Liyanage, S. (2008) *One Step at a Time: Reflections on the Peace Process in Sri Lanka, 2001-2005*, Colombo: South Asia Peace Institute.

Loescher, G. (2001) *The UNHCR and World Politics: A Perilous Path*, Oxford: Oxford University Press.

Ludendorff, E. (1943) 'The German Concept of Total War', in Earle, E. (ed.) *Makers of Modern Strategy: Military Thought from Machiavelli to Hitler*, Princeton: Princeton University Press.

Mahony, L. (2006) *Proactive Presence. Field Strategies for Civilian Protection*, Geneva: Centre for Humanitarian Dialogue.

Maren, M. (1997) *The Road to Hell: The Ravaging Effects of Foreign Aid and International Charity*, New York: Free Press.

March, J. & Olsen, J. (1989) *Rediscovering Institutions: The Organizational Basis of Politics*, New York: Free Press.

McGlynn, F. & Tuden, A. (eds.) (1991) *Anthropological Approaches to Political Behaviour*, Pittsburgh: University of Pittsburgh Press.

McKenna, T. (1997) 'Appreciating Islam in the Muslim Philippines. Authority, Experience and Identity in Cotabato', in Hefner, R. & Horvatich, P. (eds.) *Islam in an Era of Nation-States: Politics and Religious Renewal in Muslim Southeast Asia*, Honolulu: University of Hawaii Press.

Mercado, E. (2000) 'Peace and Development. The MNLF and the SPCPD Experience', in Gutierrez, E. (ed.) *Rebels, Warlords and Ulama: A Reader on Muslim Separatism and the War in Southern Philippines*, Quezon: Institute for Popular Democracy.

Mertus, J. (2004) *Bait and Switch: Human Rights and US Foreign Policy*, New York: Routledge.

Mill, J. (2002) *A System of Logic: Ratiocinative and Inductive*, Honolulu: University Press of the Pacific.

Milner, H. (2006) 'Why Multilateralism? Foreign Aid and Domestic Principal-Agent Problems', in Hawkins, D. et al (eds.) *Delegation and Agency in International Organizations*, Cambridge: Cambridge University Press.

Morgenthau, H. (1946) *Scientific Man vs. Power Politics*, Chicago: University of Chicago Press.

North, D. (1990) *Institutions, Institutional Change and Economic Performance*, Cambridge: Cambridge University Press.

Okumu, W. (2003) 'Humanitarian International NGOs and African Conflicts', in Carey, H. & Richmond, O. (eds.) *Mitigating Conflict: The Role of NGOs*, London: Routledge.

Orford, A. (2003) *Reading Humanitarian Intervention: Human Rights and the Use of Force in International Law*, Cambridge: Cambridge University Press.

Parakrama, A. (2001) 'Means Without End: Emergency Humanitarian Assistance in Sri Lanka', in Smillie, I. (ed.) *Patronage or Partnership. Local Capacity Building in Humanitarian Crises*, Sterling: Stylus Publishing.

Parsons, T. (1969) *Politics and Social Structure*, New York: Free Press.

Podhoretz, N. (2007) *World War IV: The Long Struggle Against Islamofascism*, New York: Doubleday.

Popkin, S. (1979) *The Rational Peasant: The Political Economy of Rural Society in Vietnam*, Berkeley: University of California Press

Pouligny, B. (2006) *Peace Operations Seen from Below: UN Missions and Local People*, Sterling: Stylus Publishing.

Quitoriano, E. & Francisco, T. (2004) *Their War, Our Struggle: Stories of Children in Central Mindanao*, Quezon: Save the Children UK.

Ragin, C. (1989) *The Comparative Method: Moving Beyond Qualitative and Quantitative Strategies*, Berkeley: University of California Press.

Rieff, D. (2003) *A Bed for the Night: Humanitarianism in Crisis*, New York: Simon & Schuster.

Risse-Kappen, T. (ed.) (1995) *Bringing Transnational Relations Back In: Non-State Actors, Domestic Structures and International Institutions*, Cambridge: Cambridge University Press.

Rittberger, V. (1973) *Evolution and International Organization: Toward a New Level of Sociopolitical Integration*, The Hague: Martinus Nijhoff.

Roberts, A. (1996) *Humanitarian Action in War: Aid, Protection and Impartiality in a Policy Vacuum*, London: Oxford University Press.

Roberts, D. (2002) *The Social Conscience of the Early Victorians*, Stanford: Stanford University Press.

Robinson, W. (2004) *A Theory of Global Capitalism: Production, Class and State in a Transnational World*, Baltimore: Johns Hopkins University Press.

Rodil, R. (1994) *The Minoritisation of the Indigenous Communities of Mindanao and the Sulu Archipelago*, Davao: Alternate Forum for Research in Mindanao.

Rupert, M. & Smith, H. (eds.) (2002) *Historical Materialism and Globalisation: Essays on Continuity and Change*, London: Routledge.

Rutherford, K. (2008) *Humanitarianism Under Fire: The US and UN Intervention in Somalia*, Sterling: Kumarian Press.

Santos, S. (1999) 'Islamic Diplomacy: Consultation and Consensus', in Stankovtich, M. (ed.) *Compromising on Autonomy: Mindanao in Transition*, London: Conciliation Resources.

Scahill, J. (2007) *Blackwater: The Rise of the World's Most Powerful Mercenary Army*, New York: Nation Books.

Schmidt, B. (2003) 'On the History and Historiography of International Relations', in Carslnaes, W. et al (eds.) *Handbook of International Relations*, London: Thousand Oaks.

Seneviratne, H. (1999) *The Work of Kings: The New Buddhism in Sri Lanka*, Chicago: University of Chicago Press.

Seymour, R. (2008) *The Liberal Defence of Murder,* New York: Verso Books.

Singer, P. (2006) *Children at War,* Berkeley: University of California Press.

Slim, H. & Mancini-Griffoli, D. (2008) *Interpreting Violence. Anti-Civilian Thinking and Practice and How to Argue Against it More Effectively,* Geneva: Centre for Humanitarian Dialogue.

Simmons, B. & Martin, L. (2003) 'International Organizations and Institutions', in Carslnaes, W. et al (eds.) *Handbook of International Relations,* London: Thousand Oaks.

Snyder, J. (2008) *Realism, Refugees and Strategies of Humanitarianism,* Oxford: Refugee Studies Centre.

Spillmann, K. et al (eds.) (2001) *Peace Support Operations: Lessons Learned and Future Perspectives,* New York: Peter Lang Publishing.

Stoessinger, J. (1973) *The United Nations and the Superpowers: China, Russia & America,* New York: Random House.

Subramanian, N. (2005) *Sri Lanka: Voices From a War Zone,* New Delhi: Penguin India.

Swamy, N. (1994) *Tigers of Lanka: From Boys to Guerrillas,* New Delhi: Konark Publishers.

Swamy, N. (2003) *Inside an Elusive Mind. Prabhakaran –The First Profile of the World's Most Ruthless Guerrilla Leader,* New Delhi: Konark Publishers.

Taleb, N. (2007) *The Black Swan: The Impact of the Highly Improbable,* New York: Random House.

Tambiah, S. (1992) *Buddhism Betrayed? Religion, Politics and Violence in Sri Lanka,* Chicago: University of Chicago Press.

Terry, F. (2002) *Condemned to Repeat? The Paradox of Humanitarian Action,* Ithaca: Cornell University Press.

Thommessen, B. (2003) 'Niccolo Machiavelli, The Prince (1513): Politics as the Pursuit of Power', in Gracia, J. et al (eds.) (2003) *The Classics of Western Philosophy,* Oxford: Blackwell.

Walby, S. (1990) *Theorising Patriarchy,* Oxford: Blackwell.

Walker, P. & Maxwell, D. (2009) *Shaping the Humanitarian World,* London: Routledge.

Wallerstein, I. (1990) *Transforming the Revolution: Social Movements and the World-System,* New York: Monthly Review Press.

Wallerstein, I. (1991) *Geopolitics and Geoculture. Essays on the Changing World-System,* Cambridge: Cambridge University Press.

Waltz, K. (1979) *Theory of International Politics,* Reading: Addison-Wesley.

Weaver, O. (1996) 'The Rise and Fall of the Inter-Paradigm Debate', in Smith, S. et al (eds.) *International Theory: Positivism and Beyond,* Cambridge: Cambridge University Press.

Weiss, T. (2007) 'Foreword' in Forsythe D. & Rieffer-Flanagan, B. *The International Committee of the Red Cross: A Neutral Humanitarian Actor,* London: Routledge.

White, L. (1998) *Political Analysis: Technique and Practice,* Boston: Wadsworth Publishing.

Yiftachel, O. (2006) *Ethnocracy: Land and Identity Politics in Israel/Palestine,* Philadelphia: University of Pennsylvania Press.

Journal Articles

Allison, G. (1969) 'Conceptual Models and the Cuban Missile Crisis', *American Political Science Review*, Volume 63, Number 3.

Ashworth, J. (1987) 'The Relationship Between Capitalism and Humanitarianism', *American Historical Review*, Volume 92, Number 4.

Best, G. (1999) 'Peace Conferences and the Century of Total War: The 1899 Hague Conference and What Came After', *International Affairs*, Volume 75, Number 3.

Bristol, N. (2006) 'Military Incursions into Aid Work Anger Humanitarian Groups', *The Lancet*, Volume 367, Number 9508.

Chaulia, S. (2006) 'Angola: Empire of the Humanitarians', *Journal of Humanitarian Assistance*, July.

Chaulia, S. (2007) 'International Organizations in Mindanao: To Protect or Not?', *Journal of Humanitarian Assistance*, February.

Chase-Dunn, C. & Grimes, P. (1995) 'World-Systems Analysis', *Annual Review of Sociology*, Volume 21.

Cooley, A. & Ron, J. (2002) 'The NGO Scramble: Organizational Insecurity and the Political Economy of Transnational Action', *International Security*, Volume 27, Number 1.

Cox, R. (1981) 'Social forces, States and World Order: Beyond International Relations Theory', *Millennium: Journal of International Studies*, Volume 10, Number 2.

DeMars, W. (2001) 'Hazardous Partnership: NGOs and United States Intelligence in Small Wars', *International Journal of Intelligence and Counter-Intelligence*, Volume 14, Number 2.

Desch, M. (1998) 'Culture Clash: Assessing the Importance of Ideas in Security Studies', *International Security*, Volume 23, Number 1.

Elkins, D. & Simeon, R. (1979) 'A Cause in Search of its Effect, or What Does Political Culture Explain?', *Comparative Politics*, Volume 11, Number 2.

Eriksson, M. & Wallensteen, P. (2004) 'Armed Conflict, 1989-2003', *Journal of Peace Research*, Volume 41, Number 5.

Fearon, J. (1991) 'Counterfactuals and Hypothesis Testing in Political Science', *World Politics*, Volume 43, Number 2.

Gordon, S. (2004) 'Military-Humanitarian Relationships and the Invasion of Iraq (2003): Reforging Certainties?', *Journal of Humanitarian Assistance*, July.

Greenaway, S. (2000) 'Post-Modern Conflict and Humanitarian Action: Questioning the Paradigm', *Journal of Humanitarian Assistance*, January.

Hopf, T. (1998) 'The Promise of Constructivism in International Relations Theory', *International Security*, Volume 23, Number 1.

Hultman, L. (2007) 'Battle Losses and Rebel Violence: Raising the Costs for Fighting', *Terrorism and Political Violence*, Volume 19, Number 2.

Huysmans, J. (2002) 'Shape-Shifting NATO: Humanitarian Action and the Kosovo Refugee Crisis', *Review of International Studies*, Volume 28, Number 3.

Hyndman, J. (2004) 'Mind the Gap: Bridging Feminist and Political Geography Through Geopolitics', *Political Geography*, Volume 23, Number 3.

Irwin, D. & Kroszner, R. (1999) 'Interests, Institutions, and Ideology in Securing Policy

Change: The Republican Conversion to Trade Liberalisation after Smoot-Hawley', *Journal of Law and Economics*, Volume 42, Number 2.

Keck, M. & Sikkink, K. (2002) 'Transnational Advocacy Networks in International and Regional Politics', *International Social Science Journal*, Volume 51, Number 159.

Kick, E. et al. (2000) 'Family and Economic Growth: A World-System Approach and a Cross-National Analysis', *International Journal of Comparative Sociology*, Volume 41, Number 2.

King, C. (2001) 'The Benefits of Ethnic War: Understanding Eurasia's Unrecognised States', *World Politics*, Volume 53, Number 4.

KPM. (2006) 'NGOs Help Boost Peace Process', *Kablalan Peace Monitor*, Volume 1, Number 3, February.

Krasner, S. (1982) 'Structural Causes and Regime Consequences: Regimes as Intervening Variables', *International Organization*, Volume 36, Number 2.

Kukathas, C. (2006) 'The Mirage of Global Justice', *Social Philosophy and Policy*, Volume 23, Number 1.

Lijphart, Arendt. (1971) 'Comparative Politics and the Comparative Method', *American Political Science Review*, Volume 65, Number 3.

Ling, L. & Agathangelou, A. (2004) 'The House of IR: From Family Power Politics to the *Poisies* of Worldism', *International Studies Review*, Volume 6, Number 4.

Lischer, S. (2007) 'Military Intervention and the Humanitarian Force Multiplier', *Global Governance*, Volume 13, Number 1.

Mastura, I. (2008) 'Why is the Mindanao (Moro) Conflict 'Intractable'? The Role of the International Community in its Resolution', *Autonomy and Peace Review*, Volume 4, Number 1.

Mearsheimer, J. (1994) 'The False Promise of International Institutions', *International Security,* Volume 19, Number 3.

Moravcsik, A. (1997) 'Taking Preferences Seriously: A Liberal Theory of International Politics', *International Organization*, Volume 51, Number 4.

Morgenthau, H. (1962) 'A Political Theory of Foreign Aid', *American Political Science Review*, Volume 56, Number 2.

Osgood, K. (2002) 'Hearts and Minds: The Unconventional Cold War', *Journal of Cold War Studies*, Volume 4, Number 2.

Pettigrew, A. (1979) 'On Studying Organizational Cultures', *Administrative Science Quarterly*, Volume 24, Number 4.

Price, R. & Reus-Smit, C. (1998) 'Dangerous Liaisons? Critical International Theory and Constructivism', *European Journal of International Relations*, Volume 4, Number 3.

Ramsbotham, O. (2005) 'The Analysis of Protracted Social Conflict: A Tribute to Edward Azar', *Review of International Studies*, Volume 31, Number 1.

Remollino1, A. (2008) 'US Troops Sighted During Sulu Massacre', *Bulatlat*, Volume 8, Number 2.

Remollino2, A. (2008) 'US Troops Involved in April 30 Bombing in Sulu?', *Bulatlat*, Volume 8, Number 13.

Rieff, D. (1995) 'The Humanitarian Trap', *World Policy Journal,* Volume 12, Number 4.

Rieff, D. (1997) 'Charity on the Rampage: The Business of Foreign Aid', *Foreign Affairs*, January/February.

Robles, A. (2008) 'The Elephant in the Living Room', *Development and Cooperation*, Volume 49, Number 10.

Sarkees, M. et al (2003) 'Inter-State, Intra-State, and Extra-State Wars: A Comprehensive Look at their Distribution Over Time, 1816-1997', *International Studies Quarterly*, Volume 47, Number 1.

Sackman, S. (1991) 'Uncovering Culture in Organizations', *Journal of Applied Behavioural Science*, Volume 27, Number 3.

Schein, E. (1984) 'Coming to a New Awareness of Organizational Culture', *Sloan Management Review*, Volume 12, Number 2.

Schweller, R. & Price, D. (1997) 'A Tale of Two Realisms: Expanding the Institutions Debate', *Mershon International Studies Review*, Volume 41, Number 1.

Slim, H. (2002) 'Military Intervention to Protect Human Rights: The Humanitarian Agency Perspective', *Journal of Humanitarian Assistance*, March.

Smith, S. (2002) 'The United States and the Discipline of International Relations: "Hegemonic Country, Hegemonic Discipline"', *International Studies Review*, Volume 4, Number 2.

Steering Committee. (1996) 'The International Response to Conflict and Genocide: Lessons from the Rwanda Experience', *Journal of Humanitarian Assistance*, April.

Stokke, K. (2006) 'Building the Tamil Eelam State: Emerging State Institutions and Forms of Governance in LTTE-Controlled Areas in Sri Lanka', *Third World Quarterly*, Volume 27, Number 6.

Sweezy, P. (1994) 'The Triumph of Financial Capital', *Monthly Review*, June.

Thiruchandran, S. (2003) 'Sinhala Buddhist Nationalism', *South Asian Journal*, Volume 1, Number 2.

Trice, H. & Beyer, J. (1984) 'Studying Organizational Cultures Through Rites and Ceremonials', *Academy of Management Review*, Volume 9, Number 4.

Varshney, A. (1989) 'Ideas, Interests and Institutions in Policy Change: Transformation of India's Agricultural Strategy in the mid-1990s', *Policy Sciences*, Volume 22, Number 3.

Waltz, K. (2000) 'Structural Realism After the Cold War', *International Security*, Volume 25, Number 1.

Weaver, O. (1998) 'The Sociology of a Not So International Discipline: American and European Developments in International Relations', *International Organization*, Volume 52, Number 4.

Weil, C. (2001) 'The Protection-Neutrality Dilemma in Humanitarian Emergencies: Why the Need for Military Intervention?', *International Migration Review*, Volume 35, Number 1.

Wendt, A. (2001) 'Driving With the Rearview Mirror: On the Rational Science of Institutional Design', *International Organization*, Volume 55, Number 4.

Wildavsky, A. (1987) 'Choosing Preferences by Constructing Institutions: A Cultural Theory of Preference Formation', *American Political Science Review*, Volume 81, Number 1.

Yiftachel, O. (1998) 'Democracy or Ethnocracy: Territory and Settler Politics in Israel/ Palestine', *Middle East Report*.

Newspaper, Magazine, Wire Agency and Internet Publications

AAIW, 'Philippine President Denies 'All-Out War' in Mindanao', *Asia Africa Intelligence Wire* (18 March 2003).

ABS, 'Oxfam: Humanitarian Crisis in Mindanao is Real', *ABS CBN News* (27 September 2008).

ABS, 'Surrender of MILF 'Rogues' as Precondition for Talks Dropped', *ABS CBN News* (4 March 2009)

Adriano, J, 'Arroyo's Risky Politics of Patronage', *Asia Times* (9 December 2008).

AFPress, 'JPMorgan to Invest in Philippines Mining Sector', *Agence France-Presse* (28 February 2007).

AFPress, 'ICRC Rescues 900 Civilians Trapped by Mindanao Fighting', *Agence France-Presse* (23 August 2008).

AFPress 'Sri Lanka 'Humanitarian Crisis' Draws EU Concern', *Agence France-Presse* (26 January 2009).

Almotaqa. (2007), The Moro Jihad in Southern Philippines, [Online], Available: *http://ww.almoltaqa.ps/english/showthread.php?t=6708* [14 February 2009].

ANI, 'Lankan Refugees Appeal to India to Save Tamils in Island Nation', *Asian News International* (16 February 2009).

Apps, P. 'Report Details Sri Lanka Aid Massacre, Blames Forces', *Reuters* (1 April 2008).

Arguilas, C. 'Q and A with US Ambassador Francis Ricciardone: Ops-Intel-Fusion is not Spying', *Mindanews* (28 February 2005).

AT. 'LTTE Must Renounce Violence and Stop Recruiting Child Soldiers — EU's Commissioner', *Asian Tribune* (10 March 2005).

ATa. 'TMVP Agrees to End Child Recruitment — Action Plan Signed', *Asian Tribune* (4 December 2008).

ATb. 'Expel UNICEF Representative for Illegal Meeting with Tigers — Sri Lankan Expats' *Asian Tribune* (12 January 2008).

ATc. 'European Commission Extends GSP+ Eligibility to Sri Lanka Pending Investigation', *Asian Tribune* (12 December 2008).

Avendaño, C. 'Palace: What Humanitarian Crisis?', *The Daily Inquirer* (25 September 2008).

Balachandran, P. 'Neutralisation of Tamil Moderates', *The Hindustan Times* (18 July 2006).

Bello, W. 'A 'Second Front' in the Philippines', *The Nation* (1 March 2002).

Cagoco-Guiam, R. 'The ARMM and the Peace Process: Imperatives, Challenges and Prospects', *Mindanao Forum* (22 March 2006).

Carcamo, D. 'Defence Chief Insists RP-US Balikatan Exercises to Focus on Humanitarian Help', *Philippine Star* (9 February 2009).

Carcamo2, D. 'Gov't Unfazed by ICRC Pullout in Mindanao', *Sun Star* (23 February 2009).

CN. 'UN Agencies in RP Appeal for Peace', *ABS CBN News* (15 August 2008).

CBNa. 'Government Will No Longer Sign Homeland Deal With MILF': Sources. *ABS CBN News* (15 August 2008).

Chaulia1, S. 'A Victory of Principles', *The Hindu* (16 July 2008).

Chaulia2, S. 'Civilians Caught in Sri Lanka's 'Clean War', *Asia Times* (11 September 2008).

Choudry, A. 'Bush and Arroyo: Big Brother, Little Sister', *ZMag* (6 March 2004).

Devraj, R. 'Once Bitten, India Brushes Off Sri Lanka', *Asia Times* (13 April 2002).

Dias, L. 'Casualty Count. More than 65,000 Deaths! Is it Correct?' *Tamil Week* (6 April 2007).

Dissanayake, S. 'Aid Agency Dilemma in Sri Lanka', *BBC News* (9 September 2008).

DN. 'Inquiry into Allegations against UNICEF', *The Daily News* (23 November 2007).

Docena, H. 'When Uncle Sam Comes Marching In.', *Asia Times* (25 February 2006).

Docena, H. 'How the US Got its Philippine Bases Back', *Asia Times* (28 November 2007).

Elkins, C.' Why Malaya is No Model for Iraq', *The New Republic* (8 December 2005).

Elusfa, R. 'Why 3 Oxfam Offices are Pooling Resources for Mindanao', *Mindanews* (20 July 2008).

Elusfa2, R. 'MILF Probes Kato, Bravo', *Mindanews* (10 October 2008).

Fernandez, E. 'DSWD: No Humanitarian Crisis in Mindanao', *The Daily Inquirer* (1 October 2008).

FE. 'India Should Lift Ban on LTTE: Prabhakaran', *The Financial Express* (26 October 2008).

Foster, P. 'Sri Lanka Army is Accused of Recruiting Child Soldiers for Rebel Group', *The Telegraph* (14 November 2006).

Fournier, C. 'Punishment or Aid?' *International Herald Tribune* (27 March 2009).

Gardner, S. 'Sri Lanka Probes Aid Groups for Suspected Rebel Links', *Reuters* (11 January 2007).

Gluckman, R. 'The Revolutionary has Room Service', *Asiaweek* (September 2007).

Heendeniya, K.' Truth about UNICEF and Emergency Rations', *The Island* (26 November 2007).

Hogg, C. 'Sri Lanka: Don't Abuse the Displaced', *Mainichi Shimbun* (9 March 2009).

Hutchcroft, P. 'The Arroyo Imbroglio in the Philippines', *Asia Sentinel* (31 January 2008).

IANS. 'ICRC, Sri Lanka Spar as India Hands Over Relief', *Indo Asian News Service* (20 November 2008).

IRIN. 'Humanitarian Crisis Risk in Mindanao', *IRIN News* (15 October 2008).

Jalbuena, K. 'Canada Helps Build Up Minda Peace Dividend', *The Manila Times* (22 February 2007).

Jannaral, J. 'ARMM Assesses MILF War with Military', *The Manila Times* (14 October 2008).

Johnson, S. 'The Quiet Coup', *The Atlantic (May* 2009).

Kamalendran, C. 'NGO Porn Scandal Shocks Batti, Ampara', *The Sunday Times* (23 April 2006).

Karunakharan, P. 'Indian-Led International Rights Group Quits in Sri Lanka', *Indo Asian News Service* (15 April 2008).

Keenan, J. 'The Collapse of the Second Front', *Foreign Policy in Focus* (26 September 2006).

Koh, T. 'America's Role in Southeast Asia', *The Straits Times* (17 September 2008).

Lee, M. 'In Sri Lanka, UN Still Withholds Casualty Numbers, Funds Detention Camps', *Inner City Press* (9 March 2009).

Lee, M. 'UN Official, "Elated" by Rapes, Says Corruption Watching is Up to Haiti's Preval', *Inner City Press* (24 February 2010).

Legaspi, A. 'Kids in Conflict Areas Willfully Join NPA, MILF- Study', *GMA News* (5 December 2007).

LN. 'Wanni Civilians Facing Life or Death Situation- Paul Castella', *Lankasri News* (18 February 2009).

Loftus, D. (2001) The Rise of the Victorian Middle Class. *BBC History*. [Online], Available: *http://www.bbc.co.uk/history/british/victorians/middle_classes_01.shtml* [18 December 2008].

Malalasekera, S. 'Equal Access to Justice Project is about Three Basic Principles of Hammurabi Code. *Daily News* (29 September 2004).

MC. Mindanao Still Gets Largest Share from Australian Aid. *Mines and Communities* (22 February 2007).

ME. RP Troops Secure Visiting US Navy Hospital Ship in Mindanao. *Mindanao Examiner* (27 May 2008).

ME. 'RP-US Visiting Forces Agreement Helps Build a Strong Republic, Says Foreign Affairs', *The Mindanao Examiner* (25 February 2009).

Mearsheimer, J. 'Hans Morgenthau and the Iraq War: Realism Versus Neo-Conservatism', *Open Democracy* (21 April 2005).

Merueñas, M. 'Arroyo to Bring up Child Warriors Issue to UN-Report', *GMA News* (18 September 2008).

ML. 'MILF Reiterates Policy on Child Soldiers', *Moroland* (2 May 2006).

Montlake, S. 'Where US is Helping to Make Gains against Terrorism', *The Christian Science Monitor* (15 February 2007).

Montlake, S. 'Sri Lankan Refugees Face Open-Ended Detention in Camps', *The Christian Science Monitor* (25 February 2009).

MT. 'MILF to Stop Recruiting Child Soldiers- UN Special Envoy', *The Manila Times* (13 December 2008).

MTB. 'Bring Peace in Mindanao, UN Envoy Tells GRP, MILF', *Mindanao Tulong Bakwet* (11 December 2008).

Nebehay, S. 'ICRC Says Israel Broke International Law in Gaza', *Reuters* (8 January 2009).

Nolen, S. 'Caught Between the Tigers and the Tanks', *The Globe and Mail* (23 January 2009).

Panti, L. 'Foreigners Step Up Humanitarian Aid to Conflict Areas in Mindanao: Medco Says Int'l Community Eager to Help Victims of Ongoing War', *The Manila Times* (28 August 2008).

Pareño, R. 'Abu Sayyaf Group Bares Demands for Release of Red Cross Workers', *Philippine Star* (27 February 2009).

Patranobis, S. 'To Whom Does the Country Belong?', *The Hindustan Times* (7 October 2008).

Patranobis, S. 'You are Either Wish Us or Against Us, Warns Sri Lanka', *Hindustan Times* (1 February 2009).

PP. 'Oxfam Urges House Leaders, Malacañang to Prioritise Drug Patent Rules Amendments', *Pinoy Press* (5 November 2007).

Price, M. 'It's Just War: The Politics of Humanitarian Intervention', *The National* (12 September 2008).

Ramachandran, S. 'India Chases the Dragon in Sri Lanka', *Asia Times* (10 July 2008).

Rasul, A. 'No Humanitarian Crisis in Mindanao', *The Manila Times* (6 October 2008).

Reddy, M. 'We Will Ensure the Safety of Civilians, says Sri Lanka', *The Hindu* (29 January 2009).

Reuters. (2007) Child Soldiers in Sri Lanka. *Reuters Alertnet*. [Online], Available: *http:// www.alertnet.org/LKchildsoldiers.html* [29 December 2008].

Rieff, D. (2000) Round One. *The Atlantic Unbound*. [Online], Available: *http://www. theatlantic.com/unbound/roundtable/goodfight/rieff1.htm* [22 February 2009].

Samath, F. 'Sri Lanka: NGO Scam Spotlights Cozy Funding Deals', *Inter Press Service* (18 February 2008).

Santos, D. 'WFP: No Mindanao Humanitarian Crisis', *The Daily Inquirer* (8 October 2008).

Scarpello, F. 'US, Philippines Weigh New Military Marriage', *Asia Times* (23 August 2006).

Sengupta, S. 'UN Evacuates Wounded from Sri Lanka. *International Herald Tribune* (29 January 2009).

Siddiqui, Haroon. 'Sri Lanka Links Conflict to War on Terror', *The Star* (8 May 2008).

SO. 'Oxfam Writes on Vakarai Awakening Gradually', *Sunday Observer* (27 May 2007).

SS. 'MILF Accuses Military of Burning Moro Houses', *Sun Star* (15 August 2008).

SS. 'Central Mindanao Gets First Mining Applicant', *Sun Star* (18 January 2009).

Swamy, N. 'After 25 Years, Cornered LTTE Faces Deathly Crisis', *Indo Asian News Service* (28 January 2009).

Tagacay, I. 'RP-US Balikatan 2008 in Balabac, Palawan for Humanitarian Operations', *The Palawan Times* (28 February 2008).

Taylor, R. 'EU Warns Sri Lanka Trade Depends on Rights Record', *Reuters* (19 March 2008).

TG. 'Pillayan Says He is Powerless', *Tamil Guardian* (10 December 2008).

TH. 'Military Solution in Sri Lanka Very Difficult: US', *The Hindu* (25 October 2008).

TI. 'ICRC Deputy Head Shares his Concerns with Army Commander', *The Island* (8 July 2008).

Tighe, P. & Shankar, J. 'India Urges Sri Lanka to Allow Aid Organizations Into War Zone', *Bloomberg News* (24 February 2009).

TN. 'UNICEF has Erred- Thamilchelvan', *Tamilnet* (5 March 2005).

TT. 'Red Cross Office Attacked by Sri Lanka Mob', *The Telegraph* (7 February 2009).

Weerasekera, A. (2008, December 1) Mumbai Attack- Is it a False Flag Operation?', *LankaWeb News*. [Online], Available: *http://www.lankaweb.com/news/ items08/011208-9.html* [14 January 2009].

Wijesinha, R. 'The Cluster Bomb Game', *The Island* (9 February 2009).

Wiseman, P. 'In Philippines, US Making Progress in War on Terror', *USA Today* (13 February 2007).

Wright, R. 'From the Desk of Donald Rumsfeld...' *The Washington Post* (1 November 2007).

Xinhua. 'UNICEF Says No Evidence Orphanage Casualties are Sri Lankan Tigers', *Xinhua Financial Network-Asia* (15 August 2006).

Xinhua. 'Foreigners not Advised to Leave S. Philippines Amid Kidnappings' (15 February 2009).

INDEX